UNITED STATES
NAVAL FIGHTERS
OF
WORLD WAR II
IN ACTION

UNITED STATES NAVAL FIGHTERS OF WORLD WAR II IN ACTION

by

MICHAEL O'LEARY

Line illustrations by John Batchelor

BLANDFORD PRESS

Poole, Dorset

First published in the U.K. 1980
Copyright © 1980 Blandford Press Ltd
Link House, West Street
Poole, Dorset BH15 1LL

ISBN 0 7137 0956 1

British Library Cataloguing in Publication Data

O'Leary, Michael
    United States naval fighters of World War II
in action.
    1. World War, 1939–45 – Aerial operations,
American   2. World War, 1939–45 – Naval operations,
American   3. Fighter planes – History
    4. United States. Navy – History
    I. Title
    940.54'49'73   D790

Designed by Vigo

Typeset in 'Monotype' Plantin

Filmset and printed in Great Britain by
BAS Printers Limited, Over Wallop, Hampshire

Contents

Acknowledgements

The author would like to acknowledge the people who helped make this volume possible: Robert Trimble for his tireless researches into the history of the Grumman Wildcat and the Grumman Hellcat in the 'Marianas Turkey Shoot'; Gregory Urwin for his 'Wildcats of Wake Island'; James V. Sanders for his excellent 'Brewsters of Fighting Two'; Robert Hucker for his research on Navy aces including Robert Hanson and Indian Joe Bauer; John Batchelor for his constant help and enthusiasm; and the staff of the Naval Photographic Center and Robert Carlisle whose diligent digging always turned up just the right photograph.

Special mention should also be made of two pioneer aviation historians that helped record much of the available material before it was lost to time. They are William Green and William Larkins. Both these gentlemen have recorded facts and photographs that are essential to the modern day researcher in the field of Naval aviation. Without their inspired efforts today's aviation historian would have to pursue many dead-end corridors.

Introduction

Some historians have advocated the theory that the United States did not really become 'united' until the terrible days of World War Two. The Civil War that had torn America apart on social as well as regional lines had ended less than 80 years before the conflict that was truly to circle the globe. During that time the northern states of America had grown in industrial power while the devastated south had struggled back to an agricultural economy. The western states were still regarded as 'wild' as indeed they were with the last Indian raids occurring *after* the start of the twentieth century. Americans enjoyed the policy of isolationism and little thought was given to the outside world. Even World War One, entered in spite of the furious objection of isolationists, did not broaden America's international views as the average citizen remained ignorant of the workings of international politics.

Not learning the bitter lessons of World War One, America entered back into its shell of isolationism, totally ignoring the rapid build up of the forces of Germany and Japan. After all, those countries were so *far* away. However, one of the most important technological inventions of the twentieth century, the aircraft, had the ability to shorten distances in a most dangerous way. As Europe became embroiled in the fight against Hitler's madness and, one by one, the free nations fell as the *blitzkrieg* spread its new brand of terror, American politicians and military planners slowly began to see the light. Belated production programs were hurriedly launched, most producing obsolete aircraft and equipment. Soon most of Continental Europe had fallen and only Britain stood to face the might of the Thousand Year Reich. The United States poured military equipment into England, learning from Europe's mistakes and the lessons of aerial combat over the United Kingdom. Aircraft designs began to improve and America's strongest asset began to emerge: the ability to mass produce beyond the capacity of any other country's wildest dreams.

Defense plants, bases and establishments were erected all over the United States and, when the Japanese attacked Pearl Harbor on 7 December 1941, most factories were already well on the way to gearing for a global conflict, the likes of which had never before been seen by man.

One of the few pieces of good fortune on America's part during the early days of World War Two was the fact that the Navy's few aircraft carriers had escaped the destruction of Pearl Harbor and were available for immediate strikes against the enemy that had spread its tentacles across the immense distance of the Pacific Ocean. Japanese military planners were well aware of the deadly error in letting the carriers get away and they knew that their plans for complete conquest of the Pacific were going to be slowed until the American flat tops could be neutralized.

However, the Japanese did not count on the tremendous force of mass production which soon saw newer and better carriers joining the battle-scarred veterans in the Pacific. The aircraft that equipped the American carriers, the Wildcat, Hellcat and Corsair, were also available in increasing quantity and were able to tackle anything that the Japanese could put into the air.

The island-hopping war was to be long and bloody but the final result, after the close of 1942, was never in doubt: the complete and unconditional surrender of the Japanese Empire. American Naval and Marine fighters, in the closing days of the immense conflict, ranged freely over Japan's major cities, blasting any foe that was foolish enough to rise against the marauding fighters.

It is these great fighting aircraft that this volume examines and it presents, we hope, an exciting pictorial account of the great machines that now, sadly, are virtually extinct. We have endeavored to select photographs that show the movement and excitement of the times, whether on the battlefront or in the factory. No longer was there a disparate nation. Instead there was a United States determined to further the creed under which the nation had been founded. It is to the men and women that created and flew these great Naval fighting aircraft that this book is dedicated.

MICHAEL O'LEARY *Los Angeles, 1980*

1 BUFFALO –
The Unmitigated Disaster

Stemming from a line of lackluster designs, the Brewster Buffalo was perhaps one of the worst fighting aircraft with which America entered World War Two.

To the embattled Marine pilots fighting in the hot sun above Midway, the Brewster Buffalo was not only an obsolete and poorly constructed fighter plane . . . it was also a distinct threat to their well-being!

Actually, the initial Japanese plans at the beginning of World War Two did not call for an invasion of Midway, which is located over 1,000 miles closer to Pearl Harbor than Wake Island which they did plan to invade. The task force returning from the victorious Pearl Harbor strike was to launch a massive aerial attack while on the trip home to Japan. However, actual events were to be different, *much* different.

The first aviation contact to reach Midway was during 1935 when Pan American Airways built one of its trans-Pacific seaplane bases on this location. During that year the Navy staged maneuvers at Midway that included simulated attacks by aircraft and the landing of 750 Marines. By 1939 the Navy realized the extreme importance of Midway, describing the two islands that made up the area as 'second in importance only to Pearl Harbor'. It was also realized that facilities would have to be quickly constructed. Piers were to be built and a facility for at least two patrol plane squadrons was to be established.

Working with great energy, the Navy completed the pier on 1 September 1940. A reconnaissance party of Marines arrived in May and was followed in September by a force of nine officers and 168 enlisted men to set up the 3rd Defense Battalion with one 5-inch gun battery (consisting of two guns). An Army engineer unit had been working between the two islands, Sand and Eastern, to improve the channel for shipping. The 3rd Defense Battalion was relieved by the 6th Defense Battalion on 11 September with thirty-four officers and 750 men. On 18 August the Naval Air Station was commissioned with Commander Cyril T. Simard commanding. A decision to supplement the seaplane base with an airstrip on Eastern Island had been undertaken.

On the outbreak of the war, Midway was the home of a dozen Consolidated PBY Catalina patrol boats of VP-21, situated on and around the Sand Island seaplane ramps. Two Dutch Catalinas, which had landed for fuel while on a ferry flight to the East Indies, were recalled and commandeered into the US Navy. No actual combat aircraft were present but men from VMSB-231 had arrived three days earlier to prepare for eighteen Vought SB2U-3 dive bombers that were to be flown off the *Lexington*. However, the 'Lex', upon receiving word of the Pearl attack, turned back for home base. On 10 December the pilots of VMSB-231 landed at a ruined Pearl Harbor, itching to get into battle and deal the Japanese punishment from their obsolete and highly inflammable Vindicators. Just a week later a PBY led seventeen SB2Us to Midway after an incredible overwater flight of nine hours and 45 minutes, the longest mass overwater single-engine aircraft flight up until that time. The Vindicators growled in for landing among cheers from the Navy and Marine personnel at Midway, here were aircraft with which they could do some *real* fighting. Little did they know that most of the SB2U's crews were already doomed men.

On 7 December, two Japanese destroyers dropped a few shells into Sand Island and the first casualties were taken: four Navy and Marine enlisted men were killed. The destroyers beat a hasty retreat after coming under fire from Midway's defensive batteries.

About an hour after the destroyers had retired, Captain J.H. Hamilton of Pan American Airways' *Philippine Clipper* which, after 7 December, had surely become the most dangerous airline flight ever, spotted two ships and one of them was burning intensely. The Americans on Midway had also drawn first blood from the Japanese.

The next few weeks saw a lull in action and civilian workmen were evacuated aboard the *Wright* and *Tangier*. The Japanese plan for a quick strike on Midway had not come off because of bad weather. Some of the Pearl Harbor strike force was diverted instead to Wake Island where the Japanese were suffering a loss of face from the stubborn resistance of a handful of tough Americans. Two carriers, *Soryu* and *Hiryu*, were drawn into this battle and Midway was given a reprieve of six months from battle . . . six vital months in which defenses were strengthened and more combat aircraft added.

A few hit-and-run attacks occurred during the six month period. At the end of January and the beginning of February, Midway came in for a bombardment from two enemy submarines but both attacks were routed by shore fire. On 10 March two four-engined Japanese flying boats took off from Wotje in the Marshalls. One turned for Midway while the other headed for Johnston Island. This was part of an interesting Japanese experiment to combine long-range aerial reconnaissance of American bases with refueling at sea from submarines. This could have had far-reaching effects on the early battles of the Pacific. However, on Christmas Day, Midway had finally received some fighter protection via fourteen F2A-3 Buffalos of VMF-221 that had flown off the *Saratoga*. The fighter pilots, who had been headed for the relief of Wake Island, were unhappy about abandoning their comrades at Wake, an unpopular decision among Marine aviators. The Marine pilots knew that Midway would soon be in for action and they would have a chance to avenge their friends on Wake. Another reason that the pilots were unhappy was the fact that they had been forced to hand over their new Wildcats in trade for the Buffalos so Midway was now equipped with a small air force made up of obsolete combat types.

Marine radar picked up a 'bandit' about 25 miles to the southwest and a four-plane flight of VMF-221 was scrambled to intercept. Captain James L. Neefus caught the unidentified intruder at 10,000 ft and was startled to see a four-engine Japanese flying

The prototype Brewster fighter, BuNo 0451, featured a low canopy hood which hindered pilot visibility. Note the original small fin that distinguished the first version of the prototype. First flown during December of 1937, BuNo 0451 was powered by a Wright XR-1820-22 powerplant and, from the very first, was a disappointment in performance. (BuNo 3813)

A popular method for photographing the Brewster fighter prototype was to have the pilot dive then execute a rapid zoom climb at the camera aircraft to get a photo that would give the impression of speed and power, something the Brewster was distinctly lacking. Note the openings for the machine-guns on the top of the nose cowl. Photograph was taken on 26 April 1938. (USN 80-G-3807)

boat. He was not so startled as to not immediately attack as soon as he saw the big red *hinomarus* on the aircraft's wing. Shoving the throttle forward, Neefus led his group on a firing pass. With nose and wing guns blazing, hits were exploding all over the flying boat, whose apparently startled crew members had not expected any enemy fighters. Neefus racked the Buffalo into a steep climbing turn as other members of the formation pressed home their attacks. The pilot of the flying boat nosed the aircraft down and headed for a cloud bank 7,000 ft below. The other Marine pilots made their passes but few results were observed. One of the pilots was hit in the shoulder and the Buffalo he was flying picked up a number of hits from the alerted Japanese gunners. Neefus, who had set an engine afire on his first pass, returned for another run, scoring many hits and the enemy aircraft fell aflame into the ocean. Back at Midway there was a great deal of celebrating over the victory, the first scored by an American Buffalo, and a rare bottle of bourbon was presented to the pilots. More importantly, the Japanese ex-

periment at refueling by submarine at sea was ruined. The Buffalo pilots might well be jubilant for little did they know what fate had in store for them.

By late April, the Navy had begun to expect that an attack on Midway was in the offing. Secret messages from Japan had been picked up and decoded in Washington, D.C. Preparations for attack at Midway intensified and five more anti-aircraft batteries were detached from Pearl and sent to the two islands. Protective revetments for the aircraft were constructed while two new 4,000 gallon water tanks were set up in partially buried installations. The overall base was camouflaged and sandbagged while emergency rations and medical equipment was distributed and stored.

On 26 May the *Kitty Hawk* brought in seven Wildcats and nineteen SBD-2s along with twenty-two Marine pilots (most of whom were not completely trained). Decoding of other Japanese messages now placed the attack for the first week in June which gave a little more time for preparations. This also allowed time for the repaired *Yorktown* to get in position for the oncoming battle.

At the end of May, Eastern Island bore little resemblance to the site that construction crews had begun on not that many months previously. The airfield contained four USAAF Martin Marauders converted to torpedo aircraft and seventeen Boeing B-17 Flying Fortresses that had been hurriedly brought in from Oahu to reinforce the island. Six Grumman TBF Avengers had also been brought in for the same purpose. The island could now field sixteen PBYs operated by Navy crews, nineteen Dauntlesses, seventeen

Vindicators, twenty-one Buffalos and seven Wildcats.

The twenty-eight fighters were commanded by Major Floyd B. Parks, the thirty-six dive bombers by Major Lofton R. Henderson. These aircraft consumed 65,000 gallons of fuel a day when operating and fuel became somewhat of a problem when a sailor accidentally pulled a destruct handle during an emergency drill, setting off 400,000 gallons of aviation fuel in an explosion that rocked both islands. This disaster meant that all aircraft would now have to be refueled from 55 gallon drums by hand, a thankless and backbreaking task that could become a serious problem during military operations when turn-around speed was of supreme importance.

Midway had now become a stronghold, an island bastion in the wake of Japanese aggression, a chance for American fighting men to strike back at a back-stabbing enemy. Admiral Chester Nimitz stressed the role of Marine land-based aircraft on Midway (now code-named BALSA) for offensive rather than defensive action:

'BALSA's air force must be employed to inflict prompt and early damage to Jap carrier flight decks if recurring attacks are to be stopped. Our objectives will be, first, their flight decks rather than attempting to fight off the initial attacks on BALSA ... If this is correct, BALSA's air force ... should go all out for the carriers ... leaving to BALSA's guns the first defense of the field.'

Midway was to have a formidable opponent in the shape of Admiral Yamamoto who, on the 63,700 ton battleship *Yamato*, was directing operations against both the

So disappointing was the performance of the prototype Brewster fighter that it was shipped off to the NACA full-scale wind tunnel at Langley Field, Virginia. The aircraft was supported in the slipstream on struts which transmitted the forces of the wind to the small building below the aircraft. The streamlined fairings around the struts shielded them from the airstream to eliminate extraneous forces that would act on the aircraft in flight. The airstream in this tunnel was 60 feet wide and 30 feet deep. Two 35.5 foot propellers, operated by 4,000 hp electric motors could produce a wind of up to 118 mph, a far cry from today's multi-Mach wind tunnels. (NACA)

Aleutian Islands and Midway. The Japanese Imperial General Staff and Army were reluctant to consider the attack on Midway but Yamamoto's enthusiasm was such that they soon warmed to the idea. The four carriers to head for Midway would be the *Akagi*, Japan's largest at 36,500 tons, *Kaga* (36,000 tons), *Hiryu* and *Soryu* (18,000 tons each). Three days were to be devoted to softening up the island's defenses by bombardment by carrier aircraft, two battleships, three cruisers, and destroyers. The landing force would then disembark 3,500 troops.

As it was to turn out, Marine aircraft were to play a small part in the overall Battle of Midway (which, in its entirety, is out of the scope of this volume) but the battle was also to be unique for it would be the first and *last* time that American Buffalos would be committed to battle.

On 3 June, a PBY spotted the Japanese and the B-17s droned their way from Midway to carry out a high-altitude attack against the ship. The USAAF bombers missed all targets and were soon to learn a bitter lesson: that ships are not all that vulnerable to high-altitude bombing attacks. The B-26s and TBFs were next off, to be slaughtered by the alerted Japanese. By this time the Marine aircraft on Midway were warming up and would soon join the action. Major Parks had divided his aircraft up into units of twelve and thirteen aircraft. Seven Buffalos and five Wildcats under Parks would meet attacking aircraft while Captain Kirk Armistead's dozen Buffalos and one F4F would orbit and wait for a possible attack from another direction.

Parks' group was in for a bit of luck when, about 30 miles out at 14,000 ft, they spotted a large formation of Japanese dive bombers at 12,000 ft with their Zeke escort *below* them. Apparently the Japanese were convinced that Midway would be an easy raid and so had sent the deadly fighters below the lumbering dive bombers so that the fighters could strafe and shoot up Midway's defenses.

The Marines attacked immediately and were soon joined by the orbiting group of Marine fighters. The Japanese aircraft were part of the 108 plane striking force commanded by the *Hiryu*. The twenty-five fighters hurled into the formation with typical Marine bravado but, after the initial pass, the Zekes had been warned and a deadly battle began to take place.

According to the 6th Defense Battalion, only twenty of the thirty-six horizontal Japanese attack bombers in the first wave reached Midway while a second wave of thirty-six dive bombers had been pared down to eighteen aircraft. Japanese damage to Midway was heavy for the enemy was experienced in its profession. However, the heaviest damage had been done to the Marine fighters. Fifteen of the twenty-five fighter pilots, including Major Parks, had fallen to the enemy in the heaviest losses that the Marines would sustain in a battle during World War Two. Thirteen of the Buffalos were destroyed along with two Wildcats and, of the remaining aircraft, only two were fit to take off again after they had landed. The few survivors were able to land because the Japanese had not bombed the runway, apparently thinking that their victory would be

so quick that they would not want to spend time repairing a newly captured concrete runway.

Back at Midway, crew chiefs and mechanics waited for the fighters to return until the stunning realization that the fighters were *not* going to return set in upon them. The few surviving pilots damned the Brewsters. Captain Philip R. White stated: 'It is my belief that any commander who orders pilots out for combat in an F2A should consider the pilot lost before leaving the ground.'

Other pilots said that the Brewsters should be only used as trainers while another said that he saw two Buffalos blown out of the air by a Zeke making one firing pass.

Midway's VMF-221 had been completely destroyed as a fighting unit. The personnel were reassigned to other duties, many to help fuel the surviving aircraft, especially the hungry four-engine B-17 bombers. A burning lesson had been impressed upon the surviving aircrew: American fighters were obsolete and Japanese aircraft, tactics, and pilots much superior to the lies generated by wartime propaganda.

Thus, the Brewster Buffalo had been committed to its first and last major American engagement of World War Two. It cannot even be said that the fighter acquitted itself well during the battle, for most were destroyed in the first few minutes. However,

Top left
The Brewster B-339B fighter displays its camouflage for the photographer. Six B-339Bs were on the French carrier *Béarn* when the ship made a speed run to Brest. France fell before the carrier could arrive and the aircraft were taken to Martinique where they were dumped on the beach, along with a number of SBC Helldivers, tied down with engines and cockpits covered, and left to rot. They were gradually reduced to junk by the corrosive salt air that quickly ate into their aluminium airframes. Note the US civil licence crudely affixed to the top right wing.

Center left
Photographs of Brewster in full US Navy markings are extremely rare so this view of a Fighting Three Buffalo is particularly welcome. BuNo 1398, an F2A-2, was based aboard the *Saratoga* and carries the squadron's famous insignia in black below the windscreen. The upper wing surface was painted in Glossy Chrome Yellow with the Yellow extending 5 per cent of the chord on to the under surfaces of the leading edge. The remainder of the aircraft was painted aluminium. The tail surfaces of all *Saratoga* aircraft were painted White as an identification feature. The coding on the side of the fuselage, in Black, translates to Fighting Squadron 3 aircraft No. 8 which meant that this machine was the second aircraft of the third section. (USN)

Bottom left
Excellent high-angle view of a factory-fresh Brewster showing off the compact lines of the fighter. Note the cylinder for the life raft mounted behind the pilot's headrest. Several Brewsters incurred a fair amount of damage when the life raft inflated on its own after being left in the hot sun, blowing out all the plexiglass panels and distorting the metal frames.

it did steel the surviving Marine pilots with a new respect for their enemy ... and with a desire to destroy them at the first opportunity.

★ ★ ★ ★ ★

During the middle of the 1930s it was obvious to even isolationist America that a dramatic upsurge in defense spending and development was necessary to even catch up to the rapidly rising powers of Germany and Japan. It was clear that a goodly part of the expected conflict would be fought in and from the air. Most American designs still followed the tried and true concept of the biplane developed during World War One. Streamlining was not really paid all that much attention to, yet the 1930s would be remembered in history as the age of streamline, perhaps best exemplified in the Art Deco movement. It was true that some racing and experimental military aircraft tried to boost aeronautical technology with monoplanes, slick designs, and powerful engines.

However, the general purpose biplane formed the most numerous components of the Army and Navy's air arms. The few experimental monoplanes that *were* flying deeply impressed some forward-thinking military planners in both services and proposals were soon cast that would issue forth a number of new and innovative designs.

The first monoplane fighter for the United States Navy would come from a rather unlikely company. The Brewster Aeronautical Corporation traced its roots back to 1810 when the parent company began manufacturing horse-drawn carriages. In 1935, the Aeronautical section was formed to produce a series of aircraft that were, at best, uninspired. The monoplane that Brewster was contracted to build would be a stubby single-seat aircraft capable of easily operating off aircraft carriers and would have better performance than the biplanes it would replace. It is interesting to note that a monoplane design was not specified but that only a monoplane could meet the performance specifications. It was with considerable controversy that the inexperienced company received an order for a single prototype on 23 June 1936. The military was not all that sure of the new design and another contract was placed with Grumman to produce a biplane (see the Wildcat chapter for further details).

It should be noted that Brewster immediately began to run into design problems with their XF2A-1, as the Navy designated the new fighter (the company designation was B-139), but it must be said that Brewster was treading new water with the airframe. It would be almost two years, a very long time from first order to first flight during the 1930s, before the XF2A-1 took to the air for the first time during June of 1938. The aircraft was originally designed for an 800 hp radial engine but the prototype flew with a 950 hp Wright XR-1820-22 powerplant driving a three-blade Hamilton-Standard hydromatic propeller. Construction was all-metal with flush riveting throughout. The midwing was fully cantilever. Control surfaces were fabric covered and hydraulically-operated split flaps were fitted between the ailerons and the fuselage. The landing gear, always to be one of the real weak points of the design, was hydraulically operated and was stored with the wheels slightly projecting from the sides of the fuselage, somewhat like Grumman's retractable gear design. Initial armament was typical of the period, one 0.50 caliber and one 0.30 caliber machine-gun mounted in the top part of the forward fuselage and firing through the propeller arc. Provision was also made for carrying two 0.50 caliber machine-guns in the wings, one in each wing panel.

Top

English workmen look on with some dismay as an RAF test pilot prepares to start the engine of Buffalo AS426 for a test flight. The aircraft was one of the Belgium Brewsters taken over by the RAF when that country fell before the fighters could be delivered. RAF test pilots found the aircraft unsuited for operations over Europe and the authorities recommended that the Buffalo be assigned as the standard day fighter for the Far East, a decision that was to have tragic results. Note the Grumman Martlet parked to the left of the Buffalo.

Bottom

Apparently taken at Ewa, Hawaii, after the start of the war, a Buffalo is seen in a revetment being worked on. The aircraft was assigned to VMF-221, which was the Brewster squadron that was wiped out at Midway. When the Marines attacked the initial 108 aircraft Japanese striking force with twenty-five F2As and F4Fs, disaster occurred. Fifteen of the twenty-five pilots were killed; thirteen F2As and two F4Fs were lost, clearly showing the Buffalo's weaknesses. The aircraft is painted Non-Specular Blue Grey on the upper surfaces and Non-Specular Light Grey underneath. Stripes, consisting of seven red and six white horizontal bars, were applied to the entire rudder surface. (USN/80-G-271049)

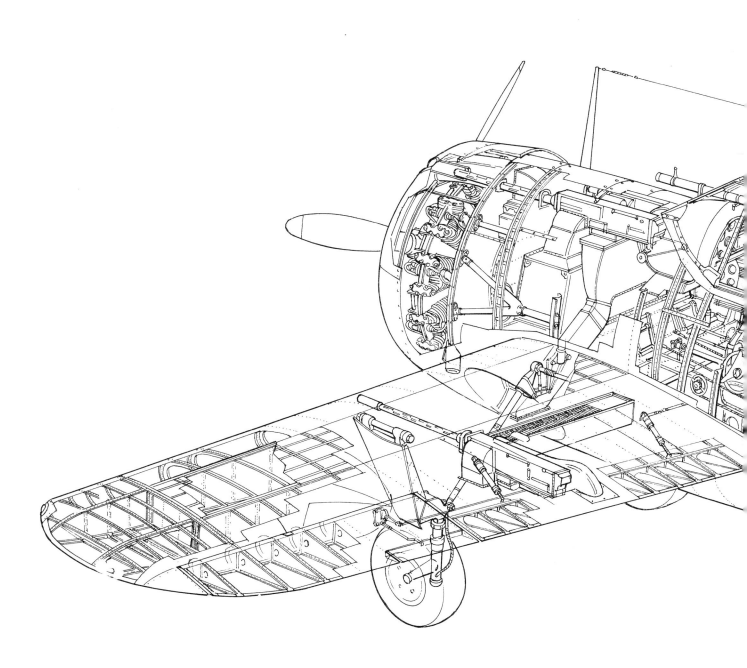

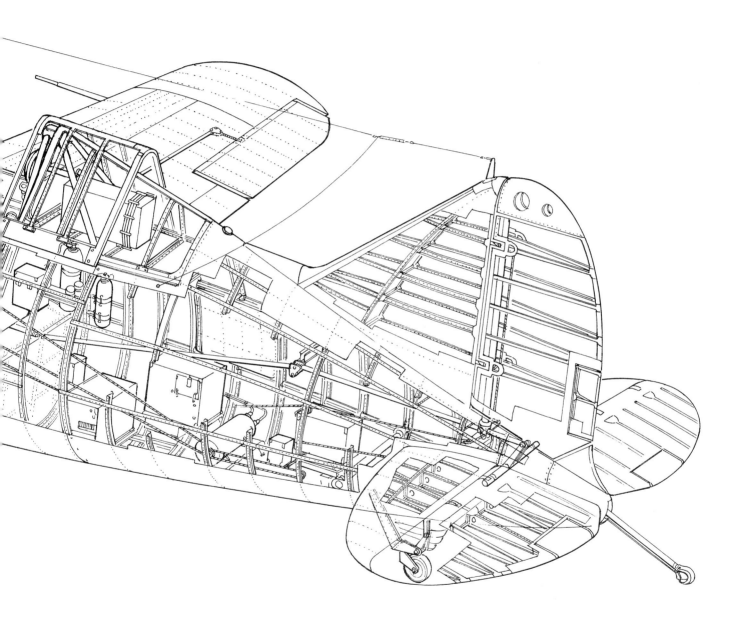

The initial flight tests were less than satisfactory and performance disappointing so the prototype (BuNo 0451) was assigned to the new NACA Langley wind tunnel where the airframe was minutely tested. A number of fairly minor modifications helped reduce drag somewhat and edge top speed to just over 300 mph at 17,000 ft. The Navy, not completely pleased with the aircraft, decided to go ahead with production and a contract was issued to Brewster for fifty-four F2A-1s on 11 June. This contract was of historic importance for the Navy for it was the first mass production contract for a monoplane fighter.

The armament on the production F2A-1s was standardized at two 0.50 caliber guns in the nose and two 0.50s in the wings. The powerplant was the Wright R-1820-34 Cyclone of 940 hp. Weight had risen to 5,043 lbs compared to the prototype's 4,835 lbs and performance took another slight drop. The weight problem was to beset the Brewster through its service life resulting in an aircraft that was unstable and took 30 minutes to climb to 21,000 ft!

The first eleven F2A-1s were assigned to Navy fighter squadron VF-3 as BuNos 1386-1396 and from that point on, all aircraft in the contract were designated as F2A-2s. The prototype had been modified and redesignated XF2A-2, flying with a 1,200 hp R-1820-40 powerplant, raised fin, and higher canopy for better pilot visibility. Finland, eager for aircraft, purchased the remaining forty-three uncompleted aircraft, allowing the Navy to concentrate on its new 'improved' version.

The first production F2A-2 was delivered to the Navy during August 1940 and the aircraft were issued to VF-2 and VF-3 as related elsewhere in this chapter. Accidents which could not be classified as normal began placing doubt on the structural integrity of the Buffalo, something that the aircraft had to live with for its short service life.

Further modifications were undertaken on the F2A-2 series to bring them up to what Brewster considered 'combat ready'. Two extra fuel tanks amounting to 40 gallons were added to the wing leading edge while a simple bomb rack was installed under each wing panel, capable of holding a 100 lb bomb, a feature that was never used operationally by the American aircraft.

The next step in the progression, or digression as one wag termed the process, of the Brewster design was the F2A-3. The -3 had a slightly lengthened forward fuselage to help the stability problem and more armor and an extra fuel tank, which helped raise the weight and once again decrease the stability!

The final 108 Navy Buffalos built now had a gross weight of 6,320 lbs, 1,500 lbs heavier than the prototype.

The Navy quickly passed the Buffalo to the Marine Corps in favor of the Grumman Wildcat and thus it fell to the Marines the task of defending Midway as described in the first part of the chapter. After Midway, the Buffalos were quickly withdrawn and sent to training units where they served for only a few more months before being withdrawn and scrapped. Not one Buffalo survives

After the disaster at Midway, all Buffalos were assigned to training units. Even in this non-combat environment, the Buffalos were still disliked and did training duty for only a few months before they were withdrawn and either junked or sent to mechanic's schools where they could be taken apart and put back together as instructional aids. Not one Buffalo survives today. These machines are seen breaking off over Florida where they were being used by a Marine training squadron. (USN/80-G-10556)

today. Oddly enough, the Buffalo's claim to fame was not with the country of its manufacture but with foreign governments whose use of the portly fighter is briefly described in the following section.

Brewsters for Finland

During the late 1930s and early 1940s, the United States had become a giant supermarket for countries frantically trying to rearm and face the threat of a rapidly expanding Germany and Japan. North American, Martin, Douglas and several other companies benefited from large contracts placed by foreign governments for combat aircraft. Brewster Aeronautical Corporation saw no reason not to benefit from this windfall of selling outdated designs so the company immediately waded into the market and, perhaps surprisingly, met with considerable success.

The little Scandinavian country of Finland was in 1939 being beset by giant Russia in a clear case of overt aggression. Americans who were dimly aware of international politics during that period seemed to be pulling for the underdog which was most definitely Finland. The remainder of the F2A-1 contract was made available to the Finns so that the Navy could proceed with the F2A-2 while keeping costs at a reasonable level. The airframes were modified with Wright R-1820-G5 engines of 950 hp under the company designation of B-239. The aircraft were crated and shipped to Sweden and flown to Finland by Norwegian volunteers, not an uncommon practice in the Scandinavian countries.

Only a few of the Brewsters had reached Finland when, on 13 March 1941, the two adversaries signed a peace treaty. As usual, the Russians were soon to break the treaty and, on 25 June, Russian forces began renewed assaults and the Brewsters were pressed into action in what became known as the Continuation War. It is most curious that the Finns operated the B-239s for three years with a fair measure of success against the Russians. Fighting in some of the world's worst weather, Brewster pilots racked up an impressive string of victories in their green and black camouflaged fighters. As soon as Germany invaded Russia, Finland was considered an enemy and supplies were cut off; the resourceful Finns adapted captured Russian engines and spares to keep their Brewsters in the air!

Finnish ace Eino Luukkanen in his book *Fighter over Finland*, states that he thoroughly enjoyed the Brewster and regarded the aircraft as quite modern compared to his earlier mount, the Fokker D.XXI:

'Early next morning we walked to the nearby airfield in the clear, spring air, still cool from the night's frost. This far south the snow had already disappeared, and the only remaining vestiges of winter were a few small frozen puddles. The single-seat Brewster B-239 fighters that we were about to collect had been relinquished by the US Navy, shipped to Sweden and assembled at Trollhattan by Norwegian mechanics working under the directions of the Brewster company's representative, Ray Matthews, test pilot R.A. Winston, the well-known Finnish aviator, Waino Bremer, and his engineer, Berger. We reached the airfield and at last, in front of us, was a modern fighter which, although born about the same time as the Fokker, had all the contemporary developments that our old D.XXIs lacked ... The B-239 fighter that I elected to fly bore the Finnish serial number BW-375, and this machine was to become my personal aircraft for more than two years, carrying me safely over some 62,000 miles.'

Luukkanen, who scored fifty-four victories, many in the Brewster, was just one of a number of Finnish aviators who racked up a number of kills with their aircraft. Perhaps the fact that the Russians were not as good or well-trained as pilots as the Japanese helped the Brewster achieve this one bright spot in its history. The Finns gave some thought to building the Brewster and went as far as to construct one prototype known as the *Humu* with a Russian engine, wooden flying surfaces and metal fuselage. This aircraft is still around, preserved in Finland. The Finns flew Brewsters, at least a few of them, almost to the end of the 1940s, making them the last flying Brewster aircraft anywhere. None of the Finnish B-239s were set aside for preservation which is unfortunate for a Brewster would have been a fine symbol for a nation that had little else but courage to fight with. 80,000 Finns died in the war with Russia and another 150,000 were disabled, terrible losses for a country so small.

Brewsters for the British

In 1939, the British Purchasing Commission, in a panic for war materials to keep Hitler out of England, made the mistake of contracting with Brewster for 170 Buffalos (serials W8131-8250 and AN168-217) to be operated as land-based fighters for the Royal Air Force. Designated B-339E by Brewster, the aircraft were basically similar to the F2A-2. All specialized naval equipment had been removed. Belgium had also ordered Buffalos (B-339B) but the country fell before the aircraft could be delivered so twenty-eight machines (AS410-437) on the contract were

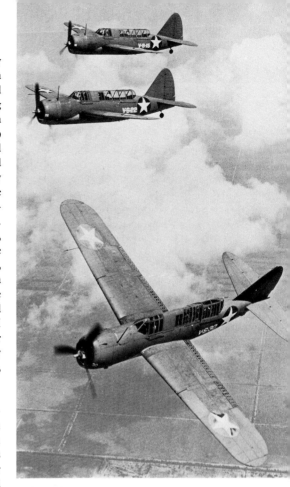

Brewster attempted to dominate Naval fighter and dive bomber categories with the F2A and the Buccaneer, a dive bomber design that has been classified as 'the worst American production aircraft of World War Two'. The aircraft was similar to the earlier B-240 design but larger. Powered by a Wright Cyclone R-2600 of 1,700 hp, the Buccaneer was capable of carrying an internal bomb load of 1,000 lbs. In 1940, the British Purchasing Commission, again making an unwise choice, ordered 750 of the dive bombers to be designated Bermuda I. The USN ordered 140 SB2A-1s. The Dutch also ordered a number of the machines but these were taken over by the Navy as SB2A-4s.

A total of 771 Buccaneers and Bermudas were built but none ever saw combat and a good many were never assigned to any operational units, in fact it is thought that many of the machines, after they were test flown, were stored until being scrapped. Brewster's dominance of naval aviation was to be a dismal failure and not the rosey picture painted for one of their posters of Buccaneers roaring off the deck of a carrier while being guarded overhead by Buffalos.

transferred to the British order.

The first Buffalos to actually reach Britain were the Belgian machines which were assembled and tested at Church Fenton. The English test pilots were vocal about the Buffalo and its total unsuitability for combat over Europe. Thus, the majority of the Buffalos were diverted to the Far East where they were to become the standard day fighter, a tragic and stupid move.

Buffalos began arriving in Singapore

where they were uncrated and assembled. Two RAF squadrons, Nos. 67 and 243, were formed to take on the tubby fighters. The English had made the mistaken assumption, as America did, that the Japanese were poorly equipped with obsolete fighter aircraft and ill-trained aircrews. From the day of the Pearl Harbor attack, the RAF Buffalos went into action. Two of the type became the first Buffalos to fire their guns in anger when they strafed Japanese landing forces on the coast of Malaya. 243 Squadron had virtually all of its aircraft destroyed on the ground, as they sat parked in neat rows, during late January when the Japanese bombed Kallang. The English realized how poor the Buffalo was and made frantic attempts to remedy the situation. All guns were replaced with 0.303 machine-guns, ammunition was restricted, and the fuel load was cut to a meagre 84 gallons but, of course, these modifications made little difference to the Buffalo's wallowing performance and the ones that were not destroyed on the ground were quickly shot out of the air by the 'primitive' enemy fighters. By May 1942, all Buffalos in Royal Air Force service had been destroyed.

When the RAF began receiving its Buffalos in the Far East, it was agreed to help bolster the aerial defenses of New Zealand and Australia by supplying those nations with Buffalos. RNZAF Squadron 488 was based at Singapore with about two dozen Buffalos which were quickly decimated when the Japanese attack on Singapore intensified.

The Australians were also misguided into preparing contracts for the purchase of about 240 Buffalos and the RAF agreed to hand some of their early deliveries over to the RAAF. Enough Buffalos were given to the RAAF to equip two squadrons in Singapore. The RAAF Buffalos, with pilots fighting heroically, lasted a few days longer than the RAF. A small number of Buffalos entered service in Australia during 1942 and thus escaped the Far East massacre. It is unusual to note that a few of these machines entered service with the United States Army Air Force in Australia whose pilots were just as dissatisfied as almost everyone else who had flown the Buffalo. Fortunately the Army pilots did not have to take the Brewsters into battle!

Brewsters for the Dutch

The Netherlands Purchasing Commission in New York was even more frantic than their English counterpart, at least England had the Channel to keep Hitler away. The Netherlands had already fallen by June 1940 but the vast Dutch holdings in the East Indies needed protection, and fast. Contracts were drawn up but engines were in short supply as US manufacturers had not scaled up production to meet demand so part of the Dutch order (B-339D) was equipped with lower horsepower powerplants. Seventy-two fighters were ordered and they arrived in the Netherlands East Indies between April and September 1941 to serve with the *Militaire Luchtvarrtafdeling van bet Koninklijk Nederlands-Indisch Leger*, a mouthful that roughly translated to Royal Dutch East Indies Air Force. Instructors were in short supply and it took quite a while to get the aircraft and crews up to strength. When fighting began, one group of Buffalos was ordered to Singapore to fight with the Commonwealth pilots but the Dutch suffered the same fate as their fellow pilots and the unit was wiped out within a few days.

The surviving Dutch Buffalos were gathered in Java to help fight the massive Japanese invasion. By 9 March, when the surrender came, it was all over for the Dutch Buffalos. Most had been destroyed in the air or on the ground. However, a small number of the fighters fell into Japanese hands. The Japanese tested a few of the machines and sent at least two back to the homeland where they made appearances in Japanese propaganda movies as 'enemy' fighter planes.

Introduction to the Brewster Fighter

by Art Reiners (Major, USAF Ret.)

By 1943, the Buffalo had virtually vanished from the US Military scene.

I first came across an operational Brewster fighter when, as a young second lieutenant during August of 1943, I found myself between assignments at NAS Fort Lauderdale, Florida. With spare time on my hands I decided to check in with the base service squadron and see if any aircraft were available for flying.

In those days it was common practice for a United States Marine Corps service squadron to maintain a small variety of aircraft that could be made available to visiting pilots or to pilots assigned to non-flying duties that had to log their required four hours per month to stay on active flight status. Unlike today, when military aircraft have become so expensive, specialized and complicated, the military pilot of 1943 usually just had to pick a machine, answer a few questions, and then roar off into the wild blue.

As I walked down the flight line, with the hot Florida sun in my face and the weight of the parachute slung over my shoulder, I checked out the various aircraft parked on the ramp. There were a couple of North American SNJ Texans, a popular and well-liked aircraft that we all trained on, a Beech SNB twin-engine hack, and, leaking oil in a large pool, a totally worn-out Brewster F2A.

Well-worn F2A-2 assigned to a training unit. The beat-up condition of the camouflage paint is noteworthy for, at this point in time, the Brewsters were not being kept in the most pristine condition. Note the outer panels of the wing, which were painted White to denote the aircraft's training role. Lieutenant Commander J.C. Clifton is seen flying the fighter on 2 August 1942. Note that the canopy was left in the full open position (USN/16054)

During flight training, when I was learning to become a torpedo bomber pilot, an occupation that suddenly had little popularity after the Battle of Midway, we young student pilots had all heard about the Brewster. Since we were Marines we occasionally heard directly from a few of the Marine survivors of VMF-221 which had been decimated at Midway while flying the Brewster. It was common knowledge that the aircraft was a poor design but we did not worry overly much about that fact since it was an aircraft on the way out, one we would not have to rely on in combat, and, besides, there were so many new and exciting designs on the way. However, a flyable Buffalo in August of 1943 was a rare machine. I had seen two or three at NAS Pensacola during the early part of 1943 where they were apparently being used as mechanic trainers.

I walked into the service squadron office, noticing that another Buffalo squatted near a hangar, appearing to serve as a parts supply depot for the aircraft on the flight line. After introducing myself I asked to be assigned the Brewster for a morning flight. The officer at the desk gave me a bit of a strange look but seemed to understand when I explained that I was trained as a torpedo bomber pilot but was awaiting transfer to a new duty, possibly as a fighter pilot. I showed him my log book, which had plenty of SNJ time along with a few hours in a TBF Avenger and a PBY Catalina (as I have stated, those days *were* different and, if one could get into an aircraft, it was presumed that one should be able to fly it). The duty officer viewed the Avenger as being 'heavy' flight time and I was duly assigned the F2A-2.

We walked out into the hot sun to survey the Brewster. It was painted in a faded and patched Non-Specular Sea Blue with white bands around the outer wing panels to denote its training role. The duty officer ran down a list of dos and don'ts that forbade any form of aerobatics, low-flying, flying over water (the aircraft had the large life raft cylinder removed because of the problems already mentioned), and a restriction on power settings and maximum speed.

I clambered into the cockpit, which was fairly roomy and comparable to the later Grumman naval fighters. Once inside the well-worn cockpit, I immediately noticed the extremely poor visibility of the Brewster, in fact the stubby little fighter was to have the worst visibility of any Marine, Navy or Air Force aircraft that I was to encounter. The fat fuselage, somewhat similar in line to the infamous pre-war Gee Bee speed racers, eliminated virtually all forward visibility and I needed two mechanics to 'walk' me out to

the runway. Once in the air the mid-fuselage wing eliminated virtually all downward view and landings were usually a matter of guessing your final few feet of altitude.

As the Brewster jolted along the tarmac of the taxiway, I soon noticed how bad the brakes were. They were extremely sensitive and prone to grabbing or sticking. It was virtually impossible to coordinate the operation of both brakes and the little fighter wobbled one way then the other as I tried to manage a decent series of S-turns as I taxiied to facilitate a better forward view over the fat fuselage. I had to hang outside of the cockpit while frantically pumping the brakes to get even a marginal view of what was going on in front of the whirling propeller. As Marines we had the feeling that we were not getting top-notch aircraft anyway (the best ones were going to the Navy to operate off carriers) and this Brewster certainly proved that fact!

Once out on the active runway, I advanced the throttle and, after a fairly short takeoff, the Brewster was in the air. The cockpit was pretty noisy as I had been instructed to fly with the canopy open as the canopy was prone to jamming and that could prove disastrous if trouble arose. Once I got the gear retracted and the aircraft up to 'working' altitude I had some time to feel the plane out. I was a bit surprised with the heavy controls and the fact that the machine was *definitely* unstable. After a few more flights in the Brewster I became a bit more familiar with the unstable nature of the fighter, perhaps this stemmed from the thick, barrel-like fuselage which could have hampered air flow around the tail surfaces. After flying the Brewster and comparing notes with a few of my fellow pilots, we came to the conclusion that we would have rather taken our trusty and responsive SNJ trainers into combat

instead of the wallowing Buffalo!

The duty officer had also pointed out that the Brewster had to be taken off and landed in a precise three-point position and he also stressed to make the landings as gentle as possible because the landing gear was weak and replacement struts were hard to get. It was common knowledge that most Brewster squadrons had been below operational strength because so many of the aircraft were down with maintenance problems. I talked to a few mechanics that worked on the Buffalo and they stated that the machines were maintenance nightmares and that spares were difficult to get.

I later went on to join VMF-221 and our commander was Lieutenant Colonel Nathan Post, one of the surviving Brewster pilots from Midway. Nothing was ever officially said about how poor the Brewster was, it was a fact that we just accepted and, by the time I was with 221, we were equipping with the Chance Vought Corsair and we knew we had a machine that could tackle anything that the Japs could put into the air.

All-in-all, I put a grand total of one hour and 40 minutes on the Fort Lauderdale Brewster which added up to a fair number of flights considering that the average flight lasted just ten to 15 minutes. At the time I regarded the F2A-2 as just another aircraft to build up some flying time with. Looking back, I probably flew the last flying example of one of the most notorious (in a historical perspective) American fighter aircraft and, as I thumb through the yellowing pages of a military log book filled with names and numbers of fighter aircraft that have long since disappeared, it is with some satisfaction when I see that brief record of one hour and 40 minutes.

The Buffalos of Fighting Two

This US Navy squadron, composed of enlisted pilots, became the second naval unit to operate the Brewster fighter.

The personnel of Navy Fighter Squadron Two watched with considerable interest as a powerful and pugnacious-appearing monoplane taxiied up and took its place alongside their tubby Grumman biplanes. The date was 7 October 1940 and VF-2 was about to become the second Navy fighter squadron to convert to monoplane fighters. The aircraft was a brand-new Brewster F2A-2, Bureau of Aeronautics number 1406.

To understand the importance of this event to Naval aviation in general and to the men of VF-2 in particular, it is helpful to recall the contemporary world situation. Thirteen months previously, Hitler had launched World War Two. Over that short period of time he had become master of Europe with only one foe remaining. At that very moment the *Luftwaffe* and Britain's Royal Air Force were engaged in determining the fate of the island nation. While the outcome was still in doubt, one factor was already certain: the day of the biplane fighter was over even though courageous pilots still went aloft in antiquated Gloster Gladiators to do battle with Bf 109s. The fast, multi-gun monoplane represented by the Spitfire and the Bf 109 had proven their superiority in the arena of aerial combat.

The need for a monoplane carrier-based fighter had been foreseen by the Bureau of Aeronautics before the war in Europe had broken out. The Grumman XF4F-2 had flown in September of 1937 and was followed by Brewster's entry into the fighter race, the XF2A-1, in December. As related elsewhere in this volume, the Brewster won out over the Grumman but Wildcat development was continued as a safeguard. The production F2A-1s entered service with VF-3 during December of 1939 but remained in service less than a year before being replaced by the F2A-2. The lessons learned over the embattled nations of Europe were carefully analyzed by the Bureau of Aeronautics. They felt that the F2A should be improved by the addition of more guns, armor protection for the pilot, and self-sealing gas tanks. These additions also meant more weight.

On 18 July 1940, a letter from BuAer directed VF-2 to prepare and fly eighteen of their old F2F-1s to Pensacola, where they were needed in the Navy's rapidly expanding flight-training program. Ferry pilots were to pick up the new F2A-2s at Anacostia and fly them back to San Diego. The eighteen F2F-1s were ready on 1 August. However, difficulty was experienced in getting Brewster to deliver the F2As to Anacostia and the

F2A-2s allotted to VF-2 (BuNos 1406 to 1423) did not begin leaving Anacostia until early October. After cross-country flights of from five to eleven days, they arrived at NAS San Diego. Seventeen had been received by 28 October. The eighteenth aircraft had experienced engine trouble and landed at Stinson Airport, Chicago, on 18 October. Delay was experienced in obtaining the replacement parts and the Buffalo (BuNo 1411) did not reach VF-2 until 28 November.

The pilots of VF-2 found the performance of their new aircraft to be an enormous improvement over their earlier biplanes (see

Top
Capturing the drama and tenseness of the early days of World War Two, an F2A-3 is hoisted aboard the USS *Lexington* during early 1942. Note the armed Navy and Marine guards. (USN/80-G-64697)

Bottom
During the early part of 1935, the Fighting Chiefs of VF-2 took delivery of Grumman F2F-1 biplanes which were delivered in full squadron markings, less insignia, as a part of the Navy Grumman contract. However, once in service only a few of the barrel-shaped fighters ever received the squadron insignia. This aircraft was assigned No. 14 which meant that it was the second aircraft of the fifth section with the top half of the cowling painted Willow Green. (USN/416179)

Table One). VF-2 did not operate the newer version of the Grumman biplane, the F3F, but the improvements offered by the Buffalo would have exceeded the performance of the Navy's ultimate biplane fighter. The F2A-2 had nearly twice the horsepower and the maximum speed was nearly 100 mph faster than the F2F. Although the gross weight of the F2A-2 was some 55 per cent greater than that of the F2F-1, the use of wing flaps on the Brewster produced a stalling speed only ten mph higher while the takeoff distance in no-wind conditions was actually somewhat less. Armament on the Grumman biplane had consisted of two 0.30 caliber machine-guns with 1,000 rounds of ammunition per gun. The F2A-2 was equipped with two 0.50 caliber guns in the fuselage each with 200 rounds and two 0.50 caliber guns in the wings with 400 rounds each.

As with most new aircraft, the F2A-2 had its problems. One problem that plagued the early Buffalos was the life raft which was mounted in a cylindrical container immediately behind the pilot's headrest. On three instances, after the aircraft had been parked in the sun too long, the rafts began to inflate on their own causing a fair amount of damage to the Plexiglass. What, if anything, the Bureau suggested to eliminate this problem is not known.

At this time, VF-2 began experiencing the landing gear troubles that would plague the F2A throughout its Navy career. The landing gear of 1410 collapsed during a simulated carrier landing on 10 December. Bent landing gear struts were found on three other aircraft during December. The landing gear was reinforced and further trouble was eliminated until actual carrier landings began to take place.

H.E. Rutherford devised his own method of avoiding landing gear problems when, on 2 January 1941, he landed BuNo 1439 on its belly. In testimony to the strength of the F2A, damage was minor and all repairs were accomplished within the squadron. Then, while landing 1413 on 27 February, he remembered to lower the gear but forgot to lock it in the down position. As he landed the gear folded back up into its wells. The engine was destroyed by 'sudden stoppage' and repairs had to be performed by NAS San Diego.

The squadron appears to have made the transition from biplane to monoplane rather smoothly. The fact that other units were having trouble is shown in a letter, dated 12 December 1940, from BuAer to the commander of VF-2:

'Information which has reached the Bureau

PERFORMANCE OF AIRCRAFT USED BY VF-2 (1940–42)

	F2F-1	F2A-2	F2A-3	F4F-3A
Sea level power (hp)	650	1000	1000	1000
Takeoff power (hp)	700	1200	1200	1200
Gross weight (lb)	3863	5447	6321	6783
Wing loading (lb/ft²)	16.8	26.0	30.3	26.1
Max. speed (mph)	231	324	321	320
Stall speed (mph)	66.1	75.2	80.7	74.8
Time to 20,000 ft (min)	12.7	7.8	9.2	9.4
Max. range (miles)	985	985	965	830
Max. endurance (hours)	8.9	7.5	7.0	5.8
No wind takeoff (ft)	375	362	508	559
25 kt wind take off (ft)	132	151	230	228

from several sources has raised the question of whether or not a service pilot, trained and skillful in the handling of biplanes, suffers a temporary loss of efficiency when shifted to a monoplane prototype.'

The commander was requested to examine the problem in his own squadron and report back but the reply has not been located in government historical files.

A potentially damaging accident was avoided on 23 January when, during a field carrier landing approach, the pilot of 1419 started a left turn with nose high and speed very low. The plane started to spin, the left wing dropped and hit the ground. The pilot succeeded in righting the aeroplane momentarily but again the left wing hit the ground. He then gave the Buffalo full throttle and pulled into the air, went around and made a safe landing realizing what a close brush with death he had experienced.

On 24 February the pilot of 1420 was not as fortunate. Experiencing a sudden loss of power due to carburettor icing, he lowered the landing gear and prepared to make a forced landing on the road adjacent to the Silver Strand State Park. At the last moment, an approaching car caused the pilot to swerve and land on the adjacent beach instead of the hard road surface. The wheels immediately sank into the soft sand and the F2A flipped over on its back, causing extensive damage.

During this time period Navy fighters were expected to also perform dive bombing chores and were accordingly fitted to carry two 100 lb bombs under the wings. Dive bombing practice proved to be hard on the Brewsters. On 29 January, C.W. Brooks was practising 45 degree dives with BuNo 1407. He had reached 400 mph and was performing a six G pullout when he felt a sudden jar. Looking out, he discovered that both ailerons were missing and that the wing tips were bent upward about 45 degrees. Failing to regain

sufficient control of this aircraft, he headed out to sea and jumped. The ailerons fell on North Island NAS while both plane and pilot went into the Pacific. Brooks was rescued but 1407 went to the bottom with only 132 hours total flying time.

The Board of Investigation gave the opinion that 1407 had not been loaded above the design specifications but that its distribution (160 gallons of fuel plus wing guns) had moved the center of gravity to the rear. They noted that NACA tests had shown that, with the center of gravity too far back, dynamic instability occurred at about 400 mph (in a test at eleven G, violent instability took place and the pilot blacked out). The board concluded that the aircraft was sufficiently strong but that the pilot did not use proper techniques in recovering from the dive with the sensitive controls that existed due to the position of the center of gravity.

During the months while the personnel of VF-2 were working up to operational effectiveness, their home carrier, the USS Lexington (CV-2), was engaged in cruises along the West Coast and to Hawaii. On 23 February, the Lexington returned to San Diego and began preparing to take VF-2 aboard. Carrier landings were undertaken and this resulted in the following two accidents:

– 26 February. Oil line of BuNo 1423 broken during raising of landing gear. Forced landing on carrier successful.

– 1 March. BuNo 1439 had landed and was taxiing forward on the flight deck under the direction of the signalman. The signalman passed the pilot on to the next signalman without first looking to see where the next signalman was or even if he was ready to receive the aircraft. The signalman was not ready and, when the pilot could not find him, he immediately applied the brakes. Before he could stop, BuNo 1439 had run into the tail of BuNo 1422.

The *Lexington* embarked its entire Air Group and set sail for Pearl Harbor during March 1941. On board were VF-2's eighteen F2A-2s and three spares assigned to the *Lex*.

For the next five months, VF-2 operated over the waters of the Hawaiian Islands, alternating between the *Lexington* and various shore bases. A sampling of the problems of this period gives some idea of the nature of this tour:

–24 March. BuNo 1413 ground looped on landing at NAB Pearl Harbor.

–31 March. BuNo 1422 landed hard and bounced eight feet before catching the wire.

–16 April. BuNo 1408 ground looped due to brake failure at NAS Mauri.

–12 May. BuNo 1423 had a failure of the propeller governor shortly after takeoff and the pilot began forced landing procedure on the *Lexington*. Just prior to cutting the engine, the governor regained control and the aircraft lurched forward and the Brewster made a hard landing.

–21 May. The outboard landing gear strut of BuNo 1419 failed during landing. Reinforcements had been installed.

–25 June. Pilot retracted landing gear on BuNo 1413 before becoming airborne from USAAF Luke Field on Oahu Island.

–30 June. Pilot had difficulty with the brakes on BuNo 1439 and ground looped the aircraft at Luke Field.

–26 July. Pilot Rutherford could not lower landing gear hydraulically on BuNo 1414 so he had to use the emergency release. On landing, the tail wheel collapsed, leading to a ground loop that the brakes could not control.

–28 July. BuNo 1408 stalled while landing. Wing and elevator scraped the ground. Pilot righted aircraft and completed landing at NAB Pearl Harbor.

It can be seen from these reports that the pilots of VF-2 were putting in a lot of flying time on their Brewsters. In July there was an exchange of aircraft between VF-2 and VF-3, five F2A-2s (BuNos 1413, 1417–18, 1421, 1435) going to VF-3 in exchange for five others (1401–02, 1414, 1436–37). The reason for the exchange is not known.

The *Lexington* left Pearl Harbor and arrived at San Diego near the end of August where VF-2 was disembarked. The last accident to its F2A-2s was reported on 5 September when BuNo 1422 lost hydraulic pressure in flight. The pilot used the hand pump to lower the landing gear but failed to pull the emergency lock and the gear retracted on landing. Total aircraft time was 341 hours.

At the beginning of September, VF-2 began turning its F2A-2s over to the Advanced Carrier Training Group (ACTG) and received F2A-3s. On 12 September 1941, the last -2 was removed from the squadron roll book. VF-3 had turned in their F2A-2s several months before. The F2A-2 served for many more months as an operational trainer for new Navy and Marine Corps pilots, first with the ACTG and then NAS Miami. Only one other Navy squadron used the Brewster fighter during this period and that was VS-201, which operated F2A-2s on the East Coast, until February 1942.

On the second anniversary of the war in Europe the situation was desperate for Britain. Hitler, frustrated in his battles with the RAF, decided that he could bring Britain to its knees without an invasion. He turned his attention to the East and to Russia. In quick succession, Yugoslavia, Greece, and Crete were overrun. The campaign in Russia proceeded smoothly and the fall of Moscow seemed only a matter of time. As part of the plan to destroy the British will and means to resist, the Germans were waging indiscriminate submarine warfare in the Atlantic. Each day might see an incident that would draw America into the war. In the Pacific, Japan, eager for the natural resources of the British and Dutch possessions, welcomed an opportunity to join its Axis partner and extend her empire.

Against this black background, VF-2 began receiving new F2A-3s in the early part of September 1941. This third model of the Buffalo fighter offered no improvement over the aircraft. Maximum speed remained the same. Gross weight was raised nearly 900 lbs, resulting in a slightly increased stalling speed. Takeoff run with no wind was increased by 66 feet. Armament remained the same. By 12 September, VF-2 had eighteen F2A-3s on hand.

VF-2 was the only Navy squadron to use the F2A-3 version and, while some would see service with Marine Corps squadrons, the majority were assigned directly to training units.

Partly because this model brought little change from previous equipment and partly because of the increasing tempo of the world situation, only a short time was allocated for training on the new fighter. Accidents were few and mostly caused by carelessness. On 2 October, two aircraft (BuNos 1527 and 1541) were damaged by a tractor which was using a bungee starter on a nearby aircraft. A few days later saw 1527 again the innocent victim of carelessness, when 1536 taxiied into the Buffalo. Both 1527 and 1541 were turned over to NAS San Diego for repairs and were left behind when, on 14 October, *Lexington* and VF-2 were on the way back to

Pearl Harbor. VF-2's complement was twelve F2A-3s and five others were assigned to the *Lex* as spares.

Lexington was west of the Hawaiian Islands on the 23rd for fleet exercises. On 27 October, the entire Air Group participated in a simulated attack on Pearl Harbor. It is not known how much VF-2 learned from this exercise but events were soon to prove that Pearl Harbor had failed to learn one important lesson: that an enemy-based attack on the Fleet in Pearl Harbor was within the realm of possibility.

During October and November there occurred a series of accidents involving the arresting gear of the *Lexington* and Buffalos of VF-2:

–25 October. Arresting wire broke and BuNo 1528 skidded into a turret.

–25 October. BuNo 1538 made a normal landing but the wire ran out to full length and the aircraft struck the barrier and nosed over.

–6 November. Pilot D.C. Barnes and BuNo 1540 made a normal landing but the wire broke and the aircraft hit the number one turret.

–18 November. While making a night landing, BuNo 1530 came in high and fast and touched down between the sixth and seventh wire. The hook bounced over the seventh and engaged the eighth. The wire parted and the plane crashed into the barrier. A flight deck crew member lost his leg to the whipping wire.

Another accident occurred on 12 November at Ford Island when BuNo 1530 made a wheels up landing due to incorrect piloting procedure.

The *Lexington* was back in Pearl Harbor for Thanksgiving. Then, on 5 December, the carrier sailed out of Pearl on a rush mission to deliver eighteen SB2U-3 Vindicators of VMBS-231 to Midway Island. Included in Task Force 12 were the heavy cruisers *Chicago*, *Portland*, and *Astoria* and the destroyers *Porter*, *Flosser*, *Drayton*, *Lamson*, and *Mahan*. As the *Lexington* steamed out of the harbor, she sailed past the orderly rows of majestic battleships anchored alongside Ford

Right
F2F-1 Nos. 4, 5, and 6 airborne over San Diego, California, on 7 July 1939. These aircraft comprised the second section of VF-2 and the cowls were painted white. The F2F was powered with the R-1535-72 engine of 700 hp and could achieve a maximum speed of 231 mph. The little fighters were very nimble, a feature that the Brewsters lacked. (USN/409229)

Island. In eight days the *Lexington* would be back but by then the mighty battle force would be destroyed and the defense of the United States would lie with the *Lexington* and its fellow carriers.

War Diary of VF-2

–7 December 1941. At 0822 the *Lexington*, under the command of Captain F.C. Sherman, was some 800 miles out of Pearl Harbor and only 400 miles from Midway when a message was received from Admiral H.E. Kimmel, Commander in Chief Pacific (CINCPAC): 'Air raid on Pearl Harbor. This is no drill!' At 0840 the call to general quarters was issued. At 0930, six F2A-3s were launched to serve as Combat Air Patrol (CAP), at 1016 these were followed by eleven more F2A-3s. VF-2 was out in near full strength. At 1218 a radar contact was reported bearing 269 degrees and at a distance of 43 miles. The CAP investigated and found a friendly PBY. VMBS-231 was to have flown off at noon but these plans were cancelled when the Force commander, Rear Admiral J.H. Newton, ordered an immediate return to Pearl. Then, on orders from C. in C. Pacific, TF-12 changed course to the south to be in position to intercept if the Japanese force which had attacked Pearl were retiring to their base at Jaluit Atoll in the Marshall Islands.

–8 December. By noon, C. in C. Pacific was convinced that the Japanese attacking force was not retiring south and TF-12 was ordered to return to Pearl. A few hours later, word was received that Johnston Island was under attack. The Task Force went charging off in that direction but before the *Lexington* could launch the air group, word was received that the report was erroneous. Course was reset for Pearl. At 1550, the *Chicago* reported a radar contact: 'Many bandits bearing 235 degrees, distance 30 miles, closing.' At 1618, the *Portland* reported being under attack. The fighters of VF-2 were sent to assist but when they arrived they found a lone PBY. In return for their assistance the F2A-3s were fired on by the *Portland's* jittery gunners (it seems that the PBY had attacked the heavy cruiser *Portland* after it had reported finding an enemy carrier 'camouflaged to look like a heavy cruiser'.) Fortunately, everyone's aim was poor and no hits were scored during this 'engagement'.

–13 December. Task Force 12 was redesignated Task Force 11. At 1357 the *Lexington* was underway with TF-11 under orders to raid Jaluit. This raid was only one part of a plan to take pressure off Wake Island. After clearing the harbor, all planes of the Air Group were landed. Aircraft taken aboard included twenty-one F2As, thirty-two SBDs and fifteen TBDs.

–16 December. At 0757, Dauntlesses 2-B-2 and 2-B-3 reported dropping two bombs on an enemy carrier at a distance of 95 miles from the *Lex*. Both bombs missed. An attack group of sixteen SBDs, thirteen TBDs and seven F2As was sent out but returned without making contact. Since the bombers reported that the 'carrier' was dead in the water, that no personnel were sighted on deck, and that no anti-aircraft fire had been encountered, it was assumed that this object was really an abandoned dynamite barge which had been reported in the area.

–20 December. On the basis of intelligence estimates of enemy aircraft and submarine strength in the Marshalls, the commander of TF-11 called off the attack on Jaluit and decided to attack the alternative target, Makin. (Not only were the intelligence estimates grossly exaggerated but an attack on Jaluit would have produced little of value for, instead of being a major Japanese base as assumed by intelligence, Jaluit was the site of only a half-finished seaplane base.) Before the attack on Makin could be launched, CINCPAC ordered TF-11 to turn northwest and join TF-14 and the *Saratoga* in an attempt to relieve Wake.

–22 December. TF-11 and TF-14 were ordered to abandon the attempt to relieve Wake and to return to Pearl.

–23 December. Wake surrenders.

–27 to 28 December. VF-2 based at Ford Island.

–29 December. Air Group returns to *Lexington*. Aircraft available: seventeen F2As, fifteen TBDs, and thirty-three SBDs.

–30 December to 2 January 1942. *Lexington* on war patrol in Oahu, Johnston, Palmyra Island triangle.

–3 January 1942. VF-2 landed at MCAS Ewa.

–4 to 6 January. VF-2 based at MCAS Ewa. Conducted training flights and stood morning and evening alerts under the control of the 7th Pursuit Interceptor Command.

–7 January. *Lexington's* Air Group back on board with seventeen F2As, thirty-six SBDs, and thirteen TBDs.

–10 January. At 1020, 2-F-11 (pilot Lt[jg] F. Simpson) and 2-F-8 (pilot D.E. Barnes) sighted an enemy submarine on the surface about 100 miles west of Johnston Island. The submarine submerged when approached. Simpson reported contact by message drop on the *Lexington* at 1057. At 1230, search groups were launched. Included were four TBDs each armed with two 325 lb depth charges set to go off at a depth of 50 ft. At 1323, 2-F-17 (pilot Lt(jg) Rinehart) in company with 2-F-10 (pilot NAP C. Brewer) made a radio report of sighting a submarine on the surface; bearing south, distance 80 miles. Rinehart and Brewer withdrew to an altitude of 8,000 ft and coached 2-T-10 and 2-T-14 (pilots Ens N. Starrie and NAP Talkington respectively) to the submarine. The TBDs commenced their approach down-sun at 2,000 ft and made a bombsight controlled run of 3,000 yards at a speed of 118 mph. The approach was from abaft the beam of the submarine which was still on the surface. 2-T-10 released two depth charges in salvo which were estimated to land at 100 ft and 124 ft astern, one in the wake and one slightly to starboard. The depth charges of 2-T-14 failed to release and the pilot went around for another try. As the submarine began to submerge, 2-F-17 and 2-F-10 made strafing attacks, opening fire with 0.50 caliber machine-guns at above 3,000 ft altitude and pulling out of their dives at 1,000 ft and 100 ft respectively. Tracers were observed striking the hull of the submarine before it got under water. Armor piercing (AP) ammunition was used with two AP to one tracer. In all, 650 rounds were expended. Meanwhile, 2-T-14 had gained a position up-sun and commenced a glide attack. The charges were released at about 1,400 ft. Observers in the other aircraft saw these two depth charges drop in salvo and estimated that they struck the water 50 to 75 ft ahead of the submarine and in line of its movement. When the depth charges exploded, the details of the submarine's superstructure were still visible indicating that it was not more than 35 ft below the surface. NAP Brewer, who was in the best position to view this attack, was positive in his statement that the bow of the submarine jerked abruptly to the right at the instant of the explosion. A small slick, different in appearance from that accompanying the first explosions, appeared on the surface. No further view was had of the submarine or of its wake. The wake, which had been visible until the last attack, ceased to show. No observer saw it reappear beyond the explosion zone. The attack aircraft returned to the carrier at 1852. The official claim was for possible minor damage. Thus ended the first and the last encounter between a Navy Buffalo and the enemy.

–16 to 18 January. VF-2 based at NAB Kaneohe Bay. No flight operations.

–19 January. At 1715, sixteen F2As, thirty-five SBDs and thirteen TBDs landed aboard and the *Lexington* was underway for an offensive patrol north-east of Kingman-Christmas Island line.

–21 January. *Lexington* ordered to attack Wake Island.

-23 January. The Task Force's only tanker, the *Neches*, was sunk by a torpedo. Since continuing without refuelling was impossible, the Wake Island attack had to be cancelled.
-25 January. VF-2 back at NAB Kaneohe Bay.
-26 January. VF-2 moved to Ford Island.
-27 January. VF-2 moved to MCAS Ewa, where they transferred eighteen F2A-3s to VMF-211 and received eleven F4F-3As from the Pearl Harbor Battle Force Pool.

The activities of VF-2 during the nightmarish month of December 1941 can be summarized as follows: **a**) Three preparations to attack enemy surface forces (south of Pearl, off Johnston Island, and off Wake Island). All cancelled. **b**) Two preparations to attack enemy land bases (Jaluit and Makin). Both cancelled. **c**) One attack launched against an abandoned barge which they failed to locate. **d**) Interception of one friendly PBY. **e**) One incident of being fired on by own forces.

On 3 December, VF-2 reported to the Bureau that they had 'ceased all operations until enemy contact became imminent. Three more F2A-3 landing struts failed on normal landings. Seventeen fighters available but with progressive failure beginning in twelve. Make expeditious delivery of reinforced struts.'

During this same period VF-2 lost three F2A-3s in operational accidents:
-4 December. Pilot AAM1C (NAP) C. Allard and BuNo 1544 hit the barrier after floating down the deck. Damage was so severe that the aircraft was beyond repair and dumped overboard.
-26 December. H.E. Rutherford and BuNo 1529 had a fuel leak develop while on antisubmarine patrol. The leak, in the cockpit, soon became a thick stream of fuel. Loss of fuel pressure caused the engine to quit and, at 1122, the pilot made a successful forced landing in the water near *Monaghan*. The Buffalo sank in 1.5 minutes and the pilot was successfully rescued. Total aircraft time 151 hours.
-29 December BuNo 1540 and Lt[jg] F. Borries Jr. hit the carrier ramp while landing at 1307. Buffalo fell into the ocean and the pilot was rescued by *Monaghan*.

The information gathered for this view of VF-2 had to rely heavily on information collected from official BuAer Trouble Reports. In the absence of the individual aircraft flight logs, these accident reports are the only source of detailed information concerning the individual aircraft. However, constant reference to these reports may mislead the reader into thinking that VF-2's experience with the F2A was nothing but

'one darned accident after another'. This situation can be brought into proper perspective by calculating the average number of accidents per aircraft flying hour. The average number of hours flown by the aircraft can be estimated from the hours reported for those that crashed near the end of the period of service. For the purpose of this calculation, a 'serious' accident is defined as one requiring more repair work than could be carried out by the squadron.

In the eleven months VF-2 operated F2A-2s, an average of eighteen aircraft were kept operational. The total flight time per aircraft was around 300 hours. One aircraft was lost and there were eleven serious accidents. An average eighteen F2A-3s were operational and the average flight time per aircraft was 200 hours. This works out to one accident for every 330 aircraft hours.

A much more important fact is that there were no fatalities or serious injuries during the entire time VF-2 operated F2As.

Buffalo finished in overall Non-Specular Light Grey. It is thought that this is one of the aircraft used by VF-2 as it was seen awaiting transfer to a training unit. All unit markings have been painted out. The photograph was taken after 15 May 1942, when the red disc in the center of the national insignia, along with the colorful tail stripes, was ordered to be removed.

Buffalo versus Wildcat

An item by item comparison of the performance of the Brewster F2A-3 and the Grumman F4F-3A fails to bring out any substantial differences between these two aircraft. However, events indicated that there was, in fact, a very great difference in their effectiveness as a fighter. The Grumman F4F, in the skies over Guadalcanal, became one of the immortal fighters of World War Two. The Brewster F2A, flown by the USMC pilots of VMF-221 participated in the Battle of Midway and lost thirteen out of nineteen aircraft. This was the only time American pilots were to fly the F2A against enemy fighter opposition.

Thus the career of the Brewster with the operational squadrons of the Navy was very limited. The speed at which the F2A was phased out of Navy service and the immediate availability of production quantities of the once 'backup' F4F is clear indication that the Bureau made the decision to replace the F2A very early. The reason for this change of heart at such an early date is not at all clear. Apparently the seviceability of the F2A left something to be desired, especially with the landing gear. It may be that the increased weight brought about by addition of armor protection, self-sealing gas tanks, and more armament seriously affected the performance of the aircraft but a fighting aircraft needs these items and this would indicate that the Brewster had been 'underdesigned'. However, the story of the Brewster of Fighting Two does not leave one with the impression that the F2A was a 'bad' aircraft but rather that it was woefully inadequate.

Serials and corresponding squadron designations

The first eighteen F2A-2s delivered to VF-2 carried Bureau Numbers 1406–1423 and the corresponding squadron designation 2-F-1 through 2-F-18 respectively. Other F2A-2s later assigned to the squadron were 1401–1404, 1428, 1431, 1435–1439. The squadron designation of these later aircraft are not known.

A total of thirty F2A-3s were assigned to VF-2: 1526–1536, 1538–1541, 1543–1545, 1547, 1549, 1551, 1554, 1556–1558, 1560, 1562, 1564–1566. Corresponding squadron designations are available for only a few: 1527 was 2-F-2, 1529 was 2-F-3, and 1540 was 2-F-5.

Camouflage and markings

The F2As of VF-2 probably appeared in three different color schemes, although definite photographic evidence is available for only the prewar scheme.

All F2A-2s were delivered to VF-2 in the standard prewar scheme of overall Silver with upper surface of the wings Orange-Yellow. The vertical and horizontal tail surfaces were Yellow to identify the aircraft as belonging to the *Lexington* Air Group. Marking details were standard for the time and mention need only be made concerning the aspects unique to the monoplanes. The chevron was carried on the upper surface of the wing, starting at the wing root on the leading edge and extending to near the inboard edge of the ailerons at the trailing edge. The individual aircraft number (1 through 18) appeared in black between the chevron and the National Insignia and was positioned to be read from the tail of the aircraft. The squadron insignia was carried just below the wind screen.

On 28 February 1941, 'An extensive modification of aircraft markings added national star insignia to both sides of the fuselage … and eliminated those on the upper right and lower left wings; discontinued the use of colored tail markings, fuselage bands and cowl markings, except the national insignia, to those least contrasted with the background.' At the same time the aircraft were to be painted overall Light Grey. While it seems reasonable to assume that VF-2's Buffalos were sooner or later painted as prescribed above, there is no photographic evidence because photos of the squadron's Buffalos are extremely rare.

In October of 1941, the order was given to paint the upper surfaces of all Naval aircraft Non-Specular Blue-Grey. A single photo exists to prove this scheme was used in the period after the Pearl Harbor attack.

Specifications

Brewster XF2A-1

Span	35 ft 0 in
Length	25 ft 6 in
Height	11 ft 9 in
Wing Area	208.9 sq ft
Loaded Weight	4832 lbs
Max. Speed	280 mph
Cruise Speed	180 mph
Ceiling	29,800 ft
Range	650 miles
Powerplant	Wright XR-1820-22 of 850 hp

Brewster F2A-1

Span	35 ft 0 in
Length	25 ft 8 in
Height	11 ft 11 in
Wing Area	208.9 sq ft
Empty Weight	4420 lbs
Loaded Weight	5643 lbs
Max. Speed	301 mph
Cruise Speed	160 mph
Ceiling	32,500 ft
Rate of Climb	2100 fpm
Range	960 miles
Powerplant	Wright R-1820-34 of 950 hp

Brewster F2A-2

Span	35 ft 0 in
Length	25 ft 7 in
Height	12 ft
Wing Area	208.9 sq ft
Empty Weight	4216 lbs
Loaded Weight	5942 lbs
Max. Speed	324 mph
Cruise Speed	165 mph
Ceiling	34,000 ft
Rate of climb	2000 fpm
Range	900 miles
Powerplant	Wright R-1820-40 of 1200 hp

Brewster F2A-3

Span	35 ft 0 in
Length	26 ft 4 in
Height	12 ft 1 in
Wing Area	208.9 sq ft
Empty Weight	4630 lbs
Loaded Weight	6321 lbs
Max. Speed	321 mph
Cruise Speed	160 mph
Ceiling	30,000 ft
Rate of Climb	2000 fpm
Range	900 miles
Powerplant	Wright R-1820 of 1200 hp

TABLE TWO

BREWSTER F2As ASSIGNED TO FIGHTING SQUADRON TWO BY MONTH (MAX./MIN.)

	1940			1941													1942	
	OCT.	NOV.	DEC.	JAN.	FEB.	MAR.	APR.	MAY	JUNE	JULY	AUG.	SEPT.	OCT.	NOV.	DEC.	JAN.	FEB.
F2A-2	17/0	18/18	20/20	19/19	18/17	19/18	19/17	18/15	17/15	19/14	19/15	16/1	1/0				
F2A-3											0		19/0	18/17	18/17	21/16	17/4	2/0

2 WILDCAT –
It Held the Line

Grumman's stubby fighter started out life as a biplane, was initially rejected by the US Navy, and turned out to be one of the toughest fighting machines ever built.

During the 1930s there was a young New Yorker named Leroy Grumman who managed to keep his small business afloat by building the retracting landplane gear for Grover Loening's amphibians. As the Depression-crippled 1930s began their long stagger, which would end in the holocaust of the World War Two, Grumman and his design staff either became more ambitious or more determined to avoid the soup lines, for they began working on a new two-place shipboard fighter which was accepted by the Navy in 1931. Designated XFF-1, the all-metal biplane incorporated a retracting undercarriage essentially identical to that of the Loenings, the wheels mounted on telescoping legs which were hauled up by turning a crank in the cockpit by hand.

Grumman and his crew moved into an empty building owned by Fairchild Aircraft Corporation. The building was located at Bethpage out on Long Island and Grumman quickly set up shop and began churning out one biplane type after another; the FF, named Goblin by the Canadians who built it under licence, being followed by the F2F and F3F fighters and the Duck series of utility amphibians. The whole class was giving way to the monoplane however, and Grumman was not about to be left behind.

In November of 1935, the Navy Department's Bureau of Aeronautics was in the market for a new carrier-based fighter. Grumman submitted another biplane under the company designation Design Number 16, this becoming the XF4F-1 when a prototype development contract was awarded on 2 March 1936, but news of competitors' efforts saw it scrapped before more than the general dimensions and appearance had been established.

Brewster's entry in the fighter sweepstakes was a monoplane with retractable gear, the XF2A-1, while Seversky was proposing a navalized version of its P-35. Never one to let

himself be shackled by reluctance to try something new, Grumman tossed out the XF4F-1 and set his crews to work on an entirely new monoplane, the Navy giving the go-ahead on 28 July. The basic designation remained the same, but the XF4F-2 did not bear the slightest resemblance to its predecessor.

Grumman had chosen Pratt & Whitney's Twin Wasp, a 14-cylinder twin-row radial known to the military as the R-1830, as the F4F's power plant. The specific model, the SC-G or R-1830-66, was rated at 1,050 hp for takeoff and was equipped with a single-stage, single-speed supercharger which enabled it to develop 900 hp at 12,000 ft. Prior to the development of the supercharger, the higher an aircraft flew the less *real* horsepower its engine developed, regardless of what its sea-level rating might be. The supercharger, driven off the engine's crankshaft or, through a turbine, by its exhaust gases was essentially a pump which sucked in more air and compressed it before vaporized fuel was injected. By this means the engine could continue to operate at high altitudes in much the same way as it did down on the deck; increased power meant increased speed and control effectiveness, vital considerations for a machine which might have to fight at 20,000 feet or higher. Two-stage, two-speed superchargers were also in the works which would allow a plane to fly even higher, but operation remained basically unchanged even as complexity increased.

With a contract in hand Grumman set the wheels in motion and the XF4F-2 took shape at Bethpage as the F3Fs rolled out of the factory doors and into the waiting hands of the Navy and Marine Corps. Late in the summer of 1937 it was completed and made a

Despite having selected the Buffalo as its new carrier fighter, the Navy felt that Grumman's airplane was worth developing, so issued a second prototype contract for a completely redesigned version, the XF4F-3. The aircraft was rebuilt, its fuselage the only part which remained essentially the same. Since it was in fact the same aircraft its Bureau of Aeronautics serial number 0383 was unchanged.

first flight on 2 September with company pilot Robert L. Hall at the controls. On 23 December, after the usual shakedown intended to bring any flaws to light so they could be taken care of before anyone else got wind of them, Hall flew the plane south to Anacostia, Maryland, where Navy pilots would proceed to thoroughly wring it out. Flights out of the proving ground at Dahlgren, Maryland, were also on the agenda, so

the plane had a busy schedule ahead of it, with periodic trips back to Bethpage for major maintenance thrown in.

As originally completed, the F4F had some design features which are worth mentioning. First, in common with most, if not all, shipboard aircraft of the day, it was equipped with flotation bags in the wings. These were to be inflated with carbon dioxide gas and would pop out of their compartments and theoretically keep the plane afloat long enough after an emergency water landing for search planes to arrive, spot it (the wing's upper surface was painted bright Orange-Yellow on all Navy and Marine aircraft specifically with visibility under this circumstance in mind), and land to rescue the crew, or at least drop rafts and survival gear to keep them alive until a ship could be summoned. The F4F's bags would figure in at least two accidents, discussed later.

Second, the F4F's armament initially was not irrevocably ordained. A pair of 0.30 caliber machine-guns were permanently mounted in the forward fuselage decking, synchronized to fire through the prop arc, with positions for two 0.50s in the wings. These could be removed to allow a 100 lb bomb to be carried, however, an arrangement which was abandoned on the eventual production machines.

Anticipating war with a renascent Germany, France ordered several types of American aircraft, including the F4F, to supplement its own industry's output. Built under the company designation G-36A, the first of these had barely begun flight tests when France was invaded, falling to Germany within a matter of weeks.

At Anacostia Naval Air Station the F4F was flown in competition with the Brewster and Seversky aircraft; the latter, designated NF-1, did not last long, but neither did Grumman's machine. On 11 April 1938, during simulated carrier trials being conducted at Philadelphia, the engine quit on final approach and the pilot had to put down in the nearest open field (which turned out to be a farm operated by the Campbell Soup Company). The plane's landing gear sank into soft ground and it turned turtle, smashing the right wing tip as it went over. The gear itself was badly damaged as were the vertical tail, propeller, and engine cowling, usual in this sort of accident. Hauled back to Bethpage, the F4F was laid up for two weeks while repairs were made, then returned to Anacostia where the Navy announced its decision later that month. The Seversky was out but, despite reaching a higher top speed, the F4F lost to Brewster's F2A, ordered into limited production the following June.

This obviously did not mark the F4F's demise, but it *did* set off a major redesign of the plane with Pratt & Whitney's uprated SC2-G being selected as the new engine. This, with the military designation XR-1830-76, developed 1,200 hp but, with a two-stage supercharger was still churning out 1,000 hp at 19,000 feet. In October 1938, a new contract was awarded for the XF4F-3, the original aircraft being completely rebuilt, the fuselage was the only essentially unchanged structure, and flying on 12 February 1939. From March to May it was again at Anacostia, returned to Bethpage for work, and then went on to the Naval Aircraft Factory to repeat carrier landing and catapult

tests. Some problems were encountered with engine overheating, Grumman engineers altering the cooling flaps, trying various spinner shapes and sizes, and adding cuffs to the bases of the propeller blades; this at last seemed to solve the problem, and became a standard feature on production aircraft. Wind tunnel tests conducted in the National Advisory Committee for Aeronautics' wind tunnel at Langley Field, Virginia, resulted in the XF4F-3's tail surfaces being redesigned.

During August 1939, while the F4F-3 was still engaged in flight tests and was being changed in response to the data thus gathered, the Navy issued its first production contract (for fifty-three aircraft) and Grumman was in the business of building Wildcats, as the fighter had been named. As events would prove, this decision had been made just in time, for the situation both in Europe and the Far East was deteriorating almost hourly, and only the most blindly optimistic still believed that a major war could be averted.

In Japan naval construction programs aimed at bringing that nation up to parity, if not superiority over, the United States and Great Britain had produced six aircraft carriers, with three more building, plus numerous capital ships and small units. Under the guidance of Adolf Hitler, a resentful German people had rebuilt their military machine in secret until, in 1935, they felt so strong that they no longer had to pretend to obey the treaty structures imposed on their country. Now, as the summer of 1939 wound down, Hitler bent on acquiring *Lebensraum*, was preparing to attack Poland as the first step in creating a German empire.

Like the F4F-3 and the 3A, the Martlet I had fixed wings and was armed with four 0.50 caliber guns. Assigned to shore-based squadrons the Martlets' arresting hooks were removed but the small, solid rubber tail wheels remained temporarily at least. (Grumman/7346)

In February 1940, the first production F4F-3 (BuNo 1844) flew, followed in July by BuNo 1845. These two aircraft were armed with two fuselage-mounted 0.30 caliber guns along with two 0.50s in the wings but subsequent machines did away with the guns in the decking and instead mounted four 0.50 calibers in wings stations along with provisions for underwing bomb racks as well. The Wildcat's service ceiling was 37,000 feet, its top speed 331 mph at 21,300, a bit more than 5 per cent. less than what the Navy really had wanted but the readily apparent qualities of the aircraft outweighed the shortcomings.

Rear Admiral John H. Towers, who had learned to fly on the Navy's very first aeroplane, the Glenn Curtiss A-1, had worked his way up to Chief of the Bureau of Aeronautics by 1940, so his opinion carried considerable weight when he came out in the F4F's camp in no uncertain terms, declaring that the test program be given the very highest priority '. . . since those airplanes are urgently needed by the operating squadrons.'

The Navy's Board of Inspection Survey pointed up a number of additional changes which were to be made, but these involved relocating controls, improving cockpit ventilation to eliminate carbon monoxide in the exhaust gases from seeping in, and generally taking care of small details, none of which affected its recommendation that the Wildcat be accepted for shipboard service.

Congress authorized the Navy to build up its air arm in May – there were only 1,741 aircraft in the inventory as of the 14th when the first bill was passed – to 4,500, then 10,000 on the 15th, and soon after to 15,000. As war became likely in Europe, commissions travelled to the United States from France and Great Britain, touring plants and examining those types then in production. Among the aircraft they selected as being the most useful was the F4F, but their orders, in addition to those placed on behalf of the American armed forces, put a system still geared to peacetime schedules and levels under an impossible strain – the time had not yet arrived when dozens of aircraft and scores of engines could be turned out in a single day – so alternative plans were laid.

At this time the French had only a single carrier but two were under construction so the F4F was not a luxury. The French Wildcat had to be adapted to take another engine, however, since Twin Wasps were in short supply. Accordingly the 1,200 hp Wright R-1820-G205A Cyclone was selected, a nine-cylinder radial with a single-speed, two-stage supercharger. Flight tests had barely begun on the first of these planes when the 'Phony War' ended and France was overrun by German forces.

With France out of the war, except for forces which fought on under the Cross of Lorraine, Great Britain took over her Cyclone-powered aircraft, naming them Martlet Is. The first of these was delivered on 27 July 1940, the Navy not receiving its Wildcats until the following month. The Wright installation had attracted official attention in the States, the third and fourth aircraft being modified to use an R-1820 as XF4F-5s and flying in July, and this was not the only other engine considered as a result of production bottlenecks. The single XF4F-6 had an R-1830-90 with a single-stage, two-speed supercharger which still gave it 1,000 hp at 12,500 feet and a top speed of 319 mph at 16,100. As a hedge, ninety-five Twin Wasp-powered fighters were ordered under the designation F4F-3A. By the end of 1941, sixty-five of these had been delivered, going to Marine squadrons where, since they could be expected to fight at lower altitudes than the Navy planes, the reduction in power would not be quite as great a handicap.

Although a total of 578 Wildcats were on order only twenty-two had been delivered to the Navy and Marines by year's end. Navy fighter squadrons VFs 4 and 7 were the first to begin trading in their F3F biplanes for the Wildcats before going aboard, respectively,

CV-4 USS *Ranger* and CV-7 USS *Wasp*. On 16 December 1940, Lt(jg) W.C. Johnson achieved the unhappy distinction of being the first pilot killed in a Wildcat, his engine failing on takeoff when he apparently switched off the main fuel valve rather than turning the control lever for the flaps, the plane crashing almost immediately.

In January 1941, *Wasp* and *Ranger* sailed for Cuba to take part in Fleet exercises, their Wildcats being involved in several accidents, fortunately without fatal results. Some new problems cropped up once the planes were involved in full-scale operations, a series of windscreen failures making a redesign necessary.

Top
The French contracts were not wasted, for Great Britain stepped in and took the G-36As over, these going to Fleet Air Arm fighter squadrons as Martlet Is. Note the curious Americanized version of a British camouflage scheme and the civil testing licence of NXG2 applied to the upper right wing. The civil licence was issued so the aircraft could not be directly identified as instruments of war since, at the time, the United States was maintaining its neutral policy.

Bottom
Grumman's Bethpage factory was literally jammed with Wildcats as this photograph, taken soon after the beginning of the war, shows. Plans were already being made to shift production from Grumman to General Motors to make way for the F6F-3 Hellcat within two months of the Pearl Harbor attack. Note the Royal Navy Goose in the foreground.

Top

Nice aerial study of an early Wildcat on a test flight from Grumman's Bethpage factory. The type of markings that this Wildcat is wearing became mandatory on 26 February 1941. Overall camouflage consisted of Non-Specular Blue Grey on all upper surfaces and Non-Specular Light Grey on all lower surfaces. Definite lines of demarcation between the two colors were avoided and the painter joined the colors in an irregular, wavy line and then feathered the colors into each other while still wet. At this time the national insignia was removed from the upper right and the lower left wing surfaces. The distance from the wing tip to the center of the insignia was to be equal to the chord length of the wing. The new order specified that the national insignia was also to be applied to both sides of the rear fuselage and the diameter of this insignia was not to exceed 24 inches. The wording 'U.S. NAVY' was reduced to one-inch black letters, moved from the rear fuselage to the vertical tail and applied as just 'NAVY' above the Bureau Number. The use of the vertical red, white, and blue rudder stripes became mandatory. As one will see from other photographs in this book that were taken during the same period, the rules were often loosely followed, especially during combat. (R. Arnold)

Center right

The *Hornet* meets its end on 26 October 1942 during the Battle of Santa Cruz. The *Hornet* had taken a number of hits from Japanese carrier aircraft, a number of its Wildcats and Dauntlesses going down with the carrier as the Pacific closed over the sinking veteran. (USN/32816)

Bottom right

With a roar of radial engines a flight of Wildcats turns up before launching for a mission. Plane handlers had to be very careful of their movements during this phase of carrier operations for the whirling invisible discs could be very fatal. (USN/80-G-17513)

During March the second fatal crash of a Wildcat was recorded, Lt Seymour Johnson probably passing out due to the failure of his oxygen system while flying at an altitude of almost 40,000 feet. With the unfortunate lieutenant unconscious, the plane edged into a vertical dive and was travelling so fast when it hit the ground that rescue crews had to dig down 15 feet to recover the mashed engine, the largest recognizable part. Later the same month, a Wildcat from newly commissioned VF-42, *Ranger*'s Scouting 41 renumbered and changed into a fighter squadron, ran into trouble when, during a dive, the flotation bags inflated without warning. The pilot was able to pull out after making the nasty discovery that the sliding hood had jammed, tearing the bags loose in the process, but ten days later another VF-42 pilot was not so lucky. In this instance Ensign Harry Howell was flying straight and level when the bags in the Wildcat popped out. He was able to tear one off but the second stayed on and the plane went out of control, killing Howell in the ensuing crash.

This dangerous problem was eventually solved by eliminating the bags entirely, counting on the natural buoyancy of the Wildcat's sealed fuel tanks and an intact skin to keep the plane afloat long enough for the pilot to make his escape. It would, of course, eventually be dragged under by the weight of the engine even if the F4F was otherwise undamaged, but providing he was also uninjured the pilot would have more than enough time to get out, deploy his life raft, and relax on the bosom of the deep until a Catalina search and rescue aircraft hove into view.

The Wildcat's landing gear caused its own share of problems, although these generally resulted in red faces and rounds of drinks for everyone at the victim's expense. Like the earlier biplanes, the F4F used a retraction system driven through chains and gears by a hand crank. As the pilot literally wound the gear up his whole body would move and it was the usual thing to see an F4F bobbing up and down as it climbed out, for he would be jiggling the stick back and forth slightly as he turned the crank handle. This also created trouble for pilots used to fixed-gear biplanes for they would forget to lower the gear and find themselves skidding along on the aeroplane's belly. Sometimes fire resulted from this mistake for part of the fuel system plumbing ran through the lower fuselage.

Deliveries picked up during 1941 with 183 F4F-3s reaching Navy and Marine units in addition to the 3As. With squadrons being renumbered, *Wasp* and *Ranger* had two Wildcat-equipped outfits apiece by the end of the year, the Marines were busily swapping

their F2A Buffalos and biplanes and aircraft were also reaching England.

No. 804 Squadron at Halston was the first Fleet Air Arm unit to receive the ex-French Martlets, turning in its Gloster Sea Gladiators beginning in October 1940. As it turned out the first F4Fs to engage an enemy were not American, a pair of 804 Squadron aircraft patrolling above the Home Fleet's anchorage at Scapa Flow, North of Scotland in the Orkney Isles, spotted an inbound bogy on Christmas Day and climbed to investigate. Lt L.V. Carter and Sub-Lt Parke mentally flipped through the recognition photographs and silhouettes as they closed with the stranger, snooping where it did not belong. Tapered wings, single vertical tail, twin radials, bulged cockpit enclosure: it was a German bomber, a Junkers Ju 88! With only three 7.9mm MG 15 machine-guns firing aft, two in the rear of the cockpit, the third in a ventral gondola, it was not heavily armed, but *could* put up a stiff fight, so neither English pilot was about to charge in as though this was another Balaclava. Weaving in through a web of white smoke trails left by tracers the Martlets opened fire, flashes indicating hits as half-inch slugs punched through the Hun's metal skin. An engine nacelle threw off chunks of dural as bullets walked across it, then dense black smoke poured out and the prop jerked to a stop. The second engine also began to falter and the Junkers headed for the deck; both Grummans hot on its tail, the German aircraft's lucky four-man crew emerging from a bent

Top and Center Right
With the throttle shoved all the way forward, an F4F-4 roars down a carrier deck and lifts into the air. Coding on the side of the fuselage indicates that this aircraft was the No. 4 Wildcat of VF-29. (USN)

Bottom right
A confusing blend of markings! A tightly grouped cluster of Wildcats and Douglas Dauntlesses display the confused application of aircraft markings during the early stages of World War Two. On 15 January 1942, a change of regulations authorized the national insignia to once again be carried in four different wing positions. The insignia was to be carried inboard from the tip a distance equal to ⅓rd of the distance from the tip to the fuselage and was to be as large as possible without extending on to the aileron. The insignia on the fuselage was to be 24 inches in diameter; if this was too large to be applied, the insignia was to be moved forward on the fuselage if necessary. Stripes, consisting of seven red and white horizontal bars, were applied to the entire rudder surfaces. The balanced portions of the rudder which extended past the hinge line were painted the same color as the tail surfaces. The national insignia and the rudder stripes were applied using non-specular colors. As can be seen, the above regulations were very loosely interpreted and many variations are recorded (USN/80-G-17532)

fuselage to find they had become guests of the King for the duration. This marked the first victory by an American type in service with the English armed forces, a convoluted accomplishment but one which was good for morale on both sides of the Atlantic.

The prop of one of the fighters involved, serial BJ562 (out of the last groups of Martlet Is to be delivered before the Martlet II appeared), was sent to the United States with an appropriate ceremony and proudly displayed in the foyer of the Navy Department's Washington headquarters.

At the same time the Cyclone-powered Martlet Is were arriving in England, flight tests of the Martlet II, equivalent to the R-1830-90 powered F4F-3A, began at Bethpage, the first example being ready for delivery in March of 1941. Like the American fighters, the Martlet II was originally built with fixed wings, but with the eleventh example, a manually-folded wing was in-troduced. Designed in response to Navy requests for an aircraft easier to store aboard ship, the wing mechanism was at first hydraulically operated but this was altered once the system had been evaluated and approved to save weight. With the introduction of this wing a new Wildcat model also entered the picture, the F4F-4, its armament increased to six 0.50 caliber machine-guns. The first example, XF4F-4, BuNo 1897, flew on 14 April 1941, going to VF-42 in May for carrier trials aboard CV-5 USS *Yorktown*. Ninety Martlet IIs were eventually ordered by England, becoming the first of the type to fly from Royal Navy carriers, with deliveries beginning in 1941. Thirty F4F-3As were built for the Greek government but they were taken over at Gibraltar, where they had been held up following Germany's invasion of that country in support of its bumbling ally, Italy, becoming Martlet IIIs. Another ten 3As were ordered directly from Grumman, bringing the total for the Martlet III to forty aircraft.

Great Britain was quick to realize the need for small carriers which could be cheaply and easily produced, based on existent freighter designs, these sailing with the convoys themselves and providing vital air cover against attacks by submarines as well as enemy aircraft. The United States would adopt this same idea early in the war, intending to use the CVE (or 'Jeep') primarily as a transport but soon realizing its value in combat roles.

A picture of Wildcat power on the open sea. The Wildcat served faithfully until the end of World War Two on the escort or 'Jeep' carriers. This mix of Wildcats and Avengers is seen on the USS *Hoggaat Bay* **(CVE-75) as four other Jeeps loaded with Wildcats and Avengers steam line astern. The photograph was taken on 2 July 1945. (USN/375480)**

Grumman F4F-3 Wildcat

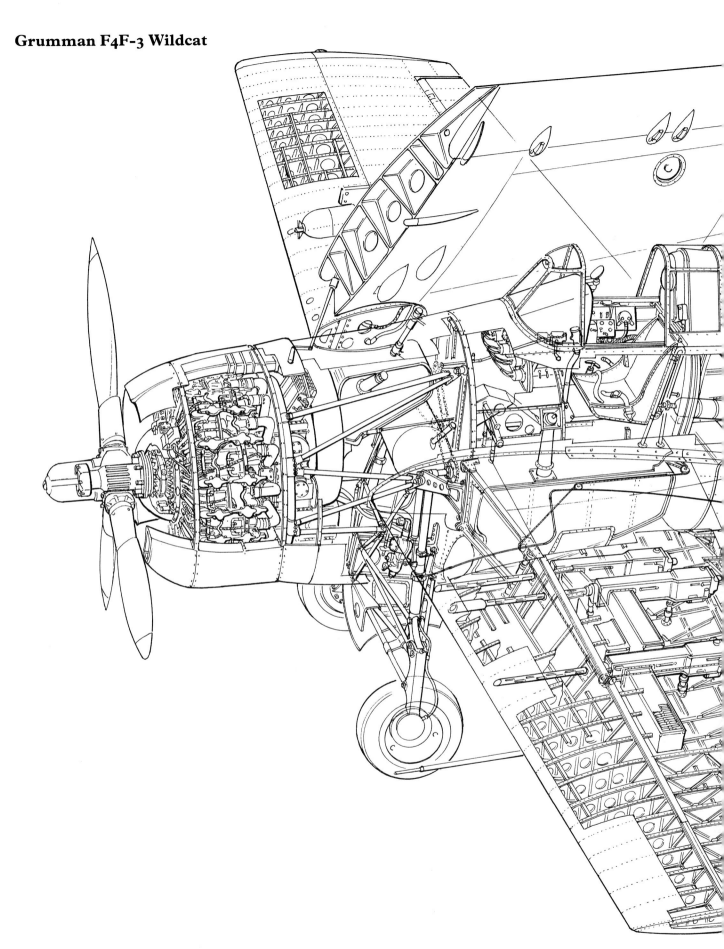

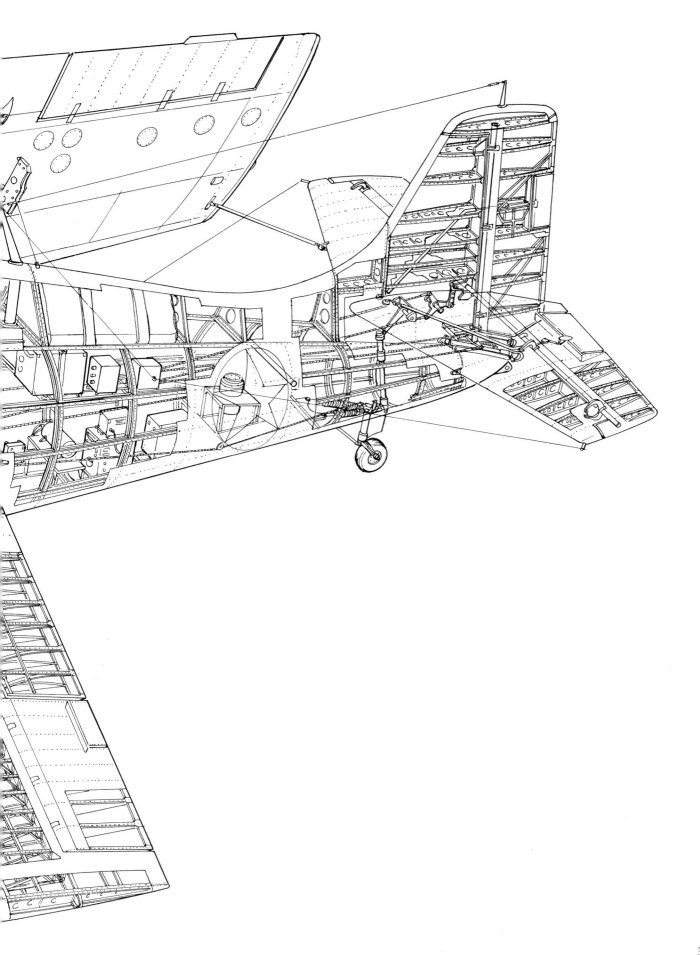

On 20 September, Martlets from the escort carrier HMS *Audacity* intercepted and destroyed a Focke-Wulf Fw 200 *Condor*, these dangerous bombers operating from bases in occupied France and Norway and making the life of the convoy's sailors hell by guiding U-Boat wolfpacks to this tempting and virtually helpless target. Earlier, Hurricanes had been catapulted from specially modified ships, but the economics of the mission which automatically meant the loss of a fighter regardless of results achieved were too wasteful. With the introduction of the 'baby flattop', German control of the Atlantic was badly weakened and, following America's entry into the war, eventually ended.

1941 was a busy year for the Wildcat's designers. Not only did they come up with the folding wing, they also developed a photo-recon. version, the F4F-7. All armament was removed, fuel tanks holding 555 gallons of 100-octane aviation gas were stuffed into the fixed wing (bringing the aircraft's total capacity to 685 gallons, claimed to be adequate to keep it in the air for 24 hours), emergency dump lines were run down through the aft fuselage and out below the rudder, a vertical camera was mounted behind the pilot's seat, and an autopilot was installed. The prototype, BuNo 5263, flew on 30 December 1941, and was at Anacostia two weeks later for service trials. On its first flight from the air station its wing tanks had been filled with water as a safety precaution, but the pilot went up to altitudes which froze the dump lines and valves. He did not realize the situation until he tried to jettison the load prior to landing to reduce weight, and was forced to divert to nearby Washington National where he made a long, hot, but otherwise uneventful landing.

The Dash Seven also figured in a flight which remained a secret throughout the war, Lt Cmdr 'Andy' Jackson covering 3,000-odd miles in an eleven hour-long hop from the East to the West Coast. Although 100 F4F-7s were ordered, only twenty-one were actually completed as such, the balance being cancelled in favor of fighters.

As 1941 drew to a close, F4Fs were rapidly replacing all other shipboard fighters, although the Marines were still saddled with some Buffalos and had a few F3F-2s and F4B-4s in service as trainers. Wildcats were already in action with the Royal Navy and it seemed only a matter of time before Japanese imperialism and American commitments in the Pacific and Far East clashed. In early December hopes for continued peace received a boost when ambassadors from the Emperor Hirohito's government arrived in Washington to conduct talks aimed at settling these differences, and some progress appeared to be in motion.

On the first Sunday of the month, passers-by noticed smoke coming from the Japanese Embassy's chimneys, but it was a cold, clear day so fires came as no surprise. The local time was 1:55 in the afternoon, if anyone happened to check a clock, but 6,000 miles to the west it was just coming up on 8 a.m. as marines, sailors, and soldiers prepared to run up the colors at military installations scattered around the islands of the Territory of Hawaii. Aboard the battleships tied up two by two along the wharves of Naval Station Ford Island, Oahu, it was just another Sunday, a welcome break from maneuvers. Attracted by the noise of aircraft engines a few men sneaked glances at the sky as they waited for the bugle calls which would bring them to attention. Who, they wondered, was

out flying this early, and on a weekend as well?

They were about to find out, and the Wildcat was going to be set on a course which would bring it long-lasting and roundly deserved fame.

There was only one thing the American Navy could be grateful for as it began a massive clean-up after the Japanese attack on Hawaiian bases: no carriers had been in port at the time, *Saratoga* was being worked on in a West Coast yard, *Enterprise* was on its way back to Pearl after delivering VMF-211's F4F-3s to Wake Island, and *Lexington* was carrying aircraft to the Marine garrison on Midway. Eleven Wildcats from 211 were strafed on the line at Ewa, a Marine Corps Air Station on Oahu, nine being destroyed or damaged, but otherwise the F4F played no part in 7 December's events.

Wake's turn was coming and would mark the first time Wildcats flown by American pilots crossed swords with the enemy. On 8 December, the Wake Island squadron was on the alert, having been notified by radio of the raid on Pearl, maintaining four-plane patrols to make up for the base's lack of radar. At 1158 (using the military's 24-hour system of time-keeping this indicates two minutes to noon), thirty-six Imperial Navy G4M1 Betty medium bombers from Roi, one of the islands

The Wildcat makes history. The first aircraft carrier takeoff using rocket assisted units was accomplished on 18 March 1944 with Commander Leroy Simpler at the controls. (USN/46501)

which make up Kwajalein Atoll, raced in from the southwest at 1,500 feet, having made their final approach under cover of rain squalls, and battered island installations. Worse, seven of the eight Wildcats on the ground had been destroyed, the survivor being damaged but repairable; in addition one plane returning from patrol smashed its propeller on debris while taxiing. Thus, within the space of a few minutes the Red Lions had only four Wildcats left, the only source for spares being wrecked. After heroic efforts, Wake fell on 23 December, victorious Japanese posed for snap-shots in front of the hulks of the well-used Wildcats.

1942 opened with the United States virtually driven from the Pacific. Every major base in the Far East had fallen, as had Wake and Guam, leaving only the Hawaiian Islands, Midway, and Samoa in American hands. The eagle wasted little time in striking back, however, both to boost morale at home and show the Japanese that they were not going to have an easy time of it after all. Those carriers the Japanese had missed at Pearl Harbor would now come into their own, raiding the Gilberts and Marshalls. On 20 February, *Lexington's* air group tore into Rabaul, on the top of New Britain; picking up an inbound raid *Lady Lex* conned a combat patrol from VF-42 on to these bandits, Lt Edward H. O'Hare splashing five Bettys by himself and earning the Congressional Medal of Honor in the process.

Fights between Wildcats and Zero-Sens, or Zekes as they quickly came to be called pointedly emphasized a number of things: first, any pilot who tried to take on the Japanese fighter in a low-level dogfight was bucking for a pine box, since the Zeke could out-turn, out-climb and out-run the F4F.

Second, the Wildcat was heavier and stronger, even though out-gunned, so if he had the advantage of altitude – and better: surprise – its pilot could pick his own time to make a diving attack, firing on the way through the enemy formation, then hightail it for the horizon, either to escape or climb back up for a second pass. Third, the F4F could absorb more damage than the Zeke and still get home. Although vulnerable from the sides and below, the Wildcat pilot sat behind a 25 lb slab of bulletproof glass and 45 lb armor plate, with another 94 lb of steel protecting his backside. In addition the Grumman 'Ironwork's' product could be put through high speed maneuvers which would severely tweak the Zero-Sen, while self-sealing tanks reduced the fire hazard considerably. As gun camera films show, the Japanese aircraft had a distressing tendency to flare like a struck match when an American began walking explosive and armor-piercing bullets over it, its pilots rarely surviving the attack long enough to take to their parachute, assuming their 'warrior spirit' even allowed them to *wear* one.

Wildcats began rolling up an impressive kill ratio as soon as their pilots had learned what they could, and could not, do. By the Battle of Midway, in June, this stood at three to one, climbing to five to one by the year's end. John Thach and Jimmy Flatley had come up with the 'Thach weave', an example of American teamwork which saw two pilots scissoring to keep an eye on each other's tail and improve the chances of spotting unwelcome company before it could do too much harm.

On 7 August, the United States launched its first land offensive, reacting to reconnaissance photographs which showed an airstrip under construction on the island of Guadalcanal; nineteen VMF-223 F4F-4s landed on this patch of dirt, hacked out of the jungle, on the 20th after being catapulted off CVE-1 USS *Long Island*. F4F pilots numbered many aces among their ranks, and not a few winners of the Medal of Honor, but the fight was not one-sided by any means, the Japanese veterans – those who were left after four carriers went to the bottom off Midway – having the edge in experience, equipment, and numbers.

Combat did not account for all the Wildcat losses either, for green pilots found the F4F a handful, and conditions on the 'Canal' were not to be believed. Even after it had been improved, Henderson Field (named after Marine Major Lofton R. Henderson, who had commanded VMSB-241 at Midway and died in his SB2U during a futile attack on Nagumo's carriers), was little more than a slightly flatter and more solid stretch of swamp. Maintenance crews had to work with limited equipment, subject to constant attacks from the air, from Japanese ships coming down the Slot, and from troops who could melt into the jungle as though they had evaporated. According to veterans, on the 'Canal' you could be in mud up to your waist and be blinded by blowing dust at the same time. Add a list of loathsome diseases, the most pleasant of which was malaria, and you begin to get some idea of what service on Guadalcanal was like.

American mass-production know-how and

Top
A sight to gladden any SBD crew. Two flights of Wildcats are seen flying a Carrier Air Patrol, prowling the Pacific for enemy ships, aircraft or submarines.

Bottom right
USS *Sable* was a converted Great Lakes paddlewheeler used for training. Note the wake from the sidewheel propulsion amidships. Also note the nosed-over FM-2. (USN/80-G-359766)

Top left
Interesting view of Wildcats from a Stateside training squadron as they display the new national insignia adopted on 28 June 1943. The directive added white rectangles on the left and right sides of the blue background circle in the national insignia. The whole insignia was also given an Insignia Red outline border. The Insignia Red outline only lasted until 4 September when it was dropped in favor of Insignia Blue but was not uncommon after the final deletion date. (USN)

Bottom left
Good use was found for war-weary Wildcats. This struck-off charge Wildcat, along with a Corsair and Hellcat, provided good training for plane captains at NAS Jacksonville, Florida, in 1944.

an ability to shift quickly from a peacetime to war footing turned the tide in the United States' favor, the island being declared secure by February 1943. 'Secure' is a relative term, however, and scattered firefights between Americans and Japanese outposts which had not been evacuated flared up for many months. The Leathernecks began receiving their new F4U-1 Corsairs at this time while Grumman's own successor to the F4F, the Hellcat, reached the first Navy squadrons to re-equip with the type; although superseded the Wildcat was nowhere near being out of the picture, nor was it only serving the Pacific.

On 8 November 1942, Operation Torch, the Allied invasion of French North Africa, began with Wildcats from CV-4 USS *Ranger* and CVE-27 USS *Suwanee* providing air cover for the invaders making the first American amphibious landing of the Atlantic War. Opposition in the air and on land was light but determined when encountered, French pilots and equipment being as good as any, but their hearts really were not in the fight and Morocco was taken by the 11th.

Back in the United States experimental work using F4Fs continued, one of the strangest programs being concerned with a study of the feasibility of *towing* fighters to increase their range as escorts. Wildcats were modified with a wire harness held to the wing leading edge by clips, this ending in a hook located out at the wingtip. In practice the fighters would close with the tow plane which trailed cables terminating in a stopper, edge in until the hook engaged, then throttle back. As the load came on the harness, the slack was

taken up, the pilot would feather his prop. and close the throttle, the Wildcat bobbing along docilely like a conventional glider. Tests were conducted using a Douglas DB-1 Havoc and a borrowed Boeing B-17 as tow planes with two F4Fs being hauled along. This proved completely practical, bridles being attached under both wings to enable the fighters to hook up in flight, cast off to do their jobs, then hook up a second time by simply switching sides.

Engine trials continued at Bethpage using the two XF4F-5s (BuNo 1846 and 1847). 1846 was re-engined with a turbosupercharged Wright R-1820-54, while an XR-1820-48 with two-stage supercharger was installed in 1847, this proving the better of the pair at low altitudes while 1846 held the edge higher up. These tests would assume greater importance later but for the time being Grumman did not pursue the matter.

The company was in the process of retooling for full-scale production of its F6F, the Wildcat's successor, and Grumman executives closeted themselves with their opposite numbers from General Motors to discuss transferring both the F4F and TBF Avenger to GM's recently established Eastern Aircraft Division. On 31 August 1942, the first Eastern-built FM-1, identical to the F4F-4, flew, less than eight months after Eastern Aircraft came into being. Kaiser Steel and Todd-Pacific were building fifty-nine escort carriers for use as convoy antisubmarine watchdogs, so there was still a need for Wildcats, one which would exist until the war's end. Other CVEs were based on converted Fleet oilers and freighters, the

The *Lexington* **and its brood receive heavy damage during the Battle of the Coral Sea. The** *Lexington* **has just taken two torpedo hits and several heavy and light bomb strikes. Debris litters the deck and smoke pours from the guts of the ship. Many of the Wildcats have sustained fatal shrapnel damage. The** *Lexington* **was doomed and, after the crew abandoned ship, the destroyer** *Phelps* **launched five torpedoes at the helpless cripple. Three of the iron fish scored hits and the carrier sank on an even keel, a tremendous explosion rocking the fleet as the ocean closed over the gallant fighting ship. Eighteen of the** *Lexington's* **Wildcats and SBDs managed to make it to other carriers. (USN/80-G-16802)**

Suwanee and *Long Island* (ex-*Trenton* and *Mormacmail* respectively) being examples of this type. As events would show, the Jeeps were used more often as tactical support ships than to carry replacement aircraft out to the Fleet carriers in the Pacific, their composite squadrons flying close support for amphibious landings beginning with Tarawa.

In a move to reduce weight and improve performance, trials of the R-1820-56 Cyclone, with a single-stage two-speed supercharger, were made, this engine being installed in the Grumman-built XF4F-8, which flew on 8 November 1942 at Bethpage. With 150 horsepower more than the Pratt & Whitney R-1830, the Cyclone developed greater torque, creating stability problems on takeoffs and go-arounds. To counteract this problem, a new vertical tail was designed, larger and higher than that on the F4Fs. The engine cowling was modified and the underwing coolers were deleted, armament being reduced to four guns. A contract for 1,265

Top left
A pilot rides in the cockpit of a Wildcat as it is raised to the ship's deck by means of an elevator. On 30 December 1940, a directive was issued that all ship-based aircraft be painted overall Non-Specular Light Grey. This Wildcat is such an example. This directive stayed in effect until 13 October 1941 when the Blue Grey/Light Grey scheme was adopted. As can be seen, the two Wildcats on the left are painted in the Blue Grey/Light Grey camouflage indicating that the photograph was taken during the change-over process to the new camouflage. The coding on the side of the Wildcat's fuselage indicates that it was assigned to VF-3.

Bottom left
A Navy pilot proudly points to a victory symbol after downing a Japanese Zero over Guadalcanal during August 1942 while operating from the USS *Enterprise*. (USN)

aircraft, designated FM-2s, was signed early in 1943, but the first production machine was not completed until that fall; 310 additional GM aircraft were delivered by year's end. In all 4,777 were built through to 1945, 340 of these being delivered to the Royal Navy as Wildcat VIs. Eastern built more Avengers than the parent company as well. Launching rails for five-inch rockets were added, three under each outer wing panel, and napalm tanks were carried on the center section stub racks for close air support missions. 100 lb bombs were hung from the stub racks when the FM-2s flew antisubmarine patrols off the Jeep carriers.

The Royal Navy received 220 F4F-4Bs, powered by GR-1820-G205A-3 Cyclones, under the designation Martlet IV. The first Fleet Air Arm squadron to take delivery of this version was No. 892, which sailed aboard two different American-built escort carriers, HMS *Archer* and *Battler*, C3 freighter hulls with flight and hangar decks replacing the normal superstructure. No. 882 participated in Operation Torch, flying from HMS *Victorious*, one of its Martlets landing on the French airfield at Blida and accepting its surrender. Operating off HMS *Illustrious* in company with No. 881, the squadron was also involved in taking Madagascar. Martlets were even engaged in the fight against the *Deutsche Afrika Korps*, No. 805 Squadron flying out of Dekheila in the Western Desert.

Encountering float-equipped Nakajima-built Zekes, called Rufes, in the Aleutians and Bismarcks the Navy, Grumman, and the Edo Corporation cooperated on the one-off 'Wildcatfish', an F4F-3 mounted on floats, small endplate rudders being added to the horizontal tail to counter the loss in stability caused by the floats themselves. The Sea Bees proved so capable of hacking airfields out of wilderness virtually overnight that, taken together with the expansion of the carrier force, there was no need to pursue the subject any further. Another F4F was fitted with full-span rather than split flaps, but the plane was lost when only one flap came down, the pilot being killed in the resulting crash. A third Wildcat was equipped with an experimental wing incorporating breakaway tips which would theoretically fail under high-G loads and save the balance of the wing itself. Although dropped on the Wildcat this was adopted on early F8F Bearcats until it caused a number of fatal crashes.

May 1943 saw a new phase of the Atlantic War begin. Escorting ASW forces had been tied to the convoys up to now, but this month Admiral Royal E. Ingersoll, Commander-in-Chief Atlantic Fleet (CINCLANT), gave his Jeep skippers free rein to follow up on any contact. On 22 May, while still riding convoy shotgun, Avengers and Wildcats from CVE-9 USS *Bogue* jumped the *U-569* in mid-Atlantic and scored the first submarine kill by an escort carrier's aircraft. Turned loose, *Bogue* and four destroyers left Argentia, Newfoundland, on the 30th. On 5 June, *U-758* was caught on the surface but managed to fight *Bogue's* airplanes off long enough to crash-dive to safety; this escape was to have fatal results for many other German submarines, for it seemed to prove that the 'fight back' doctrine of remaining surfaced and relying on the ship's battery of 20 mm anti-aircraft guns was the right one to follow. A week later, seven aircraft sank *U-118*, a tanker 'milch cow', the next kill being made on 23 July during the carrier's seventh patrol.

On *Bogue's* eighth patrol, three U-Boats went down under guns, bombs and depth charges of the carrier's planes and escorting destroyers. The pattern was set and the Atlantic, which had been the U-Boats' Happy Hunting Ground during 1942, became a death trap for these same ships. On 4 June 1944, Captain Dan Gallery's CVE-60 USS *Guadalcanal* struck paydirt when VC-8's aircraft forced a Type IX C, *U-505*, to the surface and were able to keep its crews' heads down long enough for the boarding parties to reach the boat, close its scuttling valves, and capture the top secret code books before they could be thrown over the side. A cable made fast to its bow, the sub was towed 1,700 miles to the Bahamas, then taken the rest of the way to the States. The fact of its being taken intact was not let out until after the war's end, for it was a floating gold mine for Allied intelligence officers, the codes enabling German radio traffic to be broken.

General Motors made its own experiment

with the Wildcat, proposing the XF2M-1, powered by a turbosupercharged R-1820-62. Three planes were ordered, but development was cancelled before the first was completed, the airframe being used for structural tests at the Naval Aircraft Factory in Philadelphia.

With the war's end the Wildcat was struck off the Navy's inventory almost overnight. It had, after all, been effectively obsolete even before the Hellcat entered service in 1943, and there were thousands of newer types to choose from for those squadrons, Fleet and Reserve, which survived peacetime cutbacks. Sold off for a fraction of their cost to the government, a few dozen Wildcats found their way on to the United States Civil Register, their new owners using them for purposes as diverse as crop spraying and passenger-carrying, one plane being fitted out to make room for four people behind the pilot's seat.

Today sixteen FM-2s are still carried on the books, most of them flyable or under restoration by owners who now realize the value of these historic Warbirds. Five more Wildcats are in museums, this number includes two Grumman-built machines. Not many, considering that Grumman and Eastern between them turned out 7,898 aircraft, but the Wildcat is better off in this respect than the vast majority of its contemporaries, and even its successors.

Defenders of Wake Island

Worn-out Wildcats battle with an entire Japanese invasion fleet.

It took World War Two to make Wake Island important. Before that, the V-shaped, three-island atoll had slumbered in well-deserved isolation, occasionally disturbed by wayward navigators in search of food and water. All that Wake had to offer were birds and an odd breed of rat. Naturally, no American stayed long enough to raise the Stars and Stripes, fire a one-gun salute, and claim that miserable pile of rock and coral in the Central Pacific for his country.

The United States could not find any use for Wake until the 1930s. Deteriorating diplomatic relations with Japan and the ensuing threat of a Pacific war turned Wake into a double strategic prize. From its location, it was apparent that the atoll was a vital link in America's frontier defenses; 2,000 miles west of Hawaii; 1,023 miles west of Midway; and 1,300 miles east of Guam. Wake's position also gave it offensive potential as a fixed aircraft carrier. It was within bomber range of Japan's mandate possessions, the Marshalls and Gilberts, 600 miles to the south. And it was the closest US territory to the Japanese mainland.

As is usual in such cases, a commercial interest acted faster than government agencies. In 1935 Pan American Airways built a weather station, radio transmitter, hotel, and seaplane ramp there to service its new clipper service between San Francisco and the Philippines. It took the US Navy until 1938 to recommend Wake to be developed into an airbase for long-range patrol-plane reconnaissance. And it took Congress another two

years to appropriate the necessary funds before the work finally began. As was true of the rest of America's prewar preparations, it was too little, too late.

In January, 1941, 1,100 civilian workers were landed on Wake to construct an airstrip, barracks, and a hospital. Between August and November, details of US Marines arrived to set up artillery emplacements. By 1 December 1941, Wake's garrison consisted of fifteen officers and 373 men of the 1st Marine Defense Battalion under the command of Major James P.S. Devereux. In addition there were ten naval officers and 58 seamen under Commander Winfield Scott Cunningham, the atoll CO, and one officer and five men from the Army Signal Corps. Devereux worked his Marines like dogs in twelve hour shifts to build defense installations before war broke out. In short order they dug out three batteries, one on each of Wake's islets, and placed two 5-inch guns in each of them. In support of the anti-ship batteries, they constructed three more and divided twelve 3-inch AA guns evenly among them. The Marines got their artillery pieces in place just in time, but Devereux lacked more than half the personnel necessary to man them.

Early on the morning of 4 December 1941, the last of Wake Island's reinforcements flew off the flight deck of the USS *Enterprise*. Two hours later the twelve new Grumman F4F Wildcats of Marine Fighting Squadron VMF-211 landed on Wake's airstrip. Counting the ground crews, which had arrived by

transport a few days before, VMF-211 consisted of twelve officers and forty-nine enlisted men. The commander of the fighter squadron was Major Paul A. Putnam, a hard-boiled, hard-driving career officer who had once served with Major Devereux when they were both second lieutenants in the same company in Nicaragua.

Aside from Putnam, however, most of his pilots were green and inexperienced. Only the CO and one or two others had more than thirty hours in a Grumman Wildcat. The rest had been trained to fly and spent most of their time airborne in the F3F biplanes hitherto consigned to Marine aviators. None of them had ever fired a Wildcat's machine-guns or dropped a bomb from one. They knew little about their aircraft, their propellers, and their engines. Tension mounted among his raw fliers as the clouds of war gathered but Major Putnam retained a grim brand of confidence in his men: 'They'll have to learn the hard way, which is the only way for a Marine to learn anything.'

There were many other problems. It was no secret that the Wildcat was fast becoming an obsolete aircraft. It was slower, shorter ranged, and could not climb or maneuver as well as the standard Japanese fighter, the Mitsubishi Zero. Wake's F4Fs lacked armor,

radio homing equipment, and only two of the twelve had self-sealing gasoline tanks.

Wake's airstrip was 5,000 by 20 feet. That was long enough for taking off and landing but it was so narrow that only one aircraft could safely use it at a time. No shelters or revetments had been built. Parking areas were not only unprotected, they were rough and unfinished.

Other shortages threatened to impair or even cripple VMF-211's effectiveness. All fuelling had to be done by hand, a long and laborious process. Among the entire ground crew, there was no experienced mechanic. Worst of all, Wake Island was without any radar. The only early warning system Major Devereux could offer his old friend was a lookout perched top a 50 foot water tower. Putnam tried to cut down the odds on a surprise attack by keeping four F4Fs constantly above Wake on combat air patrol. Putnam worked his pilots in relays. While four planes were on CAP, four more were to stand by as relief, and the remaining four were to undergo maintenance checks. It was an admirable system, but it was scarcely foolproof.

There was one problem Squadron 211 was able to lick with a dose of Yankee ingenuity and Marine persistence. While Putnam's

fliers were inspecting the 100 lb aerial bombs that were to be attached to the wings of their stubby fighters, they discovered that some administrator back at Pearl Harbor had made a mistake. The bombs were the wrong size! They would never fit the racks on the Wildcats. First Lieutenant John F. Kinney and Sergeant-Pilot William Hamilton gave up their Sunday off to work all through 7 December 1941 (6 December, Pearl Harbor time), on the dilemma. In a flash of true mechanical genius, they managed to improvise new bomb lugs out of sheet metal. As a small group of idle Marines crowded around to admire and compliment them on their handiwork, Kinney quipped, with just the slightest trace of false humility, 'Necessity is the mother of invention.' The remark backfired on the officer. From that moment on, he was known as 'Mother Necessity' Kinney.

Few photographs exist of the action on Wake but this is what one of the Combat Air Patrols would have looked like when the squadron was at full strength. Unfortunately, the initial Japanese attack knocked out most of the Wildcats as they sat on the ground. With additional Wildcats there is little doubt that the invasion could have been held off or, perhaps, completely repelled.

As Wake Island's last day of peace drew to a close, Major Putnam could well be pleased with the manner of spirit with which his men met their new hardships and inconveniences. But he could not help feeling uneasy. His planes were still out in the open and his pilots still inexpert. VMF-211 was in no condition to go to war. Like the other units on Wake and every other American base from Dutch Harbor to the Equator, it needed time. Perhaps it was just as well that Paul Putnam had no way of knowing that time was running out.

It was at exactly 0650 hours, 8 December 1941 (7 December Pearl Harbor time), when a breathless officer handed Major Devereux the following uncoded message:
'HICKMAN FIELD HAS BEEN ATTACKED BY JAP DIVE BOMBERS! THIS IS THE REAL THING.'

Devereux wasted no time and ordered his Field Music to sound the 'Call to Arms'. As the excited Marines scrambled with rifles to fox-holes or to man their batteries, the civilians ran to hide in the bush or to volunteer their services to Devereux. Putnam sent four planes up on CAP. The most likely origin of a Japanese attack would be from

their bases in the Marshalls, so the Wildcats were sent to scout the southward approaches. As soon as the CAP took off, Major Putnam had the other eight F4Fs drawn up on the airstrip, fuelled, armed, and ready for action at the first sighting of the enemy.

At 1100 hours a heavy rain squall burst over the atoll, blinding the Marine spotters in the air and on the ground. The storm ended in fifty minutes, but thick clouds lingered, severely restricting visibility. At 1158, VMF-211's CAP was making a northward swing at 12,000 feet for another southward sweep when the Japanese pounced on Wake.

The strike force consisted of thirty-six twin-engine Mitsubishi medium bombers, Bettys as they were commonly known. They belonged to Air Attack Force No. 1, based in the Marshalls. Flying in three tight, twelve plane Vs, the Bettys were half a mile below the American fighters at 2,000 feet. Taking advantage of the squall and clouds to come in undetected, the Japanese fliers ignored the surprised Marine gun emplacements on Wilkes and Peale Island, and headed straight for the atoll's main central islet, Wake. Their target was the airstrip and VMF-211.

Putnam's parked Wildcats never had a

chance. The Bettys pounced on them before they had a chance to get off the ground, riddling the fighters and surrounding yardage with 100 lb fragmentation bombs and machine-gun fire.

A few foolhardy pilots tried to reach the F4Fs, but their efforts proved futile or fatal. Second Lieutenant Harry 'Spider' Webb got a slug in the stomach and both his feet were crippled. Second Lieutenant Frank Holden was cut into pieces. Lieutenant George Graves managed to crawl into the cockpit of an intact Wildcat but a Betty scored a direct hit with a bomb before he could turn the engine over. He died in a sheet of flames. As Major Putnam rushed for the Wildcats, he was slowed down by a bomb fragment. Then he was knocked over and dazed by bomb concussion. Friendly hands tried to drag him to the hospital, but he refused to rest or be treated. He went back into the inferno in the

A Marine aviator warms up his Neutral Grey Wildcat in Hawaii before the start of the war. The Wildcat was intended to become the chief USMC fighter but when the war started several squadrons were still equipped with the totally obsolete Buffalo.

hope of salvaging something. The same spirit was exhibited by Lieutenant Conderman. Mortally wounded near his plane, Conderman knew he was done for before would be rescuers tried to pull him off the bullet-marked airstrip. Directing them to other wounded Marines strewn beyond him, he turned down any aid.

In a few minutes it was all over. A Japanese pilot could see his comrades grinning broadly as they departed, waggling his wings to signify *Banzai*! They had good reason to cheer. Back on Wake's airstrip, seven F4Fs were flaming wrecks. An eighth Wildcat had escaped somewhat intact, but its auxiliary gas tank had been punctured. The air-ground radio set had been damaged. Two 12,500 gallon aviation fuel tanks had been set ablaze. Numerous gasoline drums suffered the same fate. Most of the bottled oxygen had been destroyed and the squadron's few tools and spares had been shot up and partially burned.

The loss of manpower was even more severe. VMF-211 lost twenty men killed, including three pilots. Eleven more had been wounded, four of them fliers. Three of them, Putnam, Captain Frank Tharin, and Staff Sergeant Arthur, insisted they could still operate an airplane and stayed on duty. Lieutenant Webb would have liked to have joined them, but his wounds made the hospital the only place for him. His body spent the remainder of the siege in bed. His spirit did not. Medical orderlies were soon sick of his constant pestering: 'When can I get up for another crack at the bastards?'

It would take more than bravado to make up VMF-211's losses. In one fell swoop, the Japanese had robbed Putnam of 60 per cent of his men and $66\frac{2}{3}$ per cent of his planes. When those four, precious, remaining Wildcats tried to land on the bombed-out strip, an accident put one of them out of action. Captain Henry 'Baron' Elrod's F4F struck a mass of bomb debris which bent the propeller and jarred the engine.

The multiplied array of mounting catastrophe might have broken a lesser man, but Major Putnam was too much of a Marine. As his CO, Commander Cunningham, remembered:

'Paul Putnam could not shake off the terrible memory of the destruction that had visited his squadron on that first day. He continued to push himself relentlessly at the airstrip, trying to improve and extend the ground works...'

Putnam's first job was to find someone to replace the dead Lieutenant Graves, his Engineering Officer. He made the natural choice, 'Mother Necessity' Kinney. Kinney set right to work, trying to salvage parts that would make Elrod's Wildcat and the eighth surviving F4F flyable. He had to fight widespread destruction with damaged tools – all of VMF-211's manuals had been turned to ashes in the air raid. Fortunately, Kinney could rely on the mechanical instincts of his chief assistant, Technical Sergeant Hamilton, who had spent many years in all phases of Marine Corps aviation. While Kinney and Hamilton worked through the night, civilian volunteers bulldozed the holes out of the runway and the members of their squadron and more civilians completed eight bombproof aircraft revetments. By the morning of 9 December, VMF-211's Wildcats were not only safe, thanks to Kinney and Hamilton, they were ready to fly.

Flushed and overconfident by their exploits of the previous day, the Japanese bombers no longer made a secret of their approach. The second raid came from the same direction at nearly the same time, 1145 hours. Flying CAP, Lieutenant David D. Kliewer and Sergeant Hamilton came in on the flank of one of the Vs, cut off a straggler, and shot it down in flames. The 3-inch AA guns bagged another Betty. Fourteen others were hit from the ground or the air. Three of them crashed into the sea on their return flight. Nevertheless, the Japanese were still able to inflict heavy damage: the radio station was wrecked, the hospital razed, and four Marines and fifty-five civilians were killed. But the losses did not seem to shake Putnam. He knew that the air war over Wake Island had taken a new turn:

'The original raid ... was tactically well conceived and skillfully executed, but thereafter their tactics were stupid, and the best that can be said of their skill is that they had excellent flight discipline. The hour and altitude of their arrival over the island was almost constant and it was a simple matter to meet them, and they never, after that first day, got through unopposed...'

On the third day, 10 December 1941, twenty-six Bettys flew over Wake at 1045. Watching from his CP, Major Devereux saw VMF-211 rise to meet them:

'... our four Grummans attacked the Jap formation repeatedly. Captain Henry Elrod knocked down two of the big bombers before the enemy turned tail for home. A Marine watching the fury of Elrod's attack exclaimed, "Hammering Hank is sure giving 'em hell!" The name stuck. From then on Elrod was Hammering Hank!...'

Despite the punishment they were receiving from Wake's guns and planes, the Japanese fliers exaggerated their successes, claiming that they had destroyed all the US aircraft and the batteries. They convinced Admiral Sadachimi Kajioka, Commander of the Imperial Fourth Fleet, the man who had been picked to capture the atoll. On 9 December, 1941, Kajioka led his task force of one cruiser, two light cruisers, six destroyers, and two transports north from the Japanese mandates. He had been so taken in by the claims of Air Attack Force No. 1 that he provided his fleet with no air cover and only brought 450 shock troops to storm the beaches. The Japanese ships arrived off the atoll by 0300, 11 December, but an alert sentry spotted their lights. Two hours later the bombardment began. Devereux ordered his batteries not to fire until he gave the word. He wanted Kajioka to come closer so the Marines' 5-inchers could do more damage. At the same time, he telephoned Major Putnam at the airstrip: 'Don't take off until I open fire. I'm trying to draw them in, and the planes would give the show away.'

Devereux's scheme worked. Primed to imprudence by the Betty pilots, Kajioka signalled his flotilla to move in for the kill on the silent, shell-plastered atoll. At 0610 hours, the Japanese were preparing for a second firing run at Wake from a mere 4,500 yards. That was close enough. Devereux gave the order: 'Commence firing!' Four shells were instantly pumped into the cruiser *Yurabi*, Kajioka's flagship, crippling her. As Kajioka fled into a smoke-screen, Marine gunners picked and hit other targets. The *Hayate* was blown right out of the water, sinking with all hands.

Back at the airstrip, Putnam had manned his four Grummans with himself and his three most experienced fliers, Captain Henry Elrod, Captain Herbert C. Freuler, and Captain Frank Tharin. At the first salvo from Deveruex's guns, they took off and headed into the fray. Each pilot's instructions were simple. He was to drop his two 100 lb aerial bombs and empty his machine-guns into every Japanese ship he came across. Putnam's aviators obeyed with a vengeance. In all, VMF-211 made ten sorties against Kajioka's fleet, ferrying out bomb after bomb to the scattered, fleeing boats, and strafed them unmercilessly. The sky was thick with flak, but the Marines ignored it. They had a score to settle.

In the first bomb run, Captain Tharin landed a bomb on the *Tenryu*, a light cruiser, knocking out a torpedo battery. Captain Elrod hit another light cruiser. Then 'Hammering Hank' spun his machine over for a pass at the destroyer *Kisaragi*. A wall of flak was thrown up at him. Bullets and shell fragments tore through his Wildcat, cutting the main fuel line, ingiting flames. Elrod did not even swerve off course until he planted a bomb square amidships. For some strange reason, the *Kisaragi* had a load of depth charges piled on its deck. The blast from 'Hammering Hank's' bomb set off a chain reaction of explosions that were soon to send her to the bottom with all hands. Meanwhile, Elrod, completely unaware of his good luck, was trying to nurse his flaming F4F back to Wake. He almost made it to the airstrip, crashing on to the beach just a few yards too short. As his frantic ground crew raced to his rescue, Elrod, unscathed, climbed from the wreck that had once been an aeroplane. Anyone else would have been glad to be alive, but Elrod was full of regrets. 'Honest,' he told the astonished, back slapping mechanics, 'I'm sorry as hell about the plane.'

Back at the ships, Freuler managed to send a bomb whistling into a troop laden transport before AA fire pierced his oil cooler and one cylinder. Landing for repairs, he tried to take off again and cracked up. VMF-211 now had only two planes left. At that moment, Major Putnam relieved himself and Tharin, his low flying 'smokestack bomber', to give Kliewer and Hamilton a shot at the enemy. Kliewer arrived over the *Kisahagi* just in time to see it explode as a delayed reaction from Elrod's bomb. Then he and Hamilton proceeded to deliver the last instalment of VMF-211's payload to the Japanese. In all, Putnam's pilots had hurled twenty bombs and 20,000 0.50 caliber slugs at their foe.

As Admiral Kajioka's flotilla limped out of range, Wake Island rang with cheer after cheer. The Marines, gunners and aviators, had something to celebrate. Together they had caused the only unsuccessful amphibious landing attempt of the Pacific War. Not only that, they had sunk two destroyers, damaged eight other ships, and killed between 500 to 700 of the enemy. Putnam's pilots would have received a special lift if they could have read Admiral Kajioka's war diary: 'Dec. 11 – Wake Island landing after sunset (sic) unsuccessful because of fighter plane opposition.' It had been quite a day for VMF-211 and it was not even over yet.

Four hours after the landing attempt, at 1200 hours, thirty Bettys, methodical to a fault, made their daily run against the atoll. Lieutenant Carl R. Davidson scratched two of them, 'Mother Necessity' Kinney shot another apart, and AA claimed one more. Four other bombers flew out of the fracas trailing smoke. Later in the afternoon, Lieutenant Kliewer was on patrol in his F4F. He spotted a Japanese submarine, surfaced for repairs, and zoomed in for an attack. Holding

his bombs until he was so close he could not miss, Kliewer straddled the sub. Then he came back to strafe until it disintegrated.

Although the Marines had routed Kajioka's fleet, they knew it was only a matter of time before the Japanese would return. In the meantime, VMF-211 only had two planes to meet the continuing air raids. Kinney and Hamilton worked feverishly to keep at least two Wildcats flyable. They were joined by a new helper, Aviation Machinist's Mate First Class James F. Hesson. Major Putnam was amazed and delighted by how much they accomplished. After the war he wrote:

'These three, with the assistance of volunteers among the civilian workmen, did a truly remarkable and almost magical job. With almost no tools and a complete lack of normal equipment, they performed all types of repair and replacement work. They changed engines and propellers from one airplane to another, and even completely built new

One of the few relics left from the USMC stand at Wake Island. This bit of cowling and propeller was found after the war by a construction worker on Wake who erected this simple monument. Recently, the cowl was removed and added to the Wildcat that was under restoration at the National Air and Space Museum in Washington, D.C. Thus the last part of a Wildcat that took part in one of its most famous battles is preserved. (USMC)

engines and propellers salvaged from wrecks. They replaced minor parts and assemblies, and repaired damage to fuselages and wings and landing gear; all this in spite of the fact they had no previous experience and were without instruction manuals of any kind. In the opinion of the squadron commander their performance was the outstanding event of the whole campaign.'

A VMF-211 engineering report told the same story with less words: 'Engines have been junked, stripped, and rebuilt and all but created.'

VMF-211 needed all the miracles Kinney, Hamilton, and Hesson could cook up. The air raids were not only going to be stepped up in retaliation for Kajioka's debacle.

On the 12th, two four-engined Kawanishi flying boats came out of the morning sky to bomb the airstrip. Captain 'Duke' Tharin, on morning patrol got one before it got away. Later that evening, Kinney's repair crew patched a third Grumman into a state of serviceability. The next day, 13 December, started out lucky for the Marines. There was no air raid. But Wake's luck, like one of Kinney's Swiss cheese Wildcats, fell apart. While taking off on morning patrol, one of the Grummans burst its stays and bolts to crack up on takeoff.

The 14th opened with another morning raid by the flying boats. At 1000 hours, thirty Bettys arrived over the airstrip. One of them scored a direct hit on one of the two remaining Wildcats. Two of VMF-211's ground crew were killed and another wounded. It was only the beginning. The Japanese were bombing Wake three times a day now, morning, noon and evening. The endless days fused into one as the bleary-eyed Marines fought to keep awake at their posts, grabbing short, nervous catnaps between explosions and nightmares. Lieutenant Kinney got the least rest of all, as he salvaged and toiled around the clock to resurrect a second Wildcat. His self-sacrifice took a toll. A severe case of diarrhoea set in. He was so weakened that he could hardly stay on his feet, but he would not leave his post for a hospital bed.

On 21 December 1941, the morning air raid that struck Wake also sounded the atoll's death nell. At 0850 hours twenty-nine Aichi and ninety-nine Val dive bombers, escorted by eighteen Zeke fighters made a pass over the airstrip. Major Putnam drove his car through the strafing fire and managed to reach, get into, and takeoff in Wake's lone patchwork Wildcat. The Wildcat began to fall apart in the air and he had to turn back. Fortunately for him, the Zekes and Vals were exceptionally ineffective that day. But that was not important. What mattered was the fact that those Japanese planes came from aircraft carriers. That meant that another task force, considerably reinforced, was in the vicinity. Another landing attempt could not be far off. Furthermore, the presence of superior Zeke fighters over Wake doomed VMF-211's incredible career.

Undaunted, Kinney and Hamilton pulled another all night stand to ready two Wildcats for combat. When Major Devereux saw the final miracle, he marvelled at the men who 'created a plane out of baling wire and rope'.

When the Japanese carriers *Soryu* and *Hiryu* sent thirty-three Vals and six Zekes after Wake Island on the morning of the 22nd, they were greeted by the unwelcoming reception of two F4Fs piloted by Captain Freuler and Lieutenant Davidson. The Zekes veered to intercept. The Marine aviators pitched right into them; Freuler got one fighter and then went after another. He was too close to the second Zeke when it exploded under his machine-guns. Flaming flying fragments damaged his controls. Another Zeke came in behind him, pumping lead. Bullets struck Freuler in the shoulder and the spine as he managed to crash land. As Kinney and the ground crew pulled his unconscious form from out of the debris, they grimly realized that Freuler's F4F would never fly again. Lieutenant Davidson was last seen piloting VMF-211's last Wildcat out to sea with a Zeke on his tail. He never came back.

After fifteen incredible days of fighting bad luck, shortages, ships, and wave upon wave of Japanese planes, VMF-211 had finally been grounded. Yet just because they did not have any more planes did not mean the aviation Marines could not fight. They were good aviators, but they were Marines first. Major Putnam called the survivors of his squadron, less than twenty officers and men, together on the airstrip. Then he lined them up and marched them off to Major Devereux to volunteer for service as infantry.

Devereux needed all the good men he could find. At 0100 hours, 23 December, Marine sentries reported flashes of light five miles out to sea. It was Admiral Kajioka's greatly enlarged task force. In addition to two aircraft carriers and other ships, the Japanese commander had been reinforced by 1,500 men from the Maizuru 2nd Special Naval Landing Force. Keeping 500 of the marines in reserve, Kajioka promptly sent his landing parties at Wake without benefit of a preparatory bombardment. He remembered the string of Devereux's 5-inchers too well to chance another duel. Anyway, darkness covered the invaders far better than their guns would have.

At about 2400 hours, two converted Japanese destroyers, crammed with hundreds of troops, ran themselves aground in the middle of Wake Island's southern beach, right below the airstrip. There was nothing there to oppose them except for an unmanned 3-inch AA gun, which had been so damaged that it had been converted into an anti-ship weapon. Spotting the Japanese landing craft from his machine-gun nest 100 yards to the west, Lieutenant Robert Hanna raced to his gun. He was joined by a Marine corporal and three civilians. Somehow this green crew managed

to put fourteen rounds into one of the beached vessels, blowing it up. Then they shifted to the second one. It was already too late. Most of the Japanese had jumped clear and were coming straight for the American cannon, firing all the while.

Hanna and his comrades would have been overrun and killed in a matter of seconds, had it not been for the timely arrival of VMF-211. Major Putnam led his twenty wildcats cowboy style, a smoking .45 caliber pistol in each hand, in a charge that stopped and rolled back two entire companies of Japanese marines, Uchida and Itaya. The leather-neck aviators fought like demons, driving their foes far beyond Hanna's position. Inspired by their élan, a half dozen civilians picked up sidearms and went into the fight. The Japanese gave ground slowly, and as they did so, they encircled the blazing knot of Americans. When Putnam's party was completely surrounded, the Japanese counter-attacked.

Outnumbered and outgunned, the Marine aviators got the worst of it. Men began to drop. Major Putnam took a bullet in the jaw, but he would not go down. Shouting hoarsely, he led a charge back to Hanna's gun. Despite the irresistible press of numbers, thirteen Marines and civilians were able to follow Putnam down the beach. Upon reaching the 3-incher, Putnam's strength gave out. 'This is as far as we go,' he told his men as they turned to face the pursuing Japanese.

In the crazy, confused breakout mêlée, Captains Elrod and Tharin got separated from the rest of VMF-211. They ended up in a strip of brush near Hanna's gun with a squad of skirmishers, but Japanese rifle fire kept the two groups from joining forces. There was nothing the trapped aviators could do except dig in and hold their ground as their enemies took advantage of the night to encircle them. Throughout those dark hours, the pressure never let up. Uchida and Itaya Companies kept up a constant fire with knee mortars, machine-guns, and rifles. Occasionally, a Japanese squad would charge, only to be mowed down by the desperate leather-necks.

Heaps of dead Japanese grew up around Putnam's squadron. At daylight, Captain Uchida gathered his company for a hell-for-leather *banzai* charge. With amazing courage, the Japanese came forward at a run, shouting and shooting. It looked as if nothing could stop them. At that moment fury swelled and burst inside 'Hammering Hank' Elrod. He sprang to his feet, swinging and spraying a tommy gun like a movie gangster. 'Kill the sons-a-bitches!' he screamed as he emptied magazine after magazine into the snarling yellow faces. Uchida went down with a bullet in his heart and so did many of his men. The survivors broke and fled. Elrod came running after them. As he stopped to hurl a hand grenade, an enemy infiltrator, who had hidden himself among some dead bodies, sprang up and shot him. 'Hammering Hank' died instantly. So did the infiltrator.

With Elrod dead, Uchida's men came back for revenge. Three of the Americans at the gun were killed and the other nine were wounded. Only six members of VMF-211 came out of the battle unscathed. One of them was Captain Frank Tharin. After Elrod's death, he and a companion were chased into a shell hole. They were crouched at the bottom, each man clutching a Thompson sub machine-gun waiting for the end. Then a ring of enemy faces appeared around the rim of the crater and the Marines fired madly. Next morning they found the crater ringed by dozens of Japanese dead.

This was the situation Major Devereux discovered at 0930 when the Japanese brought him to VMF-211 to announce Wake Island's unconditional surrender. His old friend, Major Putnam 'looked like hell himself'. His face was a red smear from the wound in his jaw. He was hurt and tired, but he took the news of Wake's fall calmly. First and last, Putnam was a Marine. The only thing he could say to Devereux was: 'Jimmy, I'm sorry, poor Hank is dead.'

Devereux walked over to Elrod's body.

'Hammering Hank' lay where he had fallen, 'with his eyes open, defiant, and the grenade still tightly clutched in his hand'.

The Battle of Wake Island was over, but the ordeal of its garrison was only beginning. With the surviving 400 leathernecks and 1,000 civilians, the Marine aviators endured four years in Japanese prison camps in China. It was a terrible life, fraught with constant privation and the tortures of sadistic guards. The Marines fought back the best way they could, with wisecracks and petty sabotage. One member of VMF-211 even made a successful escape. Naturally, it was 'Mother Necessity' Kinney.

When Putnam's aviation Marines returned home, they found that though they had been lost, they had not remained entirely forgotten. Captain Henry Elrod had been awarded a posthumous Congressional Medal of Honor for his many exploits. President Roosevelt had also given the whole of VMF-211 a citation on 5 January 1942, for its 'devotion to duty and splendid conduct' throughout the siege. Such lavish praise was the least that Putnam's flyers deserved. They had proved themselves more than worthy of the best tradition of the United States Marine Corps. As their CO, Commander Cunningham, said of them:

'And seldom in all history, I felt, had men responded with such abandon to the challenge.'

Tontouta, 30 miles northwest of the capital of Noumea, New Caledonia, and some 300 miles south of Efate. The unit became the first USMC fighter squadron to reach the South Pacific in World War Two.

Although the field at Efate had been considered operational since the first of May, there was still considerable work to finish the living quarters and maintenance facilities. On 27 May, the squadron commander, Major Bauer, took off leading a three plane flight to land at Efate and establish a forward fighter base. The rest of the squadron then moved up and were to remain at Efate under the orders of Commander, Carriers (COMCARPAC) to blunt any further expansion by the Japanese.

Tall, dark and rugged looking, Major Bauer, because of his part-Indian heritage, was known as Indian Joe to his men. Born in North Platte, Nebraska, Major Bauer had spent almost ten years in the USMC as a flyer where his skill and leadership qualities had marked him for future high command. At the time he was aware of the serious responsibility entrusted to him with the Japanese only 600 air miles to the north. As the only Marine land-based fighter squadron in the area, the burden of stopping any aggressive moves by the Japanese would be his.

The Americans were slowly rebuilding their decimated military forces following Pearl Harbor when a chance reconnaissance flight by a lone B-17 high above the Japanese-occupied island of Guadalcanal was to greatly step up its timetable. Photographs taken by the B-17 showed the Japanese were building an airfield on Guadalcanal. When completed, long-range Japanese bombers using the field would be able to cut the sea and air shipping lanes to Australia and reach the populated northeast coast. Even the American island bases of Samoa and Fiji would be within range. The serious and potentially disastrous effect of this latest Japanese threat was too great to contemplate.

When the news of the airfield being built on Guadalcanal reached Washington the decision was made to launch an amphibious assault to take the island. Yet American military forces in the area were still far from ready to undertake such an ambitious campaign against the vastly superior air, land and naval might of the Japanese. But Washington felt it had no other choice. A landing on the island was originally set for 30 July, but numerous logistics problems were to delay it until 7 August 1942.

The Japanese on Guadalcanal, consisting mostly of laborers, were taken by surprise when the Marines came storming ashore to quickly move a mile inland and take the

Indian Joe Bauer

Dank climate, critical shortages, inferior equipment, out-numbered by a tenacious enemy ... these were some of the miseries facing Marine flyers On Guadalcanal. Yet one man with infectious confidence and enthusiasm was an inspiration to his men during those dark, early days of the war.

By the spring of 1942, Japanese expansion into the southwest Pacific had moved rapidly eastward with Imperial troops landing on Guadalcanal and Tulagi. Little foresight was needed to figure the next move by the enemy would be toward the New Hebrides and New Caledonia. It would complete the ring around Australia's shipping lanes so that country would be threatened by Japanese aircraft and naval vessels.

To counter any move the Japanese could make toward the New Hebrides, Major Harold W. Bauer and Marine Fighter Squadron VMF-212, then at Oahu in the Hawaiian

Islands, were to move to a newly-built airfield at Efate. Orders directed the squadron to leave on the first available transportation. Eleven officers and their aircraft were taken on the USS *Hornet*. Another ten officers and two enlisted men were to go on the USS *Enterprise* and the two ships left Pearl Harbor on 29 April 1942. Three days later, 2 May, the remaining squadron personnel of three officers and fifty-five enlisted men left on the USS *Pensacola*. By 11 May, the two carriers were off the coast of New Caledonia and twenty-one F4F-3s took off from the decks to land at Vila Field, located at

airfield on the first day. Work was begun immediately by construction battalions to finish the airfield, to be called Henderson Field, for the arrival of Marine air units to support the operation. It was first decided that Major Bauer's VMF-212 and recently arrived VMO-251, stationed at Espiritu Santo, were to garrison Henderson Field, but this was changed. Instead, MAG 23, composed of VMF-223, VMF-224, VMSB-231 and VMSB-232 were assigned the job. Somewhat disappointed that his squadron was not selected to take part in the first American ground offensive, Bauer also realized, should the precarious Marine landing fail and the beachhead be wiped out, his squadron would be the only fighter unit available to protect the New Hebrides.

It took the Japanese only a few hours to realize the serious threat posed by the

Top
Wildcats on the line at Henderson field. Note the anti-aircraft guns located at various points on the field to help repel the constant Japanese air attacks. (USN/80-G-41099)

Bottom right
Harold W. 'Indian Joe' Bauer in a pre-war photograph. Bauer was credited with eleven confirmed victories including four Vals on the evening of 16 October 1942, for which he was awarded the Congressional Medal of Honor.

American landing on Guadalcanal. By the afternoon of the first day a large force of Japanese bombers and fighters from Rabaul, 560 miles to the west, were on their way to hit the beachhead. Fortunately Navy fighters off the three carriers supporting the operation were able to drive the enemy planes off but not without suffering heavy losses to themselves.

The Marine's hold on Guadalcanal was to remain precarious for many months as the Japanese continued their all-out effort to drive the Americans back into the sea. Neither the Japanese nor the Americans wanted to relinquish their tenacious hold on this strategic island base. Indian Joe Bauer became more and more restive with his squadron being held in reserve while the Marines, outnumbered and hard-pressed, struggled to hold on to Guadalcanal. With losses mounting among VMF-223 and 224, Bauer was to act as a training and replacement pool, sending his experienced pilots into the fight. Concerned over the progress of the campaign and how his boys were doing, Major Bauer began making frequent trips to the island where he often joined in flying combat air patrols.

On 28 September, Major Bauer joined Marine pilots taking off to intercept a force of fifty-five enemy aircraft reported to be heading for Henderson Field. In one of the wildest and most successful air fights up to that day, twenty-three Japanese bombers and one fighter were shot down. Not one American plane was lost although four F4Fs were damaged. One of the enemy planes, a Val dive bomber, was confirmed as destroyed by Bauer. It was to be his first official victory of the war.

During another visit to Guadalcanal on 3 October, Bauer, recently promoted to Lieutenant Colonel, was with the pilots of VFM-224 when a coast watcher sent in an alert. A large group of Betty bombers escorted by Zeke fighters were reported heading for Henderson. The two squadrons of Wildcats took off to tangle with the approaching enemy formation. Catching the enemy by surprise, even though greatly outnumbered, the Marine flyers were able to knock down eleven aircraft. Four of the Zekes to go down were credited to Lieutenant Colonel Bauer, the biggest single score of any pilot for the day. American losses were an F4F shot down but the pilot was saved and another damaged F4F crashed on landing.

The next day, 4 October, Admiral Yamamoto, commander in chief of the Japanese forces in the area, put into motion an operation that had been taking shape since early in September when he realized the

Group photograph of Marine Fighting Squadron VMF-212 at Efate in the New Hebrides. Major Bauer is standing to the right of the insignia.

present troops on the island were unable to dislodge the Americans. Convoys travelling at high speed were to land a large number of troops from the Sendai Division on the island under the cover of darkness. The operation would be supported by a large surface fleet spearheaded by two battleships and incessant air attacks by the Japanese Eleventh Air Fleet. Carrier strength would be increased with the arrival of two large carriers, the *Hiyo* and *Junyo*, for a total of five carriers. It would be the largest concentration of the Japanese Fleet since Midway. Opposing this formidable force was only the tiny group of Marine pilots at Henderson Field and two aircraft carriers.

Yamamoto chose 15 October as the day to land the bulk of his troop-laden convoy. As a divergence, the Japanese Navy was to come down the slot and bombard Henderson Field at night. During the three consecutive nights of 14, 15 and 16 October, Japanese warships fired more than 1,500 large caliber shells at Henderson Field. American losses to the enemy bombardment totalled twenty-three SBDs, six F4Fs and four P-39s destroyed. Another thirteen SBDs and three F4Fs were damaged but believed repairable. There were now only thirty-four serviceable American aircraft, including only nine F4Fs, to defend the island against the onslaught of the Japanese.

More aircraft were urgently requested to be sent to Guadalcanal immediately. In response, Indian Joe Bauer was to bring VMF-212 up from Efate to reinforce the Marines on Guadalcanal. The squadron, consisting of nineteen F4Fs, was also to bring along seven SBDs, both planes and crews, from Espiritu Santo.

VMF-212 arrived over Henderson Field just before dark on 16 October. Lieutenant Colonel Bauer, always the last to land, continued to circle the field as he watched

each of his F4Fs drop down for a landing. Only a few Wildcats were still in the air waiting to land when a large formation of undetected Japanese dive bombers suddenly came plunging down from a high altitude. Their target was an old four-stacker destroyer, the USS *MacFarland*, which was unloading 350 drums of precious aviation gasoline on to a barge. The first two enemy planes missed the target with their bombs but the third plane hit dead center and the barge went up in a huge ball of orange flames and oily black smoke. Almost out of gas, Bauer still took after the Japanese formation as it turned for home. He came up from astern and within a few seconds quickly knocked down four of the fleeing Val bombers. It was a remarkable feat of flying and marksmanship taking place almost directly over the field and in full view of the men on the ground. Even though the valuable gasoline had gone up in flames, seeing Indian Joe Bauer get four of the attacking enemy planes brought cheers from the men. For skill and courage displayed in this fight, Lieutenant Colonel Bauer was to be awarded the Congressional Medal of Honor. Unfortunately he would not live to receive it.

Among the many contributions Lieutenant Colonel Bauer was to make to the beleagured and outnumbered Marine airmen on Guadalcanal, the most significant was his cheerful and optimistic outlook and his ability to inspire confidence in his men. It was no secret the Japanese Zeke was able to outclimb, out maneuver and was almost 50 miles per hour faster than the F4F. Many of the young and inexperienced pilots taking off

Left
The 'pagoda' at Henderson that was used as an operations building. It was only partially completed when the field was taken and the Marines completed the construction. Unfortunately, a few days after this photograph was taken, the pagoda was destroyed by a well-aimed Japanese bomb.

Bottom
A Marine Wildcat burns on Henderson Field as ground crewmen try to extinguish the fire. The Wildcat had been hit during a Japanese air raid shortly after the Marines had taken the airfield. (USMC/50516)

A Marine Wildcat scrambles for takeoff as Japanese bombers approach Henderson Field. Note the weather-beaten finish on the fighter. (USMC/58441)

on their first combat air patrols felt they were as good as dead if they tangled with a Zeke. Bauer was quick to knock this idea out of their heads. The stubby F4F had its faults but it also had virtues and, if used to advantage, could give them the edge in combat. In the hands of a pilot who appreciated its merits, the Wildcat could hold its own against the Zeke. The F4F had a more powerful engine and faster dive, it had greater firepower and the pilot and vital areas were protected by armor plating. A Zeke could explode in a ball of flames after a three second burst while the Wildcat would continue to fly after absorbing fifteen minutes of punishment by an enemy fighter and still bring the pilot home. The Marines were the smartest, best trained and most skilled pilots in the air, Bauer en-

thusiastically told his men and, despite the miseries, shortages and numerically superior enemy, they were going to win out.

On 23 October, Lieutenant Colonel Bauer took over as Commander of Fighters on Guadalcanal. On this day a large formation of Japanese Bettys and Zekes were reported to be heading for Henderson Field. Bauer scrambled every aircraft he had including twenty-four F4Fs and four P-39s. Just before taking off Bauer gave his men a brief fight-talk and concluded with the order they were to meet the Zeke on its own terms. 'When you see Zekes, dogfight 'em,' he told the surprised pilots.

That day was to witness the biggest and wildest dogfights ever fought in the skies over Guadalcanal. When it was over columns of black smoke were rising from the jungle around Henderson Field where enemy planes had crashed. The exact number of enemy losses is not known but the estimate was that twenty Zekes and two Bettys had gone down. But even more amazing was the fact that the F4F had been able to successfully dogfight with a Zeke, an action that would have been suicide a month earlier. It seemed that Indian Joe Bauer had correctly assessed that the enemy had lost most of their best pilots and were now using green replacements who lacked skill and experience.

Among the Marine pilots on Guadalcanal who had the highest respect for the inspiring leadership of Lieutenant Colonel Bauer was Captain Joe Foss, a member of VMF-121. Foss, who was to become the first American pilot of the World War Two to equal Eddie Rickenbacker's World War One score of twenty-six victories, often referred to Bauer as 'coach' for his habit of giving pep-talks to his pilots before a mission, much like he would to a high school football team.

The long awaited general attack on Henderson Field finally began on the night of 24 October in the middle of a torrential rain storm. The Marines recovered from the initial shock to withstand six consecutive charges during the night and into the next morning. A Japanese colonel leading a small band of men was able to work his way behind the Marines and actually reach Henderson Field. He sent out the report the airfield had been taken. Yamamoto then set in motion the naval and air forces he had been holding waiting for this word. Swarms of Japanese aircraft were soon overhead frustrating the Marine flyers huddled in air raid shelters unable to take off due to the sodden field. Only in the late afternoon were Captain Joe Foss and four F4Fs able to get into the air to tangle with the enemy, during which time five Zekes were shot down. A number of SBDs and Army P-39s then hit Japanese warships, attempting to support the offensive and to land additional troops, with devastating results. By the evening of 25 October, Yamamoto's long planned and carefully prepared offensive had been thrown back.

Even after the disaster of this offensive and the air-sea battle of Santa Cruz, in which two of his large carriers were so badly damaged they had to be withdrawn, Yamamoto did not give up on the attempt to recapture Guadalcanal. He immediately began planning another but first some 30,000 additional troops were needed and more than 30,000 tons of supplies had to be brought into Guadalcanal. With his air fleet decimated by the stubborn defense of the Marine flyers at Henderson and no longer able to protect his ships, reinforcements had to come in by night using destroyers, motorized barges and small coastal steamers. These ships made speedy trips under the cover of darkness and then scurried back into hiding as soon as the sun came up.

Marine and Navy SBDs and F4Fs maintained a constant air patrol to seek out these barges and ships hidden in coves and inlets among the many small islands that made up the Solomons group. Called the 'buzzard patrol' by the Marine and Navy flyers, it was tough and dangerous work finding these Japanese vessels and blasting them out of their hiding places. They had to go down to tree top height and often into a withering anti-aircraft fire while Japanese fighters waited above to pounce on them.

A lull in Japanese activity occurred during the first two weeks of November. Then on the morning of 14 November, a force of four cruisers and three destroyers was sighted 140 miles east of Guadalcanal heading for Shortland. This signalled the beginning of two of the most action filled days of the campaign. SBDs and F4Fs from Guadalcanal, along with Navy flyers from the carrier Enterprise, went into action. Then an even bigger prize was sighted. Eleven transports and cargo ships screened by twelve destroyers, were seen steaming down the slot near the Russell Islands. All day long Marine, Navy and Army flyers hammered away at the Japanese ships, sending many to the bottom. Lieutenant Colonel Bauer was kept busy getting every available aircraft into the air to join in the fight.

Late in the day Bauer took off leading a flight of F4Fs which included Captain Joe Foss and Lieutenant Coot Furlow. The three men were to provide high cover for a mixed force of SBDs and TBFs sent to hit the transports. After the bombers were through, Bauer violated one of his own rules and it was to cost him his life. He had cautioned his men to always be alert and wary of high flying Zekes but Bauer could not resist joining in the fight. He signalled Foss and Furlow to follow him down to make strafing runs on the burning and sinking transports. As the three F4Fs were shooting up the transports, two Zekes came down on their tails. Bauer pulled around in a tight turn to face the Zekes and, after a short burst, one suddenly exploded. Foss and Furlow went after the other Zeke but lost it when they had to dodge the anti-aircraft fire of a Japanese destroyer.

Foss and Furlow flew back to join up with Bauer but when they got to the area there was only a big oil slick on the water with a figure in a yellow life jacket swimming in the middle. Foss dropped down and recognized Bauer in the water. Circling around and coming back, Foss attempted to drop his life raft to Bauer but repeated pulling on the trigger mechanism failed to release it. Bauer waved at Foss and pointed to the southeast indicating Foss and Furlow should return to Guadalcanal. On the way back to the field Foss repeatedly tried to reach Henderson by radio to get a rescue plane into the air but was unsuccessful.

Within five minutes after landing Joe Foss was in the rear cockpit of the Grumman Duck used for rescuing downed pilots. At the controls was Lieutenant Joe Renner who taxiied out to takeoff as the last trace of daylight was already beginning to fade. Just at that moment a squadron of B-26 Marauders was preparing to land, almost out of gas from their long journey from New Caledonia. Since landing aircraft had preference over ones that were taking off, all Foss and Renner could do was wait. Finally after more precious minutes of daylight had ticked away the Duck was able to take to the air.

It was pitch black when Foss and Renner reached the area where Lieutenant Colonel Bauer had gone down. The two men searched the inky black waters with the horizon weirdly lit up by five Japanese ships, attacked that afternoon, still burning. Now and then a brilliant light would flare up followed by a low rumble as a load of ammunition in one of the ships blew up. The Duck continued to circle over the area looking for Bauer until its fuel supply ran low and there was no choice but to head back for Henderson Field.

The next morning every aircraft and ship that could be spared was out searching for Bauer but without success. The air and sea search continued for the next four days. Russell Island natives were alerted to scour among the many small and uninhabited islands in the area on the chance Bauer was able to swim to one. Yet despite the diligent search no trace of the colonel was ever found. He may have been wounded in the fight with the Zekes, succumbed to exhaustion or been attacked by sharks. Whatever his fate it has remained a mystery. All that is known is he had died in the bright blue waters north of Guadalcanal which had already claimed so many American and Japanese lives.

The loss of Indian Joe Bauer had come just as the end of the bloody Guadalcanal campaign was in sight. After the vicious and costly battles of 14 and 15 November, the Japanese made only feeble and sporadic attempts to maintain their hold on the island. Although Guadalcanal would not be officially secured until 9 February 1943, by this time the main battle area had already moved far to the north.

Wildcat Wrecks

It is an unfortunate fact but the majority of destroyed USN fighter aircraft were lost not to combat but to training and operational accidents.

Top right
The short-coupled Wildcat gained a reputation for being a 'flipper'. This particular machine caught the cable while travelling at a higher than recommended speed and flipped on to its back. Due to the Wildcat's rugged construction the pilot escaped with only a few bruises. (USN)

Bottom left
Night flying accidents were not uncommon at the large US Navy flying training base at NAS Sanford. This FM-2 flew into the ground during a night training exercise on 13 August 1945. Aircraft was painted Glossy Sea Blue.

Bottom right
Pilot of this FM-1 found that his landing gear would not lock up or down so with a great deal of care he brought the machine down on to Sanford's runway. The gear gently folded into its wells as the Wildcat ground to a halt with crewman spraying foam to reduce the chance of fire.

Top left
Aircraft carriers are, at the best of times, hazardous locations with a number of gremlins just waiting to raise their ugly heads and take a snap at the unwary pilot. The pilot of this VF-8 Wildcat found himself literally hanging by a thread although in this case the thread was the arresting cable which can be seen tautly stretched from the Grumman's tail hook. The pilot managed to scramble back to the relative safety of the flight deck after the aircraft had veered sharply on landing. The unhappy deck crew is left with the less than exciting prospect of hauling the fighter back up on deck. (USN/80-G-11800)

Top right
Loss of power brought this Wildcat down on a beach near NAS Sanford. There were no permanent air units stationed at Sanford. Rather, pilots with ratings in lower horsepower aircraft were shipped to Sanford to be checked out in high-performance fighters. To aid in accomplishing this end, a mock carrier deck was painted on a cleared area between the Air Station and one of the lakes and the air and ground crews worked together to perfect landing techniques. The pilots would generally execute a touchdown to simulate a landing and arrester hook engagement, then give the engine the gun and go around again. Unfortunately, many of these overworked aircraft suffered partial power losses or complete engine failure during the climb out and many a young airman spun into a swamp in the process.

Center left
A totally destroyed FM-2 in a swamp near NAS Sanford. This accident occurred on 11 April 1944 after the engine cut out and the pilot had to put the aircraft down immediately. The cockpit section was about the only part of the Wildcat that was not destroyed and the pilot walked away with a cut on his hand. During peak training periods Sanford had one serious or fatal Wildcat accident every eight days, giving some idea of the tremendous aircraft losses suffered by military aircraft.

Bottom left
Glossy Sea Blue FM-2 sinks beneath the surface of Lake Monroe near NAS Sanford after the pilot bellied the fighter in when the engine failed. Accident occurred on 19 November 1944.

On His Majesty's Service

Grumman's Martlet/Wildcat put the Royal Navy back into the fighter aircraft business.

Right
AJ115 was one of a group of fifty-four Martlet IIs ordered by the Royal Navy. The aircraft is seen being positioned by the deck crew after landing. Space on British carriers was, at best, restricted and aircraft were closely packed together during operations. The Grummans and Swordfish were tightly positioned until they could be transferred to the elevator for storage in the flight hangar below deck. The rough, weather-beaten condition of the Martlets is noteworthy. Aircraft on carriers were always subjected to the corrosive effects of salt spray.

Bottom
A Martlet II is positioned on the deck of HMS *Illustrious*. On 10 January 1941, the *Illustrious* suffered heavy damage in the Mediterranean when it was attacked by Axis aircraft based out of Sicily. The *Illustrious* was well-known to the Axis for its spectacular attack on the Italian fleet at Taranto on 11 November when aircraft from the carrier destroyed half the fleet. The *Illustrious* escaped to the USA where repairs were undertaken and this photograph shows the deck crew working up to the ship's next combat cruise.

Top right
A batsman brings a Martlet into land aboard the *Illustrious*. The *Illustrious* was completed during August of 1940 and shortly thereafter joined the Mediterranean Fleet where its armored flight deck and radar were welcomed as very modern additions to the art of warfare. British pilots had to change their thinking a bit when flying the Wildcat series of aircraft for they found the cockpit layout very 'unBritish' but were soon to enjoy the logical simplicity of the Wildcat's controls.

Center right
Martlet II taxiies to its parking position. AM966 carries an unusual insignia directly behind the cockpit canopy. British carrier-based aircraft rarely carried any form of personal marking which was in direct contrast to the USAAF units in England whose aircraft were virtually flying art boards.

Bottom
Royal Navy pilots were not fond of the Grumman's narrow tread landing gear and they were quick to form a 'wingtip club' for pilots who managed to dent a wingtip during landing. AM988 was one of a batch of forty-six Martlet IIs for the Royal Navy. Of this batch (serialled AM954–AM999) AM954-963 were delivered non-standard with fixed wings which were later replaced with standard units. The first of the Martlet IIs began to arrive in England during August of 1941. This version was similar to F4F-4 and had six 0.50 caliber wing guns. The Martlet II was about 1,000 lbs heavier than the Martlet I but the forward view was improved a bit because of the different cowling. The Martlets quickly began to build up a score against the Fw 200 whose crews gained a healthy respect for the stubby little fighter.

Wildcat Versus Zeke

The following information is reprinted from a U.S. Navy manual covering the performance of Navy fighters against enemy aircraft.

The Zeke (Zero) is superior to the F4F-4 in speed and climb at all altitudes above 1,000 feet and is superior in service ceiling and range. Close to sea level, with the Wildcat in neutral blower, the two aircraft are equal in level speed. During dives the two aircraft are also equal with the exception that the Zeke's engine cuts out in pushovers. There is no comparison between the turning circles of the two aircraft due to the relative wing loading and low stalling speed of the Zeke. In view of the foregoing, the F4F-4 type in combat with the Zeke is basically dependent on mutual support, internal protection, and pullouts or turns at high speed where minimum radius is limited by structural or physiological effects of acceleration (assuming that the allowable acceleration on the F4F is greater than that of the Zero). However, advantage should be taken where possible of the superiority of the Wildcat in pushovers and rolls at high speed, or any combination of the two.

Five Down in Five Minutes!

The American public was hungry for a hero and Lieutenant Butch O'Hare was the answer.

Early in 1942 America needed heroes in the worst way. The war in Europe was going poorly with the British forced out of a number of key positions but it was the war in the Pacific that really had most Americans worried. For the immediate post-Depression American citizen, the Pacific was a confusing place. Its names were unpronounceable and few citizens really had any idea of the actual location of Pearl Harbor. Americans of the 1920s and 1930s were products of the curious illness called isolationism. The United States had advocated a policy of cutting itself off from the outside world and concentrating on the many problems that beset the country. Therefore, the outside world was completely neglected and anything foreign was immediately under suspicion.

The attack on Pearl Harbor had suddenly thrust the outside world very violently upon the average American and, even though he did not have any idea where the news reports and bulletins were coming from, he did know that the situation was extremely bad and that something had to be done to stem the tide of the perfideous Japanese military.

Newspapers and radios broadcasted item after item proclaiming victories for the Japanese steamroller that was sweeping over

the Pacific. A gloom settled over the nation as news of the defeats spread. The gloom intensified as tens of thousands of young men were drafted to fight a war they knew very little about. The government tried to keep down the constant rumors that ran rife about the country. Every day brought news that the Japanese were landing on the West Coast or that Japanese bombers were attacking Los Angeles or that Japanese submarines were shelling Southern California oil refineries (which really *did* happen). Bright news was a limited item and the government tried as hard as possible to search out any ray of hope on the vast battlefield and transmit it to an anxious public.

Far out in the Pacific, the remnants of the once-proud Pacific Fleet played a cat and mouse game with the Japanese. Afraid to commit the precious carriers to full-scale combat with a numerically superior enemy, Fleet commanders settled for 'hit and run' raids until a clearer battle situation could be assessed.

Admiral Bill Halsey, as did many other American commanders, felt disgust at not being able to challenge the enemy directly. However, the wise commander knew that the day for retribution would have to be coming

and he prepared himself and his men for the sweet satisfaction of hitting back. Halsey and his carrier *Enterprise* had been ordered to sweep north and east of Oahu and search for enemy submarines. This was a dangerous task for a target as big as the *Enterprise* and indeed, on two occasions, torpedoes nearly found their mark but the Big E did have a measure of success when the carrier's air group found and destroyed *I-170*.

The *Enterprise* and *Lexington* continued their dangerous patrols and they were soon joined by the *Saratoga* which had been steaming out of San Diego for Wake Island with a load of Wildcats for the Marine garrison. However, the commander of the *Saratoga* knew that Wake was under attack by Japanese carrier aircraft and that the situation was in doubt so, rather than risk the loss of a precious carrier, Vice Admiral Pye decided to let Wake fall. The *Saratoga* was hit by enemy torpedoes on 11 January 1942 and put out of action for six months anyway. The Japanese, who were acutely aware that they had missed the carriers at Pearl, were jubilant. Newspapers proclaimed that 'the exploit was equivalent to sinking three enemy battleships'. The Japanese, flushed with the recent success of sinking the British *Prince of Wales* and *Repulse* mistakenly identified the *Sara* as the *Lexington* and presumed that the torpedo damage would have been enough to sink the big ship but the *Sara* managed to steam back to Bremerton, Washington, for repairs and modifications.

The unremitting flow of bad news into Washington caused concern for the Pacific Fleet but the Fleet's new commander, Admiral Chester W. Nimitz, had other plans. Nimitz brought a new vitality and optimism to a badly dejected Navy. Individually he began to strengthen the spirit of the American fighting man. Nimitz knew that his strategy would have to be basically defensive and he knew that Midway should be strongly defended to protect the vital Hawaiian western approaches. To take pressure off Midway, Nimitz would have to have a diversionary attack on the Marshall Islands. Wisely, he selected the fire-breathing Halsey to form Task Force 8 with the *Enterprise* and *Yorktown*.

.

Opposite
This striking portrait of O'Hare perhaps best typifies the American fighting spirit during the early days of World War Two. The photograph was used as a model for several recruiting and patriotic posters during that time period. This view is also an excellent illustration of a Naval officer's flight gear. (USN/80-G-10562)

The Marshalls were a strongly defended area 2,000 nautical miles from Hawaii. All the important coral atolls were within air distance of each other so that the Japanese could count on moving air support to any threatened atoll with a minimum of trouble. The Americans did not have much up-to-date information regarding Japanese defenses and emplacements so a decision was made to attack all known targets at the same time. The SBDs and obsolete TBD Devestators from the carriers made surprise attacks on the Japanese targets including airfields and ports. The aircraft met strong opposition from the Japanese in the form of anti-aircraft and fighters. A number of the SBDs and TBDs were lost at sea when they tried to return to the carriers while low on fuel. The carriers beat a fast 'retirement' to avoid any Japanese reprisals. The *Enterprise* had the misfortune to run into a tenacious enemy in the form of a flight of Nells that pressed home a heroic attack but the *Enterprise* got away with a minimal amount of damage.

On 6 February the *Enterprise*, wearing its battle scars, steamed back into Pearl Harbor. The military personnel working on salvaging the ruined Fleet cheered the big carrier and Halsey who stood on the bridge. In actuality, the amount of damage done by the American attack was much less than originally thought and a dozen aircraft had been lost but, to the Americans hungry for revenge and good news, the first of many blows to avenge Pearl Harbor had been struck and, for the Japanese, the full threat of the undamaged American carriers had been revealed.

However much publicity the Marshalls surprise strike had received in the newspapers, it was still not enough to cover the fact that February 1942 had been the worst month of the war for the Allies with many defeats and bitter battles and heavy losses in the Pacific.

The Netherlands East Indies were about to fall to the Japanese onslaught but Admiral Nimitz realized that it could well be a futile gesture to send the carriers to the aid of the beleaguered Dutch. Instead, much planning went into another surprise carrier strike, this time against Rabaul in the hope of relieving pressure on Port Moresby in New Guinea. The *Lexington* under the command of Captain Frederick C. Sherman was to be the main part of the strike force.

On 20 February, as the *Lexington* plowed through smooth seas 400 miles northeast of Rabaul the nerve-racking klaxon sounded its strange wail. A Japanese Mavis flying boat had been spotted and Wildcats of VF-3 were scrambled after the invader. The Mavis was intercepted by Lieutenant Commander John Thach and destroyed by the intrepid pilot who noted that the Japanese crew made no attempt to bail out and fought to the very last, the turrets of the Mavis spewing out 20 mm leaden death right up to the last second when the flaming flying boat impacted with the ocean. It was to be an unpleasant sign of what was to come.

Even though the Mavis had been sent to join its ancestors, it had performed its mission; radioing the position of the *Lexington* back to home base. Late that afternoon, nine Mitsubishi Betty bombers came looking for the *Lex* with a vengeance. The bombers approached in perfect formation at around 11,000 ft and the *Lex*'s Wildcat CAP tore into the formation. Four of the Bettys fell in flames but the others continued on course. Captain Sherman kept his cool and waited until the bombers had released their load of death before he executed a sharp turn. The bombs exploded harmlessly in the water.

Much to their horror, the radar operators, who thought that danger had passed, observed another flight of nine more Bettys roaring in on an attack course. At this point only two Wildcats were in position to intercept the Japanese and one of the stubby fighters was flown by Lieutenant Edward H. 'Butch' O'Hare who was to become the Navy's first air war hero.

O'Hare later stated that his first thought was to attack, with little regard to the superior numbers and heavy armament of the Bettys. He knew that the fate of the valuable *Lexington* could well hang on his actions and reactions during the next few minutes. Sweating in the afternoon sun, O'Hare shoved the throttle of the Wildcat to the 'wall' and felt the little fighter buck under the increased horsepower. Pushing the nose down, O'Hare roared into the Japanese formation whose gunners immediately began putting up streams of gunfire. On the first pass, two of the Bettys shuddered from the bullets of O'Hare's attack and fell out of the formation trailing smoke which was soon to blossom into brilliant tongues of flame as the Bettys' unprotected fuel tanks torched. O'Hare racked the Wildcat into a high-G turn and roared back into the depleted formation. Another bomber burst into flames, lighting the indigo ocean with a lurid color. Then another and another. O'Hare had knocked down five of the Bettys in just over five minutes, accompanied by cheers from the sailors in the task force who could see the action in the clear and languid skies of the late afternoon. Thach was also up for the action and pursued the remainder of the enemy far out to sea and claiming several more victories for Fighting 3. The squadron claimed nineteen out of twenty attacking enemy aircraft. A close examination of wartime records reveals that the Japanese lost thirteen of the seventeen Bettys in the attack plus another two that were forced to crash land. Three of the Mavis flying boats were also lost. Thach was later quoted as stating that the squadron's victories came from constant gunnery practice and 'making every bullet count'.

Lieutenant O'Hare had instantly become an ace and, even though the surprise attack on Rabaul had been called off when the essential element had been lost, the United States gained a tremendous propaganda victory from the brief battle and O'Hare's photo and name was in every newspaper in the US. For his heroic determination in protecting the *Lexington* from enemy attack O'Hare was awarded the nation's highest honor, the Medal of Honor.

'Butch' O'Hare, with his all-American good looks, became an instant recruiting poster for Naval Aviation but his good luck did not last through the war. O'Hare, a 1937 Naval Academy graduate, had used his acedom as a springboard to a successful career. O'Hare added to his score over Wake when he destroyed a Zero and two bombers while flying the new Grumman Hellcat. During the Gilberts Operation, O'Hare had been promoted to Commander of Air Group 6 on the *Enterprise*. The Navy was worried about single or small groups of Japanese bombers stalking the carriers at night and trying to hit them when their defenses were the least potent.

O'Hare and other pilots of the Air Group came up with an innovative idea to counter the Japanese. The *Enterprise* had one of the new radar-equipped Grumman TBF-1C Avengers and it was planned that the Avenger would take off and orbit the carrier while two night-qualified Hellcat pilots would form up with the torpedo bomber with one fighter flying on each wing of the Avenger.

On 26 November 1943, the unwieldy formation joined up in the black skies over the *Enterprise*. The Avenger was flown by Commander John Phillips of VT-6 while O'Hare and Ensign Warren Skon flew the Hellcats. The radar aboard the *Big E* vectored the trio towards a blip that was thought to be an enemy aircraft. The Avenger, being much slower than the Hellcats, began to fall behind. Suddenly, the radar on the *Big E* reported another enemy aircraft, close to the lumbering Avenger. Phillips spotted the exhaust flames from the other aircraft's engine and opened up with his fixed 0.50 caliber guns from a radar reading distance of

Top

After O'Hare scored his amazing five victories he was sent to NAS Kaneohe in the Hawaiian Islands for a series of 'propaganda' photographs that were to be distributed to newspapers and magazines in the United States to give the 'folks back home' a needed bit of good news. The aircraft used in the photographs was not the same Wildcat that O'Hare had been flying during the combat mission but rather a line machine that had been recruited for the session. Photographers are seen setting up their gear while a mechanic warms up the Wildcat's engine.

Right

O'Hare in full flight gear before a Wildcat. Note the taxiing Vought Kingfisher in the background. Today, O'Hare is remembered through the name of Chicago's international airport, the world's busiest airfield.

only 200 yards. As he drew even closer, Phillips wildly banked the Avenger to give his rear turret gunner a chance to spray the sighting with fire from his single 0.50 caliber gun. The target turned out to be a Betty bomber and, as it passed under the Avenger, the twin-engine bomber burst into flames and dropped into the sea. The new idea worked.

Two more Bettys were spotted by the radar on the *Big E* and Phillips gave pursuit, shadowing one of the fast moving bombers. O'Hare came on the radio and asked Phillips to blink his navigation lights for he was in the area and was afraid to fire in case of hitting a friendly aircraft. Phillips complied but the Japanese pilot spotted the lights and dove for more speed. The two Hellcats made a firing pass without success and it was left for Phillips, whose Avenger was radar equipped, to stalk the aircraft. He caught up with the bomber and a well-aimed burst turned the Betty and its crew into a fireball.

Phillips' gunner thought he spotted another aircraft and snapped off a burst. At this time, controllers aboard the *Enterprise* were becoming concerned about their three charges. They requested that the aircraft turn on their lights and formate. The lights came on and the three aircraft joined in an easy formation.

Suddenly it seemed to Phillips and his crew that another aircraft was passing into their formation. The rear turret gunner snapped off a burst and it appeared that the unknown aircraft pulled up and disappeared. To Skon it seemed that the stream of tracers passed between his aircraft and O'Hare's when, without warning, O'Hare's Hellcat skidded into an out-of-control turn and disappeared from the formation. Repeated radio calls failed to find a reply from O'Hare and Skon closed up with Phillips and both began to search for O'Hare. Both Bettys were still furiously burning on the surface of the ocean but no trace of another aircraft could be seen. The aircraft then returned to the *Enterprise*.

There are two theories as to what happened to 'Butch' O'Hare. One is that an enemy aircraft slipped into the formation and nailed O'Hare before he had a chance to react. The other, and more probable theory, is that Phillip's rear turret gunner fired on the Hellcat by mistake or fired on an enemy aircraft and accidently hit O'Hare.

No trace was ever found of O'Hare or his Hellcat and the nation mourned the loss of one of their first air heroes of World War Two. Today, the gallant pilot's name is perpetuated by O'Hare Field in Chicago, Illinois, the world's busiest airfield.

Mr Thach and his Weave

This innovative aviator created one of the most important maneuvers in confronting the dreaded Zero series of fighters.

The complete slaughter of the Douglas TBD Devastator torpedo bombers at the Battle of Midway proved that many of the aircraft types with which the United States Navy entered World War Two were totally incapable of performing their mission in the fact of enemy fighter opposition or determined anti-aircraft umbrellas. Japanese fighters pounced on the Devastators of VT 3, 6 and 8 wrecking havoc and not one ship was hit by the torpedoes that a few of the TBDs which got through the defensive line of Zekes could launch. Into this mêlée roared two Wildcats from Commander John Smith 'Jimmy' Thach's VF 3. These two out-gunned and out-numbered fighters were the only help that the doomed TBDs were to receive. Of the forty attacking American torpedo aircraft, only six survived and not *one* managed to score a hit. This was not due to the courage of the crews but rather the outdated aircraft and tactics and the virtually useless Mk.13 torpedo which was so slow running most ships could easily outturn the weapon provided it was spotted in time.

At the time of the Devastators' attack, Thach was leading four of VF 3's Wildcats on a high altitude patrol and they were cut off from going to the dive bombers assistance by a large gaggle of Zekes. One Wildcat fell in flames during the initial attack but Thach quickly regrouped and put into effect a simple maneuver that he had invented. This maneuver, later dubbed the 'Thach Weave', was so successful that it transformed the Wildcat from an outdated fighting platform into a machine that could cope with, and destroy, the dreaded Zeke. The Wildcats, usually in pairs, would sharply turn into each other, causing great aiming difficulties for the Japanese pilots and allowing each of the swerving pilots to take a shot at the Zekes that were attempting to fasten on to his wingman's tail. The results of the experiment were electrifying: three Zekes fell to Thach's guns. The Wildcats survived the battle although they did not dare break their 'weave' until the Zekes broke away from combat.

Thach's Weave became the mainstay tactic for the Wildcats. Even some of the dive bombers got in on the act. A flight of five

This classic photograph illustrates Commander Jimmy Thach, in Wildcat F-13, flying with Lt Butch O'Hare as they pose for publicity photographs off the Hawaiian Islands. (USN/80-G-10613)

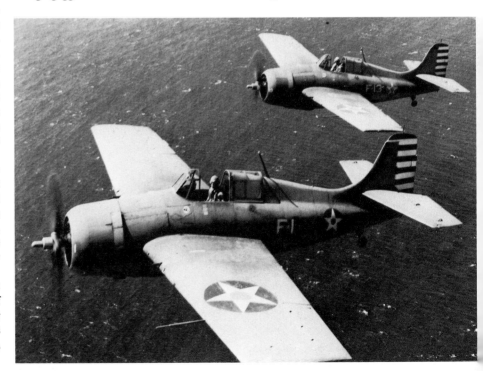

SBD Dauntlesses, their slow speed making them easy targets, went into the weave when attacked by a large number of Zekes. By doing this, the Zekes were subjected to the massed firepower of the two rear firing machine-guns in each Dauntless plus the forward firing armament. The Zekes quickly broke off their attack and went looking for easier prey.

Commander Thach was typical of the American pilots in the early days of the war who had to make do and stay alive with the equipment on hand. Their tactics were to cause damage and confusion among the Japanese who were much more conservatively trained in the rules of aerial combat and the day was soon coming when American pilots would be able to face the enemy on faster, tougher and superior mounts.

Wildcat Ace Supreme

Captain Joe Foss was one of the Marine Corps' finest fighter pilots in the Pacific during World War Two.

During the early part of World War Two many American combat aviators were wondering who would be the first to break the aerial victory record of Captain Eddie Rickenbacker. During World War One, Rickenbacker had amassed twenty-six victories while flying a biplane Spad fighter.

The record fell (and the Congressional Medal of Honor was awarded) to USMC Captain Joseph Jacob Foss who gained all his victories, flying a Wildcat, in the short period of three months part of which time he was suffering acutely from malaria!

Foss started out life on 17 April 1915 near Sioux Falls, South Dakota. His parents were simple hard-working farmers of European ancestry; the type of people that harvest most of America's 'Grain Belt'. As a boy, Foss picked up hints from his father on shooting and marksmanship and, by the time he entered high school, Foss knew virtually everything about firearms. During this time his father was killed in an auto accident and the double burden of continuing his education and running the farm fell on Joe's shoulders. After several periods of ups and downs, the crop failed during a drought and Joe went to work as a janitor to support himself and his family and pay his way through college.

Foss took his first aircraft flight during 1934 and, whenever he could get a few dollars ahead, he would go to the local airport and take flying lessons. After graduation from college in 1940, Foss went to Minneapolis, Minnesota, and enlisted in the United States Marine Corps. Foss was put through flight training and won his wings during March of 1941. After this he was made an instructor and sent to San Diego, California. His aggressive nature bridled at being stuck in what he considered a dull position but Foss was told by his superiors that he was too old to fly combat aircraft.

Repeated requests eventually made the higher-ups realize that Foss was serious and he was made Executive Officer of VMF-121 at Camp Kearney, California, on 1 August 1942 and, by the first of September, Foss and his outfit were on their way to the South Pacific.

VF-121 was equipped with sixteen Grumman Wildcats and Foss led eight of these while the Squadron Leader took the other eight. The men liked Foss and called him 'Old Foss' even though he was not *all* that much older than his charges. VMF-121 was assigned to the hell-hole of Henderson Field on Guadalcanal and Foss was soon to find the action that he craved.

On 13 October 1942, while on patrol, Foss encountered Japanese Zekes and a fight ensued during which time Foss was able to bring one of the enemy down. The Japanese

Foss flew several patrols each day from Henderson Field. The trying pace of combat flying and the rough living conditions at Henderson took their toll on Foss. (USN)

pilot had surprised the Wildcat from 6 o'clock high but his opening burst went wide of his target. The Zeke roared past the Wildcat and Foss, with his quick reactions, pressed the trigger on the Wildcat's control stick, and the Zeke exploded in a ball of flame. Three more Zekes tore into the combat and pounced on Foss. Their heavy cannon and machine-gun fire blew holes in the Wildcat's wings as Foss tried every trick in the book to escape his blood-hungry pursuers. More shells found their mark and the Wildcat's engine nearly shook itself off the mounts and the propeller froze to a stop. Foss managed to keep his wits and made a dead stick landing at Henderson Field while the Zekes kept up their attacks. With Foss on the ground, the Henderson anti-aircraft batteries opened up and drove off the attackers. Foss knew he had had a lucky escape and vowed always to keep a look-out while flying. From this action he earned yet another nickname: 'swivel neck Joe'.

VMF-121 was kept busy while at Henderson Field. In between Japanese attacks the squadron escorted SBDs and TBFs on missions against enemy shipping. During the afternoon of 23 October, Captain Foss took off for his second mission of the day to intercept one of the frequent formations of Betty bombers that would roar in trying to blast Henderson Field out of existence. Five of the Zeke escort fighters went after Foss and his flight. Just before contact with the enemy Foss noticed a further twenty of the Mitsubishi fighters joining in against the drastically outnumbered Marine aviators. Foss got off a snap shot at a Zeke that was on the tail of another Wildcat and, to his surprise, the Zeke exploded. A few seconds later he caught another Zeke on the top of a loop and sent it down in flames. Coming out of the loop, another Zeke crossed the gunsight of the Wildcat and the enemy fighter fell into the ocean in flames. Yet another Zeke fell to the unerring marksmanship of Captain Foss before the mission was over.

Joe Foss' ability to score so many victories in such a short period of time was attributed to the fact that he was an excellent marksman. In fact, it appeared that once an enemy aircraft was within shooting range of Foss, he was doomed. Foss, in many instances though, had to break away from combat because of plane damage, shortage of fuel, or lack of ammunition. In fact, he was so sure of his shooting abilities, Foss usually used only four of the Wildcat's six 0.50 caliber machine-guns to conserve ammunition.

Foss attacked the Japanese over Guadalcanal with a fury. On 25 October he shot down a further five Japanese aircraft. Five of

VMF-121's Wildcats were attacked by a flight of six Zekes and Foss quickly jumped on the tail of one of the attackers and forced the pilot to parachute from the damaged machine. Before all the pieces had crashed into the sea, Foss had fastened on to a second victim and sent it down in flames. A third Zeke exploded from Foss' guns and the burning engine nearly took off the wing of Foss' wingman. A Zeke singled out the ace and fired a long burst which went wide of its intended target and as the enemy sped by Foss got in a burst that sent the fighter down out of control.

By this time, the fighters of VMF-121 were low on gas and ammunition. Returning to Henderson Field, the Wildcats were jumped while landing by a superior number of Zekes. One of the Wildcats fell in flames but Foss managed to shove his throttle forward, get the landing gear back up, and climb into a nearby 'friendly' cloud. After gaining a bit of speed Foss emerged from the cloud and attacked two of his antagonists and, with his last remaining bullets, felled one of the Zekes, his sixteenth kill of the war.

On 7 November, Foss destroyed two Japanese recon. aircraft and another Zeke. After the fight he became separated from his squadron and found himself in the midst of violent thunderstorms that drove the Wildcat far off course. The engine malfunctioned and Foss was forced to crash-land the stubby fighter in the ocean. The impact with the surface of the water was extremely rough and the Wildcat broke apart with Foss trapped inside the cockpit. As the wreckage rapidly sank, Foss kicked himself free and swam to the surface. Using the chlorine containers on

his life vest, Joe managed to ward off attacks by sharks. A group of natives from a nearby island had seen the crash and they rowed far out into the ocean in a wooden canoe in search of the downed ace.

The natives took him to a desert mission on the island where he was cared for until a PBY Catalina could find the island and land. When Foss returned to Guadalcanal, he loaded his Wildcat with razor blades, chewing gum, tobacco, cigarettes and magazines, and dropped his bundles over the mission in thanks for the natives' kindness to the downed aviator.

Admiral W.F. Halsey presented Captain Foss with the Distinguished Flying Cross on 9 November. The captain's Wildcat flight became known as 'Joe's Flying Circus' and went on to score seventy-two victories during Foss' command.

While on a patrol, shortly after the award ceremony, Foss felt himself becoming ill. As he headed back to Henderson he could feel his strength rapidly leaving. By the time the Wildcat was on the ground Foss had to be lifted from the cockpit. The doctors quickly diagnosed Joe's high fever as a symptom of malaria. On 19 November Foss was evacuated in an Army C-47 to New Caledonia and by 30 November he was in a hospital in Sydney, Australia. During his illness Foss lost 37 pounds and suffered from many side effects of the disease.

Foss was soon back in action and, although still not himself, he flew a combat patrol on 15 January and ran into a very rough dogfight

This Wildcat at Henderson Field was credited with nineteen Japanese victories. Foss flew this particular machine for several of the kills. Few Marine pilots were assigned a personal aircraft. Plane Captain R.W. Greenwood points to the victory symbols. (USN/80-G-37932)

In six weeks of combat flying, Foss shot down twenty-two Japanese aircraft including sixteen Zeke fighters. (USN/34232)

over new Georgia. Malaria did not impair his marksmanship and Foss nailed three more Zekes, bringing his total victories to twenty-six enemy aircraft destroyed.

Base medics could tell that Foss was not a well man and they accordingly ordered the Captain back to the United States. On the trip back home, the malaria flared up again and several times Foss was very near death but, as before, he managed to shake the disease off. On 19 April 1943, Foss arrived to a huge welcome and acclaim as America's 'Ace of Aces'. A trip to the White House in Washington, D.C., followed and, on 18 May, President Franklin Roosevelt awarded the Medal of Honor to Captain Joe Foss.

Foss, in view of his considerable combat expertise, was appointed as tactical advisor to the USMC along with the rank of major. Foss, with his restless nature, did not like the idea of a desk job and constantly agitated for a combat posting. He was given command of a Corsair squadron and, after training on the type at Goleta, California, was sent off to the Pacific. On many missions Foss flew with Colonel Charles Lindbergh who, as technical representative of the Vought Sikorsky Company, was conducting proving flights with the Corsair under combat conditions. On one of these missions Lindbergh managed to bag a Zeke becoming probably the only civilian pilot of World War Two to score a combat victory.

After the end of the war Foss started a flying outfit with one aircraft and this quickly grew to a fleet of fourteen machines. Joe resigned his commission in the USMC to become a lieutenant colonel in the United States Air Force Reserve and then proceeded to organize the South Dakota Air National Guard whose commander and chief of staff he became. Foss then entered politics and was elected state representative.

When the Korean War reared its ugly head Joe immediately volunteered for combat duty but a USAF rule prohibiting Medal of Honor winners from flying combat missions prevented the ace from getting back into action. Foss went to Washington and tried to get a waiver on the rule, even offering to give back his medal, but he was refused.

In 1953 Foss was promoted to the rank of brigader general in the Air National Guard and the following year he was elected Governor of South Dekota. Joe Foss established the reputation of a man who cared about his country and he aspired to the American dream of a farm boy rising to high military and political rank. He was certainly one of the most successful fighter pilots in American military history.

Wildcat Bureau Numbers

XF4F-2/XF4F-3:	0383	
XF4F-3		
F4F-3:	1844–1845; 1848–1896; 2512–2538; 3856–3874; 3970–4057; 12230–12329	
F4F-3A:	3905–3969	
XF4F-4:	1897	
F4F-4:	4058–4098; 5030–5262; 01991–02152; 03385–03544; 01655–12227	

XF4F-5:	1846–1847
XF4F-6:	7031
F4F-7:	5263–5283
XF4F-8:	12228–12229
FM-1:	14992–15951; 46738–46837
FM-2:	15952–16791; 46838–47437; 55050–55649; 56684–57083; 73499–75158; 86297–86973

Martlet Serial Numbers (UK Air Ministry)

Martlet I:	AL236–AL262; AX725–AX738; AX824–AX829; BJ507–BJ527; BJ554–BJ570
Martlet II:	AM954–AM999; AJ100–AJ153
Martlet III:	(BuNo 3875–3904)
Martlet IV:	FN100–FN319
Martlet V:	JV325–JV636
Wildcat VI:	JV637–JV924; JW785–JW836

WILDCAT PERFORMANCE AND SPECIFICATIONS

Military Designation	Engine (Take off hp)	Super-charger	Prop.	Span	Length	Wing Area	Armament	Empty Weight	Gross Weight	Max. Speed Altitude	Service Ceiling	Range	No. Built
XF4F-1	XR-1670-02 XR-1535-92 (875)	I I	HS/CP	27-0	23-3	250	(1).50 (1).30	3320	4594	264/10500	29400	853	0
XF4F-2	R-1830-66 (1050)	I	HS/CS	34-0	26-5	232	(4).50	4035	5386	290/10000	27400	740	I
XF4F-3	XR-1830-76 (1200)	3	CE/CS	38-0	28-0	260	(2).30 (2).50	4863	6099	334/20500	33500	907	I
F4F-3	R-1830-76, 86 (1200)	3	CE/CS	38-0	28-9	260	(4).50	5238	7065	331/21300	37000	860	285
F4F-3A	R-1830-90 (1200)	2	CE/CS	38-0	28-9	260	(4).50	5216	6876	312/16000	34300	825	65
XF4F-4	R-1830-76 (1200)	3	CE/CS	38-0	28-9	260	(4).50	5776	7489	326/19500	34000	—	I
F4F-4	R-1830-86 (1200)	3	CE/CS	38-0	28-9	260	(6).50	5766	7964	318/19400	33700	—	1169
F4F-4A	To be powered by R-1830-90 engine. None built.												
F4F-4B	Redesignated Martlet IV.												
XF4F-5	R-1820-40 (1200)	2	HS/CS	38-0	28-10	260	—	4887	6063	306/15000	35500	—	2
XF4F-6	R-1830-90 (1200)	2	CE/CS	38-0	—	260	—	4985	7065	319/16100	34000	—	I
F4F-7	R-1830-86 (1200)	3	CE/CS	38-0	29-10	260	None	5456	10328	310/19400	26900	3700	21
XF4F-8	XR-1820-56 (1350)	2	HS-CS	38-0	—	260	(4).50	5365	7080	321/16800	36400	—	2
FM-1	R-1830-86 (1200)	3	CE/CS	38-0	28-9	260	(4).50	5732	7404	Perf. sim. to F4F-4			839
FM-2	R-1820-56 or 56W (1350)	2	CE/CS	38-0	28-11	260	(4).50	5542	7431	320/16800	35600	—	4127
Mart. I	GR-1820-G205A (1200)	2	HS/CS	38-0	—	260	(4).50	Weights and perf. sim. to XF4F-5				930	81
Mart. II	Twin Wasp S3G-4G (1200)	2	CE/CS	38-0	29-1	260	(6).50	5345	7512	293/13000	31000	890	100
Mart. III	R-1830-90 (1200)	2	CE/CS	38-0	28-9	260	(4).50	Weights and perf. sim. to F4F-3A					30
Mart. IV	R-1820-40B (1200)	2	HS/CS	38-0	28-5	260	(6).50	5773	7904	298/14000	30100	—	220
Mart. V	R-1830-86 (1200)	3	CE/CS	38-0	28-9	260	(4).50	Weights and perf. sim. to F4F-4, FM-1					312
Wildcat VI	R-1830-56 or 56W (1350)	2	CE/CS	38-0	28-11	260	(4).50	Weight sim. to FM-2		314/13252	Sim. to FM-2		340

Notes:

HS—Hamilton Standard
CE—Curtiss Electric
CP—Controllable pitch
CS—Constant speed

Supercharger
1—Single-stage, single-speed
2—Single-stage, two-speed
3—Two-stage, two-speed

3 HELLCAT –
Spearhead to Japan

While the Wildcat had held the line with the Japanese, the new Hellcat was to start the drive to Japan, a drive that the Japanese could not stop.

Leroy Grumman and his staff of engineers knew that their Wildcat fighter was outdated from the day it entered combat but the sturdy little aircraft displayed a number of virtues that helped it to hold its own against the Japanese Zekes. Grumman knew that the Wildcat could perhaps be updated if its best points were retained and new features added. The Wildcat needed a more powerful engine, increased range and a better landing gear that would not make ground handling so tricky. After the Battle of Midway, the United States Navy sent a report to Grumman that concerned the Wildcat's performance against the Zeke: 'Our F4F is markedly inferior to the

Zeke in speed, maneuverability, and climb. These characteristics must be improved but not at the cost of reducing the overall superiority that enabled our fighter squadrons to shoot down about three Zeke fighters for each of our own lost. However much of this superiority may exist in our splendid pilots, part at least rests in the armor, armament, and leak-proof tanks of our planes.'

The designers at Grumman set to modifying the Wildcat into a more advanced fighter but, by the time their initial sketches were finished, they saw that an entirely new aircraft was about to be born. However, little

did they know that the aircraft on their drafting tables would account for an amazing 75 per cent of US Navy's aerial victories over the enemy!

The proposal that was to emerge from Grumman was as sturdy looking as the earlier Wildcat but it was also larger and more powerful. The designers had fitted a Wright R-2600 Cyclone radial of 1,600 hp to the front of their new design and a Naval contract was issued on 30 June 1941 under the

F6F-3 Hellcat gets the take-off flag from Lieutenant John M. Clarke during the attack on the Marshall Islands on 23 November 1943. (National Archives/80-G-44605)

designation XF6F-1. Grumman and William Schwendler had carefully listened to the recommendations of Naval pilots that had flown the Wildcat in combat just as they had kept a close watch on all the data coming in from Naval intelligence on what little information was available concerning the structure and performance of the Japanese warplanes that the Americans had been encountering. All this information was fed via their slide rules into the new design. The last vestiges of any resemblance to the Wildcat were finally disposed of and the design team felt that they had a winner in the big rugged-looking bird that emerged from their efforts.

The best word, perhaps, to sum up the XF6F over the Wildcat was *more*. The new design had more of everything ... more fuel, more ammunition, more weight, more armor, more horsepower, more range, and more ability to meet and destroy the enemy over his own territory. For a Naval fighter the XF6F had an immense wing with the largest wing area of any American World War Two single-engine fighter plane. The large wing was needed to carry the heavier weight while keeping wing loading at a reasonable level. The XF6F had an unusual 'sit' in the air as it appeared to be flying tail down. Well, it *was* flying tail down due to the fact that the wing was mounted to the fuselage at the minimum angle of incidence to reduce drag while the powerplant featured a negative thrust line thus giving the XF6F its rather disconcerting stance. The unusual sit of the aircraft helped

pilot visibility by giving an improved view over the nose, something that the Corsair was distinctly lacking.

On 26 June 1942, Grumman test pilot Selden Converse gingerly eased the throttle of the R-2600 forward and the XF6F-1 felt air under its wings for the first time as the rather stubby fighter lifted from the Bethpage runway. The XF6F-1, left in its bare metal finish, could not have been called a classic looking design when compared to other fighters such as the Mustang, Spitfire, or Corsair yet, as was typical of Grumman's designs, the machine was functional and efficient. The Grumman engineers did not compromise with the construction of the XF6F; it was heavy, well-armed, and well-armored. Grumman and Schwendler had spent hours debating over the merits of Japanese construction techniques. They knew that the enemy's preference for light construction was also at a total disregard for the life of the crew. True, the enemy had achieved splendid results from their designs but they had also backed themselves into a rather deadly topping out of the performance curve. Grumman and Schwendler came to the conclusion that the new XF6F could not incorporate any of the Japanese design philosophies and that the new aircraft would have as much power available as possible with pilot protection and firepower being predominant. The Grumman design team wanted the XF6F and all other future Grumman fighters to be machines that could

Carrier decks are always a busy, and dangerous, place during air operations. An early production Hellcat in the Non Specular Blue Grey upper surfaces and Non Specular Light Grey lower surfaces is seen being positioned for launch.

blast their way through the best that the enemy had to offer and return to base to fight again another day. It was a decision that they were never to regret.

The Navy was concerned about the choice of the R-2600 powerplant as they wanted the new fighter to have more power. To this effect, Grumman's president, Leon Swirbul, made a lightning trip to Pearl Harbor shortly after the decisive Battle of Midway. Swirbul met with a number of Naval officials including the master of Naval aerial tactics, John Thach, who had done so much to develop the Wildcat into a fighter that could meet and defeat the superior Zeke. The closed door meetings were intensive and productive and the final results were to drastically change the future of the XF6F design.

The Wright R-2600 powerplant was dropped and replaced with the Pratt & Whitney R-2800 which was to become the most famous and perhaps best radial engine ever built. The selection of the R-2800 offered an increase in power that came near 25 per cent. Also, the engine would mean a commonality with the powerplant in the Corsair, thus helping to reduce confusion in the massive overseas supply-line effort. Thus, on 30 July 1942, the second XF6F thundered airborne

Top
Early production Hellcats cavort during a training mission over Southern California. Young pilots found the Hellcat straightforward in operating procedures and handling qualities, unlike the Corsair which, rumors told them, was a pilot killer. (USN)

Center right
An early model F6F-3 in flight. The Hellcat was the only Allied fighter that remained virtually unchanged during its entire production run, a statistic that spoke well of the success of Grumman's design team.

Bottom right
Suicide attacks were perhaps the biggest threat that American carriers had to face during 1944. Hellcats were used to fly cover from the carriers but some of the aggressive Japanese pilots managed to get through. This kamikaze is seen impacting on a carrier full of Helldivers and Hellcats. Another kamikaze can be seen crashing into the sea. The Navy wanted a fighter faster than the Hellcat to intercept these raiders and the F2G Corsair and F8F Bearcat were the result. (National Archives/80-G-270739)

from Bethpage, this time powered by the R-2800, the change in engines also giving a new designation: XF6F-3.

The aircraft was soon given the name Hellcat, a name that it was to live up to in ways never thought possible. Final armament was standardized on six 0.50 caliber Browning machine-guns mounted three in each outer wing panel with 400 rounds per gun. Armor plate covered many of the vital areas and contributed a bit over 200 lbs in weight. Construction of the Hellcat followed that of the Wildcat with the Grumman welding technique providing an exceptionally smooth external finish that helped performance. The 250 gallons of fuel were carried in a massive tank directly under the cockpit. This gave the pilot the highest possible position on the aircraft, affording a good view. The turtledeck cut down on visibility but Grumman engineers apparently never considered the possibility of a bubble canopy on the Hellcat design. In fact, design changes were so few that the last Hellcat was different from the first XF6F-3 only in small updates and modifications. The Hellcat was to be the least modified of any Navy fighter during its production run.

Intensive flight trials found that the Hellcat was a bit too stable, a trait that was not desirable in a fighting machine that had to be called upon to produce some outlandish aerial maneuvers during combat. Also the test aircraft was 'red-lined' far below its maximum speed as tail flutter had cropped up. Quick modifications soon eliminated the stumbling blocks. The Hellcat had been ordered into series production on 23 May 1942, and a pre-production line was set up in the Grumman plant while work went on around the clock to complete a new production facility that would be devoted to churning out Hellcats. Grumman builders scrounged materials from junkyards to finish the new building and Hellcats were on the new production line while the walls and detail work on the plant were still being finished. The enthusiasm of the Grumman employees to produce weapons for the military machine was so high that it was commented on very favorably by the press and government. All this praise fell on deaf ears because Grumman was turning out aircraft so fast that they did not have time to listen.

The -3 Hellcat had a leaner look than the -1. The spinner and landing gear fairings had been discarded, a new cowling added, and the Curtiss Electric propeller had been replaced with a Hamilton Standard unit. The first production Hellcat was in the air on 4 October 1942, an amazing feat considering that the prototype had flown for the first time

Grumman F6F-3 Hellcat

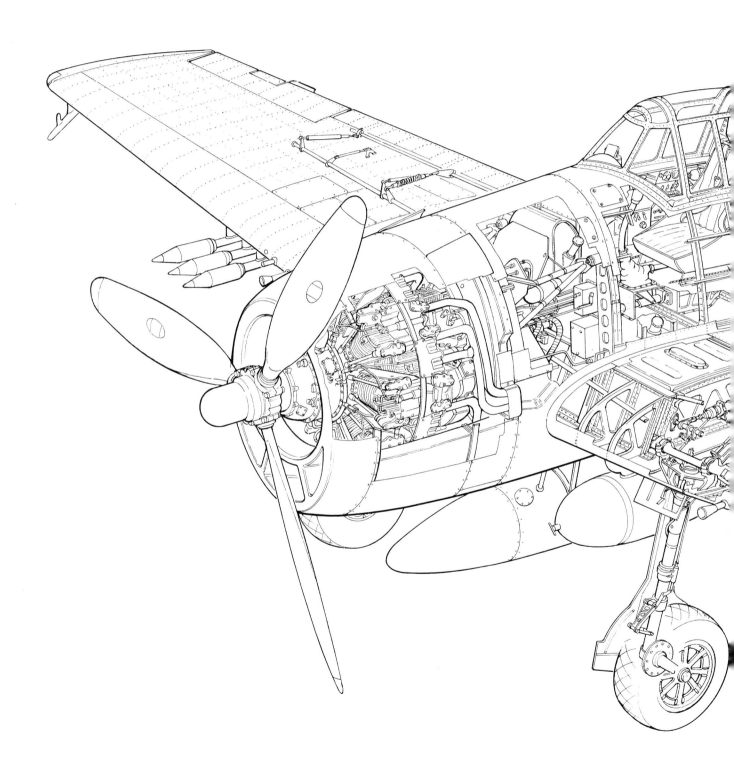

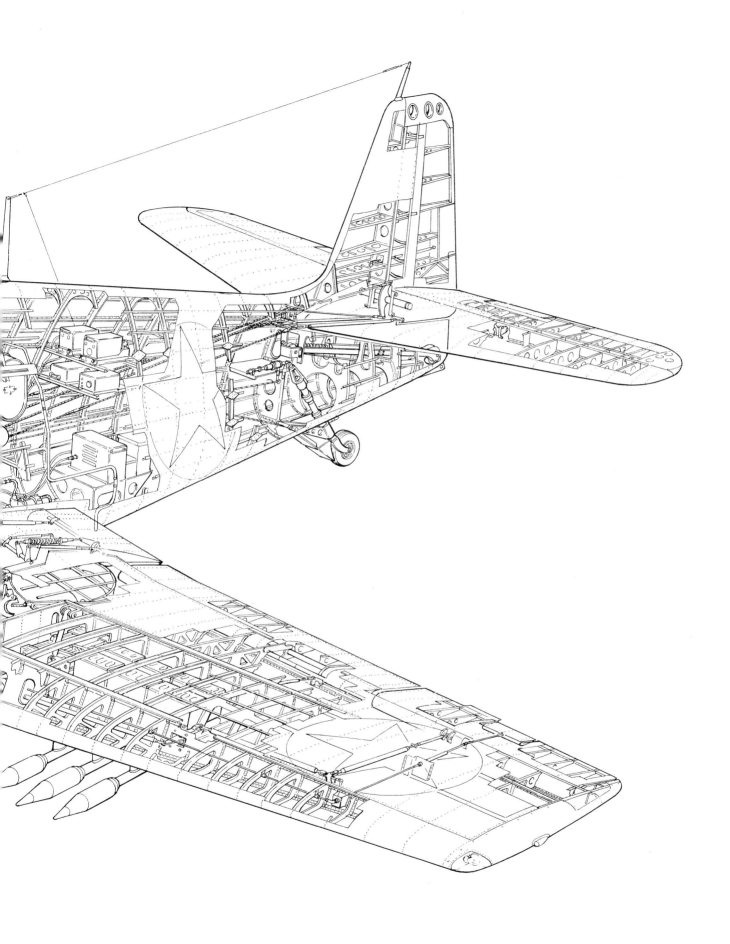

on 30 July! The Navy began taking the first aircraft as quickly as possible and pressing the machines into the rigorous duty of carrier qualifications. Some problems were encountered with the rear fuselage structure when tail hooks pulled out and the structure itself failed. Back at the factory the engineers quickly introduced modifications that would strengthen the rear fuselage and test work continued on after the brief delay. The Hellcat was found to have outstanding handling qualities on the carrier deck, much better than those of the Wildcat and infinitely better than those of the Corsair. The carrier qualifications proceeded without further delay and the new fighter was cleared for unlimited operations by the Navy.

The Navy wanted to build up Hellcat squadrons and rush them to the Pacific as soon as possible so training of young aviators that would pilot the new machines was speeded up. It is interesting to note that the much superior Hellcat would not completely replace the older Wildcat. The Wildcats were put on the small Jeep carriers where they operated with another Grumman product, the Avenger, in searching out enemy shipping and submarines. The Wildcat would stay in service until the end of the war although it was quickly replaced by the new Hellcat in the fighter role.

The first Hellcats reached VF-9 during the middle of January 1943 and the squadron embarked on the USS *Essex*, the pilots having few problems with their new mounts. The aviators enjoyed the new freedom of all the extra horsepower from the Pratt & Whitney R-2800 and found the new power a particular advantage when launching with a heavy load from the carrier's pitching deck or during a go-around approach when the extra power was quite often able to extricate the fighter and pilot from what could have been an embarrassing situation.

The Hellcat saw its first action with VF-5 aboard the USS *Yorktown* on 31 August 1943 during the attack on Marcus Island. Marcus Island was to be a training ground for the island-hopping war that America was to wage against Japan. Hellcats flew cover and ground strafing missions against the Japanese garrison.

The era of the powerful 'task force' was now with the US Navy as new carriers and other ships were completed to carry the war to the enemy. The Hellcat immediately began to distinguish itself during the beginning of the island war, meeting the Zeke on its home ground and decisively defeating the enemy. The power of the task force was something that the Japanese had not expected. The Navy's original hesitancy to operate more than one carrier in a single formation had been overcome as the American ships had proven able to defend themselves against enemy attack. By experimenting and finally perfecting the maneuvering of carriers in consort, Naval officials had created a mobile air force of overwhelming strength that the enemy would never be able to seriously challenge.

This rapidly developing time period also saw the appearance into the task force of the escort 'Jeep' carrier. These makeshift little vessels had only been employed in transport and convoy assignments except for one combat mission in the support of the North African landings. When introduced to the Pacific theater, the Jeep carriers were able to distinguish themselves while letting the larger fast carriers operate as deadly offensive weapons. The first deployment of the task force concept was known as Task Force 50 (and later as Task Force 58 and Task Force 38) under the command of Rear Admiral Pownall. This huge force comprised six fast carriers, five light carriers, eight escort carriers and about 900 aircraft. The development of this concept placed importance on the involvement of naval aircraft in amphibious operations while suggesting that the air units would be the principal factor in the control of sea areas. On 13 November 1943, aircraft from this force began raiding Japanese installations in the Gilbert and Marshall Islands, the first step to a long and deadly battle towards Japan. Hellcats from the squadrons aggressively attacked the enemy and established air control over an enemy that was willing to fight to the death.

The long period of new construction on ships and aircraft, training, and sweat and blood really began to pay off during the early part of 1944. During the next year and a half the Navy was to score one victory after another as they smashed the enemy on the long road to Japan. The invasion of the Gilberts had been a taste of what was to come and the island campaign started in earnest with the invasion and conquest of the Marshalls during the early part of 1944. The efficiency with which the Marshall Islands were neutralized from the air, bombarded from the sea, and captured by American soldiers and Marines made it a model amphibious operation.

One of the most daring carrier operations was the attack against Truk. Truk had always been a symbol of Japanese strength and it was with some anxiety that Vice Admiral Mitscher led his units on a sortie against the island on 12 February 1944. Intelligence information concerning the target was limited, a fact which heightened the island's reputation

The Marines, like Navy pilots, were always at the mercy of landing on aircraft carriers and, like their Navy counterparts, they had their share of mishaps. This damaged Marine Hellcat has fallen off the deck of a carrier and a fire has resulted. Note the deck crewman jumping up on the blazing tank which has detached from the aircraft, to rescue the pilot. (USN)

as a dangerous enemy stronghold.

16 February saw the task force 90 miles off Truk after an approach that apparently had not been detected by the enemy. A fighter mission of seventy Hellcats took off and completed a sweep over the island during which time fifty-six enemy fighters were destroyed in the air and about seventy finished off on the ground. Four Hellcats were lost in the action. This attack swung the balance of airpower in favor of the Americans and the only real threat to their aircraft from this point in time was from the many anti-aircraft guns located on the island. Air attacks on all the airfields with fragmentation, clusters, incendiaries and delayed action bombs were so effective that no Japanese aircraft were seen in the air on the second day of the attack. After the initial sweep, launches were staggered between carriers to provide a continuous flow over the target. With the destruction of enemy air power, shipping became a primary objective but few Japanese combat vessels were found contrary to previous intelligence reports. However, the anchorage area was found to be full of small auxiliaries which were attacked and virtually eliminated.

What had been viewed as an attack into a hornet's nest had turned out to be an outstanding victory for Naval airpower. Over 270 enemy aircraft had been destroyed in the air and on the ground, forty-seven enemy ships and vessels were sunk, and installations and buildings were ruined in bombing attacks. The Truk action displayed the power and versatility of the F6F-3. American losses amounted to thirty-five aircraft through enemy action and accidents. The most serious damage to American forces occurred on the night of 17–18 February when a Japanese aircraft slipped a torpedo into the *Intrepid*, forcing the carrier to withdraw with a heavy escort.

Hellcat pilots had no trouble in engaging with the Zekes. They felt that the Hellcat was superior in all aspects to the enemy fighter except in some areas of maneuverability.

A group of Marine F4Us taxi by the Hellcats of VMF(N)-534 at Orote. The coral-covered airstrip was put into operation just 24 hours after its capture from the Japanese. It is interesting to note that the Navy put $280,000,000 worth of installations on to Guam but the enemy left the base virtually untouched. MAG-21 which had seen so much action during the war was now destined to see only one more enemy aircraft. An intercepted message indicated that a very important enemy would be a passenger in a seaplane en route from Truk to Iwo. Four F6F-5Ns from VMF(N)-534 were summoned up to Saipan from Guam, and a destroyer took on board controllers from AWS-2 who would act as fighter directors. When the Myrt showed up—in daylight instead of darkness – two of the Hellcats intercepted and Lt Brett E. Roueche made the kill 110 miles northeast of Saipan. Marine historian Robert Sherrod speculates that the aircraft was carrying a message rather than a VIP, because VIPs were usually transported in twin-engine aircraft. (USMC/92396)

The Hellcat could walk all over the Zekes and enter and break off combat at will. The Hellcat could follow the Zeke through most maneuvers but tight loops and tight turning were still difficult and care had to be exercised so that the Hellcat would not stall during these maneuvers.

Improvements took place on the Hellcat production line during January 1944 when, from that date, about 60 per cent of all the Hellcats were equipped with the R-2800-10W powerplant with water injection that boosted horsepower to 2,200 for short spurts of power. Beginning in April, as more of the powerful engines became available, all Hellcats were so equipped. The next step in Hellcat upgrading came on 21 April when the F6F-5 was introduced to the production lines. This variant of the Hellcat was also equipped with the -10W engine and

featured some streamlining efforts that had been tested out on an F6F-3, a flat windshield that eliminated distortion and scratching, and deletion of the small aft windows on most of the production run. Other improvements included such things as an increase in armor, a once-again strengthened tail group, racks for bombs or drop tanks on the wing center section, stubs for six rocket rails on the folding wing panels, new cowling, and a number of other small but useful improvements.

The production run of F6F-3s included 4,402 machines that featured a number of interesting variants. The original XF6F-1 which had been converted to the second XF6F-3 was yet again modified to the XF6F-4 with the addition of a R-2800-27 with a two stage supercharger. The F6F-3E and -3N were early attempts at modifying the

Hellcat into a night fighter. The Hellcat was not an ideal single-engine night fighter, if indeed any aircraft of that period would have made an ideal night fighter, but eighteen -3E Hellcats were constructed from standard -3 airframes by the addition of AN/APS-4 in a fiber radome attached to the right wing. The -3N used the improved AN/APS-6 radar and 150 of these machines were delivered. It was during an early experiment with Hellcat night fighters that famed ace Butch O'Hare was killed.

The British were also interested in the Hellcat for their carriers and, early in 1943, 250 F6F-3s were supplied to the Fleet Air Arm. The aircraft were originally named Gannet Is but this was soon changed to the American name for standardization reasons. The British had the Hellcat I enter service with No. 800 Squadron during July 1943. The F6F-5 was also supplied under Lend-Lease with just over 900 aircraft being designated Hellcat II. Twelve Fleet Air Arm squadrons were eventually equipped with Hellcats including two that were equipped with F6F-5Ns under the designation Hellcat NF. II.

The F6F-5 series of Hellcats had remarkably few variants as it was so successful in its standard form. Two airframes were modified as XF6F-6s with R-2800C Double Wasps with 2,450 hp benefit of water injection and was the fastest of the Hellcat series with a top speed of 420 mph. Almost 1,700 of the machines were contracted for but the end of the war cancelled all development. The only other variants of the F6F-5 were the -5N night fighter and -5P photo recon. aircraft. The -5N was similar to the earlier Hellcat night fighters with the AN/APS-6

radar being located in a pod on the right wing. A total of 1,435 F6F-5Ns were produced. This variant was quite efficient and, in one instance, replaced a Black Widow night fighter unit because of its better rate of climb and superior handling qualities.

From 1945 on, the Vought Corsair, which had finally gained approval to operate from the Navy's carriers, had begun to supplement the Hellcat as the Navy's primary fighter. However, the Hellcat was to play a major role in Naval fighter forces right up to the end of World War Two. It is interesting to note that, during the Hellcat's combat service, the Japanese had introduced fighters of superior performance to the Hellcat but the trend was too late to reverse the huge victory that the Hellcat had been rolling up.

The Navy had decided to standardize on the Corsair as its primary fighter bomber but Hellcats were not immediately phased out of service at the end of the war. Hellcats continued in active service for several years after the end of the conflict and many were transferred to the Naval Air Reserve where they soldiered on for a few years more. Hellcats were also supplied to a number of foreign nations in small numbers and a few flew on until the late 1960s. Happily, a few Hellcats still take to the air in the hands of private owners who have restored the veteran warriors to their former military glory.

In retrospect the Hellcat was an important milestone for both the US Navy and Grumman. For Grumman the Hellcat established that company as the leading supplier of advanced Navy combat aircraft of which the Mach 2 F-14 Tomcat is the latest product. For the Navy, the Hellcat proved that aircraft could control large areas of the sea and

establish absolute aerial superiority.

The facts speak for the Hellcat's greatness with the final victory tally: 4,947 enemy aircraft were destroyed in aerial combat by carrier based American Hellcats while 209 other enemy aircraft were destroyed by land-based USN and USMC units for a total of 5,156 enemy aircraft destroyed. This figure is even more amazing when it is realized that this number represented almost 75 per cent of *all* USN aerial victories. Not bad for an aircraft that was originally envisaged as an updated Wildcat.

Turning its back on a destroyed Mitsubishi Betty, one of the first Marine VMF(N)-534 Hellcats to land on Orote Field stands ready for the next mission. The squadron was commissioned on 1 October 1943 at Cherry Point. Arrived at Espiritu on 4 May and in Guam on 4 August. The squadron flew its first CAP on 7 August. In May of 1945 part of the squadron was based at Kober Field on Saipan to provide night air defense of the Saipan-Tinian area while another part was sent to Eniwetok to assume the same role in the Gilberts-Marshalls. The squadron continued to operate at Guam, Eniwetok, and Saipan until the war ended. (USMC/93361)

Hellcat Bureau Numbers

XF6F-1:	02981
XF6F-3:	02982
F6F-3:	04775–04958; 08798–09047; 25721–26195; 65890–66244; 39999–43137
XF6F-4:	02981
F6F-5/5N:	58000–58999; 69992–72991; 77259–80258; 93652–94521
XF6F-6:	70188, 70913

Specifications

Grumman XF6F-1

Span	42 ft 10 in
Length	33 ft 10 in
Height	14 ft 5 in
Wing Area	334 sq ft
Empty Weight	8480 lbs
Loaded Weight	11,629 lbs
Max. Speed	375 mph
Cruise Speed	200 mph
Ceiling	35,500 ft
Rate of Climb	2350 fpm
Range	1500 miles
Powerplant	Wright R-2600-16 of 1700 hp

Grumman F6F-3

Span	42 ft 10 in
Length	33 ft 10 in
Height	14 ft 5 in
Wing Area	334 sq ft
Empty Weight	9025 lbs
Loaded Weight	13,221 lbs
Max. Speed	391 mph
Cruise Speed	200 mph
Ceiling	39,400 ft
Rate of Climb	3100 fpm
Range	1850 miles
Powerplant	Pratt & Whitney R-2800-10 or -10W of 2000 hp

Grumman F6F-5

Span	42 ft 10 in
Length	33 ft 10 in
Height	14 ft 5 in
Wing Area	334 sq ft
Empty Weight	9060 lbs
Loaded Weight	12,598 lbs
Max. Speed	410 mph
Cruise Speed	200 mph
Ceiling	38,800 ft
Rate of Climb	3150 fpm
Range	1900 miles
Powerplant	Pratt & Whitney R-2800-10W of 2000 hp

Top left
Hellcat Combat Air Patrol (CAP) prepares to
launch off the *Bunker Hill* CV-17. Note that the
F6F-3s are all carrying the large centerline drop
tank. (USN)

Bottom left
Not all Hellcats were destroyed in training
accidents or aerial combat. Parked Hellcats were
ripe targets for *Kamikazes*. The elevator for this
carrier has been blown out and a Hellcat that had
the misfortune of being parked nearby sits in
shredded ruins near the smoldering opening.
Damaged aircraft such as this were immediately
dumped over the side as there was little or no
room to store the aircraft until they could be
repaired or stripped for spare parts. Note the
numerous hoses brought forward to fight the fire
by various damage control parties. (National
Archives/80-G-700654)

Top right
As Air Intelligence Officers take notes, flight
crews from the *Yorktown* refight their strikes
against Wake Island in October of 1943, checking
reports against reconnaissance photos hastily
patched together into a composite map of the
sand spits and coral reefs which link the island
together. Note the hard rubber recognition model
of a Japanese Val hanging from the ceiling, a
common feature of the ready rooms.
(USN/432598)

Bottom right
Built as a response to the need for large numbers
of carriers in the shortest possible time, the light
carriers were converted from nine uncompleted
light cruisers. CVL-26 USS *Montery* started life
as CL-78 USS *Dayton*, but in March 1942 was
renamed and completed as an aircraft carrier.
Launched on 21 February 1943, *Montery* was in
action by November, taking part in raids on
Makin Island and the Marshalls. The ship's air
group was involved in the Marianas Turkey Shoot
but, after sending strikes against numerous
Japanese targets, *Montery* was caught in a
typhoon and had to return to Bremerton,
Washington, for repairs. In WESTPAC again, the
ship, part of TF 58, attacked the Home Islands and
was preparing to hit targets in Tokyo when word
came down that Japan had surrendered on 15
August. This ship is seen with its complement of
Hellcats and Avengers tied down on deck.
(USN/290628)

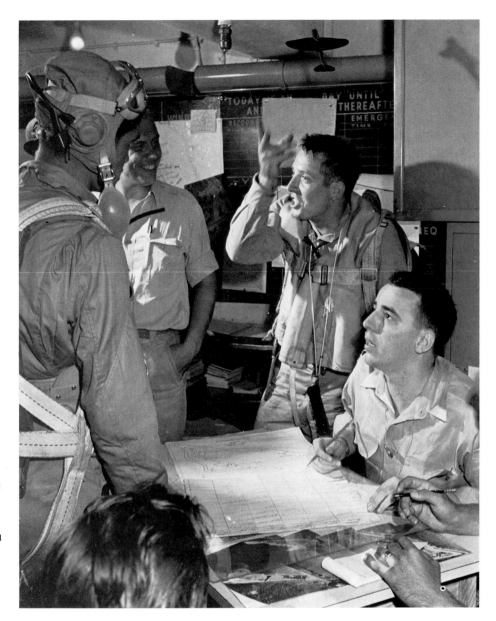

Top left

American production capacity was the one great factor in winning the war. During the 1930s the time required to build a carrier averaged four years; after the inevitable bottlenecks and confusion were reduced, if not eliminated, the Essex-Class ships took 19 months, from laying the keel to launching. CV-16 was named *Lexington* in honor of the old 'Old Lex', lost at the Battle of the Coral Sea in 1942. Surviving the war *Lexington* served off Korea. A combat air patrol (CAP) prepares to launch in this photograph taken in November 1943. The F6F-3s show the effects of over painting a Red surround specified to be used on 29 June 1943 and at the same time White side bars were added to the insignia but replaced on 14 August by Blue to reduce the possibility of confusion with the Japanese *hinomaru*; the tendency being to fire at the sight of red paint and check the target's identity afterwards. In this instance the surround has been repainted with a lighter shade of Blue than was used on the circular field of the insignia; however, only the lower portion is visible, contrasting with the planes' Intermediate Blue sides, so it appears that Non-Specular Sea Blue was used, the upper part of the surround simply being blended into the fuselage spine. (USN/473081)

Top right

USMC F6F-3 Hellcats on the captured airfield at Munda, New Georgia. Not how the Red surrounds have hurriedly been painted out. (USMC/61756)

Center right

Pilots from VF-8 aboard the *Bunker Hill* talk over a mission. Note the rugged center section construction of the Hellcat. In many cases, after a crash landing, the only part of the Hellcat left more or less intact would be the center section, leaving a dazed pilot to thank his good luck in the tough birds from the Grumman 'Ironworks'.

Bottom right

Disaster aboard USS *Cowpens* CVL-25. An out of control Hellcat has avoided the deck crash barrier and travelled for'ard to smash into a group of parked Hellcats with the net result being at least four destroyed fighters. Note the *Cowpens* markings of two White bars on the vertical tail surface and two White bars on the upper right aileron. (USN)

Top left

Two carriers, loaded with the best from Grumman – Hellcats and Avengers – steam into an American port after a combat tour. The sailors are decked out in their whites and the ship has been put in the most presentable condition possible. The aircraft are completely buttoned up and tied down. In these quiet minutes before docking the crew can pause and reflect on their months in combat and their hard-won victories.

Top right

One Hellcat on deck and another in the air, this scene was typical of F6F action off Formosa during 1945. The aircraft in the air has just received a wave-off and is banking steeply for another approach to the carrier. The wave-off phase of landing was one of the most dangerous as the aircraft was going at very slow speed and the sudden addition of the power could cause the fighter to snap over with absolutely no chance for recovery before impacting with the surface of the ocean. (National Archives/80-G-284464)

Center left

A scene that would not set well with one affected by sea-sickness. Waves break over the bow of a carrier off Iwo Jima on 19 February 1945. Note how the Hellcats are securely lashed to the deck of the ship.

Bottom left

The F6F-5 featured a new cowling that helped improve streamlining while increasing air flow over the P & W R-2800-10W. This aircraft painted overall Glossy Sea Blue is carrying the drop tank from a machine that had been finished in the tricolor camouflage scheme. Note how much better the visibility over the nose was compared to the Corsair. (National Archives/80-G-469416)

Top left

Disaster was always around the corner on the deck of a World War Two carrier. An explosion in the wing of this landing F6F-5 created a large blaze which the damage control crew is busily trying to control. Note how several small blazes have sprung up on the carrier's deck.

Top right

USS *Bennington* CV-20 joined Vice Admiral Marc Mitscher's Task Force 58 in February 1945 and, as the lead ship of Task Group 58.1, provided air support for the Marines as they fought their way on to Iwo Jima, a miserable chunk of lava selected for capture because it could serve as a base for air strikes on Japan. Off Okinawa on 24 March, *Bennington* had a brush with a *Kamikaze*; the weather was perfect for the attack but after a barrage of anti-aircraft fire put up by the ship, the pilot departed the area at high speed with his bomb still attached. The most serious damage the ship suffered was caused by the weather, a typhoon raising seas which buckled the forward section of the flight deck. Here F6F-5s from Air Group 1 launched strikes against Japanese airfields which destroyed eighty-five aircraft. (National Archives/80-G-468990)

Center right

During the war the services were constantly transferring aircraft back and forth. This Grumman F6F-5N is an excellent example. The machine was photographed at the USMC base on Peleliu on 25 September 1944 as part of the First Marine Division. However, closer inspection will reveal a number of interesting points. Firstly, note the designator on the fuselage side. It reads 'F(N)59'. A quick check of Marine Corps night fighter squadrons will reveal that no night fighter unit was designated 59 during the war. The original print reveals the BuNo 58801 on the fin and the designation F6F-5N on the rudder in bright, clear white paint. However, looking at the service designator on the fin 'Marines' appears to have been hastily painted over with a wash of light blue paint. Checking into Navy files one will find VF(N)-59 listed; thus we have an example of a Marine night fighter being transferred back into the Navy. (USMC/97569)

Bottom right

Powerful F6F-5N night fighter was a deadly opponent for Japanese intruders. The -5N was fitted with AN/APS-6 in a fiber pod on the right wing and over 1,400 were constructed. (Grumman)

Top left

Designated a night fighter carrier, *Enterprise* **dropped the identifying White triangle in favor of this outlined arrowhead. The pilots felt that the White triangle made their aircraft stand out. Painted in overall Glossy Sea Blue, these F6F-5Ns burn following a** *Kamikaze* **attack off Okinawa on 18 March 1945. (USN)**

Top right

Ensign Ardon R. Ives survived one of the more harrowing flight deck accidents on 25 February 1945, following a strike against Tokyo in support of the Marines' landing on Iwo Jima. Damaged, his F6F-5 lost its auxiliary fuel tank following a hard landing on *Lexington* **(a blown tire on the right main mount did nothing to help); the tank had come loose and smashed into the propeller which neatly severed the nose cone of the tank splashing high octane gasoline across the deck towards the crewmen in the gun tubs who are ducking in anticipation of what could happen next. The fuel burst into flames as crash crews ran towards the plane, dragging hoses fitted with fog nozzles and foam generators. Ensign Ives unstrapping in record time jumped off the right wingtip to safety. The diagonal White bands were** *Lexington's* **G symbols. The rudder was a replacement part which had been in storage for some time and was still in Intermediate Blue, being uncrated and installed without benefit of a coat of Glossy Sea Blue to match it to the rest of the plane. (National Archives/80-G-268186)**

Center left

Space aboard carriers was at an absolute premium, every foot being utilized for parking aircraft, gasoline tanks, and bombs and ammunition. These Glossy Sea Blue Hellcats carrying the G symbol markings of USS *Langley* **CVL-27 and are parked as far back on the stern of the flight deck as possible to make room for flight operations.**

Bottom left

The 10,000th Hellcat off Grumman's Bethpage production line. The Hellcat was one of the few fighters to go through the war with hardly any airframe changes, the last examples being virtually identical to the first examples. (Grumman)

Top left
Hollywood goes to war. Actor Wayne Morris joined the Navy Reserve and became a Hellcat driver and an ace. Unfortunately, the war seemed to have been the stopping point for his rising career and Morris never regained his pre-war popularity and he died in obscurity in the early 1960s. (USN/258657)

Bottom left
The Navy's top-scoring ace, Commander David McCampbell finished the war with thirty-four confirmed victories and the Congressional Medal of Honor. Here he is seen aboard the *Essex* in the cockpit of one of his Hellcats, an F6F-3 painted Glossy Sea Blue overall with the name 'Minsi III' painted in White, after bringing his score up to thirty kills. (USN/258198)

Top right
A classic photograph of the 'Fighting Lady', the USS *Yorktown* CV-10, as the famous ship recovers a flight of Hellcats. (USN/414666)

Center right
The last Hellcats in Navy service finished their life in a rather ignominious duty, that of target drone. Designated F6F-5Ks, these aircraft served as remotely controlled targets for guided missiles. The last of the World War Two veterans was blown out of the air in the early 1960s.

Bottom right
After the end of the World War Two, many Hellcats were transferred to the Naval Air Reserve as was F6F-5N BuNo 79889, assigned to New York NAS Floyd Bennett Field. Naval Air Reserve aircraft were identified by an Orange band painted around the fuselage. Note the 20 mm cannon fitted to this aircraft. (R.T. O'Dell)

Marianas Turkey Shoot – The Hellcat's Finest Hour

Yamamoto was dead, ambushed by a flight of Army P-38s over the fetid jungles of Bougainville, the charred corpse found with its head blown apart by a heavy machine-gun slug. Koga, his successor, was also dead, victim of a flying accident. Now the mantle of Commander-in-Chief of the Japanese Combined Fleet had descended upon the shoulders of Admiral Soemu Toyoda, who barely had time to shuffle his desk around to his satisfaction before having a particularly hot potato dropped in his lap.

The stubborn Americans – who refused to give up even though the gods themselves were against them – were battering their way into the Bismarcks and north towards the Philippines. Of course it was only a matter of time before the Japanese soldier's sacred spirit of *bushido* turned the tables on these light-skinned devils with their funny round eyes, but they *were* proving far more stubborn than pre-war thinking had led anyone to expect. Now MacArthur, roaring back from Australia, was clipping one piece after another off New Guinea's eastern, Japanese-held coast. Wake was taken on 19 May 1944 and, to speed operations, MacArthur ordered the next assault to be made against Biak, an island which could be used by 7th Air Force Liberators as a forward airfield.

Toyoda's strategic plans called for a major fleet action at mid-year, and heavies flying from Biak could put a serious crimp in this schedule. Accordingly Rear Admiral Naomasa Sakonju was ordered to land 2,500 men from a force of destroyers on Biak to reinforce its garrison, but the admiral's own warrior spirit seemed to be taking a vacation, for he allowed himself to be panicked and chased back to Mindanao in the Philippines without a fight. Determined to stiffen New Guinea's defenses Toyoda called in the twin super battleships *Yamato* and *Musashi*, capable of rolling over the cruisers which made up 7th 'Phib's fire support force without even noticing the thump. Three days before this armada was to steam for New Guinea the admiral, evaluating intelligence and contact reports, decided that Raymond Spruance's Fifth Fleet was going to hit the Marianas and pulled all of his ships back north into the Philippine Sea to await further developments.

The Combined Chiefs of Staff did not pull names of islands out of a hat nor were they dedicated to the idea of staging bloodbaths, as had been charged after Operation 'Galvanic' – the assault on Tarawa and Makin staged the preceding November which had produced what seemed to be enormous casualties – each chunk of real estate being carefully selected on the basis of genuine strategic value. Saipan and Tinian, in the Marianas, were needed for bases for the B-29, Boeing's superheavy which some advocates held was capable of bringing Japan to its knees single handed. Toyoda was as convinced of the Superfort's capabilities as were the Americans, thanks to the Empire's efficient intelligence service, and knew what dangers enemy airfields held this close to the Home Islands. The choice he faced was not an enviable one, but in the long run the Marianas were of greater importance, and New Guinea's defenders were abandoned to their inevitable fate.

The major islands which make up the Marianas group – Guam, Tinian, Rota, and Saipan – lie in a near-perfect line, running north-northeast from a point 13 degrees above the equator. Of these Guam was the best known, having been lost on 10 December, only three days after Pearl Harbor, when its 365-man garrison was swamped by a Japanese landing force of 5,000 troops. Like Wake, its recapture was a matter of restoring national pride as well as establishing another base to support the drive towards Tokyo. On 23 February canny old Marc Mitscher's Task Force 58 paid the first visit to the islands since Guam's fall. Although intended to gather information on what the Japanese had done in two and a half years, carrier aircraft and lurking subs teamed up to put 45,000 tons of shipping on the bottom of the sea.

Operation 'Forager' began taking shape on 12 March when the Joint Chiefs picked the Marianas as America's next target in the Central Pacific. Although most available troops were being shifted to Europe in anticipation of Overlord, the invasion of France, the Marines still had three full divisions in the Pacific, the Army two, and the Navy had hauled itself up by its bootstraps after Pearl Harbor to field the largest surface force the world had seen, its backbone formed by the fast 'Essex' Class Fleet carriers, light flat-tops built on cruiser hulls, and the ubiquitous Kaiser-built freighter-hulled 'Jeeps', originally intended for use as transports but proving themselves the equal in spirit, if not size, of their companions. The nearest friendly base was Eniwetok, 1,000 miles from the Marianas and still showing the scars of its recent change in ownership, but already well along in its transformation by the Seabees into an important advanced base. If the Navy had not established control of the Pacific through its carrier groups and submarine wolf packs, 'Forager' would have been impossible; that it was set in motion is the most convincing proof that the ocean had become an American lake.

On 11 June, four days before landings on Saipan were scheduled to begin, TF 58's four fast carrier task groups began carrying out strikes against Japanese airfields and coastal defense positions. Toyoda slipped his carefully husbanded force's leash and Operation 'A-Go', intended to trap the unsuspecting Americans and annihilate them, was underway. Throughout the war the Japanese exhibited an unshakeable belief that the United States Navy would make just the blunders required to lead to its destruction. Prior to Midway a staff war game's results had been reversed when the officer assigned to take the American part did not play by the rules and sank four Imperial carriers; the proper outcome was a crushing Yankee defeat and nothing would be allowed to contradict this. Now, two years later, Vice Admiral Jisaburo Ozawa, who had replaced Nagumo, the victor of Pearl Harbor, set out fully confident that *this* time all would go according to plan. Ozawa had nine carriers – three large Fleet flat-tops (veterans *Zuikaku* and *Shokaku* and the new *Taiho*) and six light units; the super heavy *Yamato* and *Musashi*, the largest and most powerful battleships in history; four older battlewagons; eleven heavy cruisers; thirty-four destroyers; and six oilers. Preparations for 'A-Go' started on 3 May, before Spruance's fleet invested Saipan, since it took the Japanese even longer, thanks to American submarines and roving carrier task groups, to move from one point to another. By 16 May Ozawa's forces had linked up and were riding at anchor at Tawi Tawi in the Sulu Archipelago, where they were spotted by a pair of snooping subs, the *Puffer* and *Bonefish*; another sub, the *Ray*, reported surface units in Davao Gulf, sighting which convinced Spruance that the planned landings on Guam should be postponed and preparations carried out to prepare his ships for battle.

First blood in the long-planned decisive battle was drawn by the Americans, *Bonefish* attacking a group of tankers and destroyers on the night of the 14th and sinking one of the latter; *Puffer* put two tankers down; and *Harder* sank three destroyers. A force of twenty-five RO-class submarines was stationed on the 'NA' line to bar the Americans from areas which the Imperial High Command wanted to lure them into at a later date, but seventeen of these were sunk by hunter-

killer destroyer groups, the *England* alone accounting for six – victims of the newly-introduced hedgehog rockets. On 15 June, when word of the attacks on Saipan reached him, Toyoda issued the orders which finally launched Operation 'A-Go', frantic Japanese sailors and airmen cheering wildly now that the waiting was over. Ozawa had three things going for him: he would be within range of land-based Japanese aircraft on Marianas airfields; his carrier-based planes had the edge in range over the heavier American machines with their armor and self-sealing gas tanks; and he would be sailing into the wind, which meant he could launch and recover aircraft without loss of time. All the unfortunate Americans could point to were superior aircraft, better pilots, greater numbers, and a murderous desire to kill Japanese which had been fuelled by two years of war!

All through the 18th the Japanese and American scouts probed for each other's ships, Ozawa taking fullest advantage of his planes' superior range to stay just out of sight over the horizon. Spruance left the actual tactical disposition to his subordinates, Mitscher with the carriers and Vice Admiral Willis A. Lee who commanded the Battle Line of battleships and cruisers which were to engage the Japanese in a surface action if they closed. By 0415 hours on 19 June, Ozawa felt his dispositions were complete and prepared to launch 300 planes against the American carriers, unaware that Spruance, still in ignorance of the Japanese position, had turned east and was steadily opening the range. The day promised to be a splendid one with nine to twelve knot winds generally from the east, light clouds melting away until, by mid-morning, ceiling and visibility were unlimited. The American ships were grouped in circles by Task Groups, the carriers forming an inverted 'L' while Lee's cruisers and battleships lay in the angle to provide covering anti-aircraft fire in the event of an attack. Tirelessly, radar antennaes swept the empty brilliant blue sky, operators in darkened compartments watch-ing as thin lines of bright green light spun hypnotically around receiver screens. In CICs talkers settled their headsets more comfortably, juggling fluorescent crayons as they awaited the first reports of inbound bogeys; pilots in Ready Rooms made final notes before heading for the flight decks and their waiting planes. The stage was set for one of the most savage battles in the history of aerial warfare.

Three Air Groups were divided among the Japanese carriers: the 601st, aboard *Taiho, Zuikaku* and *Shokaku*, was made up of pilots who averaged six months of training (Americans were not expected to be ready for squadron assignments until they had two years in their log-books); the 62nd, assigned to the *Hiyo, Junyo* and *Ryuho* of Carrier Division 2 had received three months of training; while those unfortunates aboard *Chitose, Chiyoda* and *Zuiho* (Carrier Division 3) as the 653rd could look back on only two. Japan had begun the war with the best carrier pilots in the world, men who had survived an unimaginably brutal training program and years of combat in China, but hundreds had died during the desperate fighting during 1942 when Japan's carrier force was cut to pieces; more hundreds, transferred to shore bases, being killed the following year as American production lines poured superior aircraft into the hands of waiting squadrons. Marines flew the Navy's one-time orphan, the F4U Corsair, which carrier pilots felt was too hot for shipboard operations with its 400 mph plus top speed and difficult landing qualities, while the Navy had a new product from the Grumman 'Ironworks', the F6F-3 Hellcat. The Japanese Navy was still wedded to the Mitsubishi A6M *Rei Seiten*, known variously as the Zero or Zeke. While a formidable opponent in capable hands up to the very last day of the war, the Zeke was totally outclassed, outperformed and outgunned by the Hellcat. The Japanese pilots would pay the price.

The American carriers lay approximately equidistant from Guam and Saipan on the morning of the 19th, Hellcats from the light carrier *Belleau Wood* picking up trade during a sweep over Guam around 0830 and engaging in a running fight for several minutes until recalled. Something of greater importance had come up.

At the same time that *Belleau Wood's* F6Fs were poking a stick into the ant hill at Guam, Ozawa launched the 653rd, the 3rd Carrier Division sailing some 100 miles ahead of the main body. At 0959 the battleship *Alabama*

picked up the first traces of this strike, sixty-four aircraft strong and 130 miles out, the carriers *Cabot* and *Enterprise* confirming this within four minutes. The recall went out to *Belleau Wood's* fighters, 'Hey, Rube!' bringing them back hotfoot to refuel and rearm. Mitscher immediately ordered all of his torpedo planes and dive bombers to launch and take up stations well to the west of Guam, where they were to orbit and stay out of the way to keep the American decks clear for the Hellcats. Turning into wind, TF 58's carriers put up nearly 200 Hellcats within fifteen minutes, the blue painted fighters setting off towards the Japanese position, which had remained unchanged all this time as the strike leader and his followers orbited for a final briefing.

At 1035 hours eight F6F-3s from *Essex's* VF-15 jumped the lead Japanese elements 55 miles out. With a 6,000 foot height advantage the Americans had surprise on their side and could take time to set up their attacks. Rolling inverted to keep his target, a Zeke armed with a bomb, in sight, the squadron skipper, Commander C.W. Brewster closed to 800 feet before opening fire. It was common practice to harmonize a fighter's six machine-guns so their fire converged at a range of 300 yards; the dark green aircraft was hit by a hail of half-inch explosive and armor-piercing bullets, exploding in a ball of flame. His wingman firmly in place off one wingtip, Brewster dove through the formation, hauled the nose of his Hellcat up, and lined up on a

second Zeke whose startled pilot was communing with his ancestors before he had a chance to decide on a course of action. Within moments the Yasukuni Shrine in Tokyo had two more boarders, but nothing lasts forever, and Fighting Fifteen had to make room for twenty Hellcats from *Hornet* and *Princeton* after only three minutes of having the show all to itself.

So far twenty-eight Americans in Hellcats were diving and skidding as they chased the surviving Japanese but, by 1043 hours, this had escalated to forty-two as planes from the *Cowpens* and *Montery*, throttles to the firewall, jumped in with both feet. The once-pristine sky was now streaked by oily black smoke from burning Japanese aircraft, unprotected fuel tanks flaming as steel-jacketed slugs tore through without hindrance, their pilots jumping like khaki-clad puppets as they were riddled in their unarmored cockpits. Scattering in the face of unbroken attacks by their tormentors, reinforced a second time by Hellcats from *Cabot's* VF-28, more from VF-31, flying off *Monterey*, and the *Bunker Hill's* Fighting Eight, the Japanese pilots refused to retreat, pressing on in ones and twos toward their targets. Four selected Lee's TG 58.7, not a wise choice under the best of conditions but definitely a bad idea now, since *Enterprise's* VF-10 dropped on them without delay and turned two into oil slicks. Two Jill torpedo bombers tried to slip their tin fish into one of Lee's battlewagons but their concentration

... crew begin to run towards a Hellcat that has
... anded for additional fuel and ammunition
... g the Turkey Shoot.

... right
... natic gun camera view of the deadly combat
... took place during the fight that became
... n as the Turkey Shoot. A Hellcat pilot is
... y destroying a Zeke with a few well-aimed
... s, the Hellcat's gun camera faithfully
... ding the action, when another eager Hellcat
... suddenly cuts in front to fire his guns at the
... dy burning enemy, a distinctly dangerous
... edure as the other Hellcat was still firing!
... that the second attacking Hellcat has still not
... ped his auxiliary fuel tank. (National
... ives/80-G-46981)

... left
... F6F Hellcat landed aboard the USS *Essex*,
... ng its tail hook out of the fuselage in the
... ess. As can be seen, it ended up in the crash
... er which contributed its own share of the
... age. *Essex* played an important role in the
... anas operation called 'Forager'. (USN)

was disturbed by a pair of F6Fs from VF-10 who flamed one from point-blank range. The only Japanese plane to succeed in its endeavors managed to put a bomb into the *South Dakota*, killing twenty-seven men and wounding another twenty-three, but the battleship continued to blacken the sky with anit-aircraft fire.

Somehow evading the trigger-happy Americans, the Japanese survivors straggled back to their carriers and counted noses: of the sixty-four planes which had taken off with such high hope, forty Zekes–eight fighters and thirty-two hastily rigged dive bombers–and two Jills had been destroyed, taking three Hellcats with them. Before the first strike had reached Spruance's position, Ozawa launched his second wave, forty-eight Zekes flying cover for fifty-three Judy dive bombers and twenty-seven Jills. The submarine *Albacore* got a torpedo spread off at *Taiho*, trying to send more Sons of Heaven to meet their ancestors. One of the Jill pilots saw the wakes and tried desperately to save his ship by diving into the sea in an attempt to detonate them, but his sacrifice was in vain, the carrier being hit fatally. Eight more planes were lost when their own ships opened fire on them, another ten being damaged so badly that they were forced to return to their carriers. At 1107 hours the massive formation showed up on American radar screens, the leader repeating his predecessor's move by going into an orbiting pattern in order to brief his crews, and again giving the Hellcats time to get off and set up their interception. Aboard *Lexington* Lieutenant (jg) Charles A. Sims, who had listened in on the first wave's radio traffic and provided a running translation, settled himself at his radio, finely-tuned the knobs and began feeding the attack leader's instructions directly to CIC and the fighter controllers. The 601st, from Carrier Group 1, may have had the best-trained (to stretch a point to breaking) pilots but its luck was no better than that of the 653rd's tyros. 129 Hellcats were in the air in *addition* to those already tearing the first attack to bloody tatters, thirty-three more being scrambled as soon as the second raid was detected. At 1126 three divisions – a dozen planes – from VF-15, led by Air Group (CVG) 15's leader (or CAG) Commander David McCampbell, were vectored toward the inbound trade, sighting their prey 13 minutes later, 40 miles west of TG 58.7. Flying at 25,000 feet, McCampbell and his men had a 5,000 foot edge on the Japanese and, leaving four men behind to guard their tails, he led three sections down in a high-side attack on a formation of Judy's. McCampbell's plan to bounce on a Judy from above, then dive under the formation and take on another from its low, or blind side, fell foul of Japanese construction and design when the first aircraft blew up, the survivors immediately breaking for safety in every direction with their rear gunners enthusiastically firing at equally startled Americans.

Again the fight turned into a general mêlée as Hellcats from *Wasp*, *Lexington* and *Princeton* dropped in, the Japanese pilots picking targets of opportunity and boring in by elements and divisions with F6Fs from *Bataan* and *Yorktown* scrambling to intercept their piecemeal attacks against Lee's battleships. By 1151, 26 minutes after McCampbell first engaged it, the 601st had been reduced to a shattered mob. TG 58.7 continued to soak up the bulk of their efforts, one Jill crashing into *Indiana*'s hull but doing little more than gouging the heavy belt of armor protecting its waterline. *Iowa*, *South Dakota* and *Alabama* were all attacked but with no effect. Six Judys got through to the carriers of TG 58.2, a phosphorous bomb exploding above *Wasp*'s flight deck, wounding a dozen men and killing the unlucky thirteenth. Two more went after the *Bunker Hill* but that ship's ordeal was still to come and the best the enemy could do was a near miss which killed three men, wounded seventy-three more, and started a few small fires which damage control parties easily controlled and extinguished. TG 58.2 escaped unscathed, torpedo runs on *Enterprise*

Top left and right

Rocket carrying Hellcats attacked enemy airfields during the Turkey Shoot. Sometimes they returned with unlaunched rounds as did this Hellcat which, in the first photo, is seen catching the arresting wire. The force of the landing jars two rockets loose and they go bounding down the deck, creating a hazard for everyone on the ship. However, quick thinking deck crew grab the finned missiles and toss them overboard. Typical of the countless unsung heroic actions that took place during a conflict such as the Turkey Shoot, this one just happened to be caught on film. (USN)

Bottom right

Guns are manned and ready as a Hellcat lands on the USS *Lexington* during the Turkey Shoot. (USN/236955)

Top left
These are the Hellcat pilots that defeated the best that the Japanese could put in the air. This group of F6F pilots is seen doing a bit of last minute talking before heading to their aircraft for yet another mission over the Pacific. (USN)

Top right
An F6F-3 Hellcat of VF-1 runs up just prior to releasing brakes to launch from the USS *Yorktown*. The date is 19 June 1944. The American fighter will soon be able to pick from several hundred attacking aircraft. (USN)

Center right
Grim evidence of the aggressive American spirit displayed by the Navy's Hellcat pilots, this Japanese dive bomber lies wrecked near one of the landing beaches as the Marines storm ashore in the Marianas. An amphtrak gives a tow to an incoming jeep in the background. (USN)

Bottom right
Lieutenant (jg) A. Vraciu, USNR, after returning from a combat patrol during the Turkey Shoot. Vraciu destroyed a number of enemy aircraft during the Marianas action. (USN/236899)

Top left
This Hellcat pilot took an AA hit in his left ankle during a raid over Guam, applied a torniquet above the wound and flew 300 miles to return and land on his carrier, the USS *Essex*. (USN)

Top right
A Hellcat piloted by Ensign H. Crabb of VF-1 attempted to come aboard the USS *Yorktown* with flaps up, the resulting high speed impact completely breaking off the aircraft's tail section. Luckily, no one was hurt. (USN)

Center and Bottom
Flight accidents cost the US carrier forces almost as dearly as enemy action. Ensign L.I. Cyphers of VF-1 approaches the *Yorktown* for a landing during the Turkey Shoot. He realizes too late that the F6F which landed ahead of him has not cleared the flight deck. In a desperate attempt to turn away, he pulls up his landing gear and applies full throttle – only to crash into the sea ..... fatally. (USN)

and *Princeton* drawing a complete blank. Of the 117 aircraft which had launched from Ozawa's first division only twenty-three returned to their ships, four Hellcats being lost in a prolonged battle; out of the four American pilots, three went down with their fighters while the fourth was able to step over the side and take to his life raft once he had hit the water and worked out of his chute harness, being picked up later no worse for wear.

Up to this point the 2nd Carrier Division had been standing on the sidelines but, between 1000 and 1015, the 652nd's first raids were launched, sixteen Zeke fighters, twenty-six Zeke dive bombers, and seven Jills heading in the wrong direction due to an error in the position report relayed by a scout aircraft. A corrected position was sent out but neither the dive bombers nor the Jills received it; their fighter cover did, however, and for some reason did not notice that the bombers were still heading for a spot some 60 miles north of TF 58. Hellcats from *Hornet* and *Yorktown* intercepted the Zekes and shot down seven without loss. At 1100 Ozawa sent off the fourth and last attack wave, drawn from the 601st and 652nd reserves – which were nothing to brag about. In all ten Zeke dive bombers, twenty-seven obsolete Val dive bombers, six Jills, nine Judys, and thirty Zeke fighters were thrown into this last-ditch effort to recoup something from the disastrous day. For a second time in the battle a false position report sent the planes haring off after phantoms, this time to a point 100 miles southwest of Guam.

This was too much even for the duty-conscious Japanese, who split up according to their air groups, eighteen heading back for the *Zuikaku* while fifteen aircraft from the 652 diverted for Rota, the balance picking Orote airfield on Guam as their destination. Taking these flights one at a time, ten of the Zekes on their way back to the carriers ran across a three plane search team from VT-16, off the *Lexington*, the pair of TBM Avengers and their escorting Hellcat knocking three Zekes out of the air! The 652 Judys and Zekes sighted southern-most TB 58.2 and made an ineffectual glide-bombing attack on *Wasp* and *Bunker Hill*, recovering their fighters at the time and so caught at a decided disadvantage, but heavy anti-aircraft fire dropped five of the dive bombers and drove the survivors off. The remaining forty-nine reached Guam and were in the traffic pattern for Orote,

preparing to land, when forty-one Hellcats from *Cowpens, Essex* and *Hornet* caught them with their pants down and shot thirty planes out of the air. Of the nineteen which managed to get down not one was left in flyable condition and it is doubtful if any were put back into the air.

In the course of four raids Ozawa's air groups had launched 328 out of the 430 aircraft they had flown aboard; of these 220 were lost, either in combat or through operational accidents, as were another twenty-three of his scouts. Seven Hellcats were lost in the air battles off the Marianas, nine more over Guam, and an additional six through accidents. Seven dive or torpedo bombers were shot down by Japanese fighters and ground fire in the course of attacks on Guam, two more being lost in accidents. No combat operations, before or since, have been as one-sided, nor has a victory been bought at such a low price. The green Japanese pilots proved so inept that the Americans who had quite literally slaughtered them coined a name for the day's action: it went into the history books as the Great Marianas Turkey Shoot and was a tribute to the fine fighting qualities of Grumman's Hellcat. After this action the Imperial Navy's aviation branch ceased to be a factor in the war until, backs to the wall, the Japanese loosed the Divine Wind against the Americans and their Allies.

Head on view of the USS *Cowpens* (CV-25). Named after a small town in South Carolina near which a US victory was recorded during the Revolutionary War, the rather strange name did not hinder this escort carrier from running up a distinguished record during World War Two. Commissioned during May of 1943, it was on hand a little over a year later for the Great Marianas Turkey Shoot in which its Hellcats accounted for a number of the Japanese aircraft destroyed. (USN/74269)

Left
A Hellcat from the USS *Lexington* prepares to launch while one of Admiral Lee's new battlewagons escorts in the background. The credit for the overwhelming victory scored during the Turkey Shoot clearly goes to the aggressive young fighter pilots of the fifteen US carriers on hand for the Marianas operation. Note the victory marks painted under the windscreen. (USN)

4 CORSAIR –

They Called it Whistling Death

It was up to the Marine Corps to prove that the F4U was World War Two's greatest naval fighter

On 29 May 1940, a relatively clear day, Naval Aviation history was made in the sky over Bridgeport Municipal Airport, Stratford, Connecticut, as Vought-Sikorsky's Chief Test Pilot Lyman A. Bullard eased the prototype XF4U-1 into the air. Bullard advanced the throttle for the big Pratt & Whitney XR-2800 and felt the airframe of the new fighter quiver with anticipation as the build-up of over 1,800 horsepower began to gallop from the three-blade propeller and the radically new fighter picked up speed as it progressed down the runway, watched by factory employees and curious onlookers who all stood with fingers crossed.

The concept for the XF4U-1 began during February of 1938 when the United States Navy initiated a design study for a totally new single-seat fighter for carrier use. The fighter was to have exceptional speed and handling characteristics. Chance Vought, long a sup-

plier of naval and military aircraft, decided to submit a proposal to the Navy. The engineering department knew that, in order to be successful, a totally new aircraft would have to be created.

The engineering staff was led by Rex B. Beisel and, under his supervision, several designs were drawn up for possible submission. Finally, in April of 1938, two designs were approved by Chance Vought for entry into the Navy fighter contest. The first design was given the company designation V-166A and was to be powered by the readily available Pratt & Whitney R-1830 Twin Wasp. The other design was designated V-166B and carried the most powerful piston engine that would be available, the Pratt & Whitney XR-2800 Double Wasp radial engine.

During the 1930s a distinct difference had cropped up between Navy and Army Air

Corps aircraft and the trend was more apparent as World War Two approached. The Navy was sticking to radial air-cooled engines while the Army was going for liquid-cooled inline powerplants, especially for the fighting aircraft. There were several reasons behind this split. Firstly, there was the serious problem of inter-service rivalry, an unfortunate problem that still exists today. Whatever the Navy had, the Army would not want and vice versa. In effect each service was sticking to the position that whatever item they used had to be better than the one used

The prototype Corsair during an early test flight. This view shows off the nose and wing gun positions to advantage. Note the canopy which is farther forward than on production versions. When the main fuel tank was moved from the wings to behind the firewall, the pilot's position had to be moved to the rear, decreasing visibility. Prototype was finished in overall Silver with Yellow wings. (Vought)

by the other service. Secondly, the Navy felt that the radial engine was more rugged and lent itself very well to long flights over vast stretches of ocean. However, the Army claimed that the liquid-cooled inline power-plant offered much less frontal drag because of its reduced area and that high speed aircraft could be built only with liquid cooled engines. The sad fact is that both services were right to a degree, the radial was more reliable and the liquid cooled engine was more streamlined. However, the time and expense frittered away in this see-saw contest only polarized the factions even more.

The Navy had been concerned about getting more power out of the radial engines, especially since they had seen the new Allison and Rolls-Royce powerplants that seemed to offer the ultimate in power and streamlining. The famous engine firm of Pratt & Whitney had developed an experimental twin-row engine that promised over 2,000 horsepower along with a two-speed, two-stage super-charger. Thus the Navy would be able to have an engine that would be both reliable and extremely powerful. An added plus was that the drag-causing frontal area was not

that much larger than radial engines currently in use.

Four proposals were eventually reviewed by the Navy and the V-166B came out most favorably. Even though it was a radical design, the other concepts presented to the Navy reviewing board were even more unusual and some were downright unworkable. With the engineering and structural knowledge of the day, the airframe of the V-166B was the smallest one that could be attached to the most powerful engine. As we shall see in a later chapter, the Grumman Bearcat also attempted the same formula but, at that time, technology had added a number of changing factors to the formula. To absorb and transfer the power generated by the R-2800 a very large propeller was called for and Hamilton Standard completed a three-blade, 13 foot 4 in diameter unit. The propeller would need a great deal of clearance and, if a conventional wing were used, cause an unacceptably high angle of attack while in landing or takeoff configuration. Vought engineers accordingly fitted their design with what was to become its most famous trade mark – the inverted 'bent' gull wing. The inverted gull wing had a

Early formation flight of three F4U-1 fighters. The relocation of the main fuel tank moved the pilot's position back three feet. The narrow canopy with its low hood did not increase visibility and the small quarter panels were more for style than for any practical purpose. (Vought)

number of advantages beside propeller clearance. The structure also gave improved pilot vision since the pilot would have a 'dip' in the wing to look past. Since the folding part of the wing would be at a lower height than normal, the folding portions would take up less height which was a particularly good advantage for a shipboard fighter where room was of paramount importance. Another factor in favor of the inverted gull configuration was a drop in the drag factor.

The Navy board was very excited by the paper fighter presented by Vought and, on 11 June 1938, a contract was issued for a prototype aircraft to bear the designation XF4U-1. By 10 February 1939, a full-size mockup of the fighter had been constructed for wind tunnel tests and for inspection by the Navy. A similar project for a current jet fighter has been known to take years to develop rather than months!

Top left

By 1942 the Vought factory was busily churning
out Corsairs as this publicity still illustrates. The
aircraft in the photograph are equipped with new
canopies that included a small bubble over the
pilot's head that helped visibility during landing
and take off to only a marginal extent. These
aircraft are finished in the Non-Specular Blue
Grey upper surfaces with Non-Specular Light
Grey lower surfaces. (Vought)

Top right

Excellent view of an early F4U-1 at the Vought
factory in Stratford, Connecticut. The blending of
the camouflage points is shown to good advantage.
Gun ports housed three 0.50 caliber Browning
machine-guns in each wing. Note the extremely
fine job of cowling the massive Pratt & Whitney
R-2800 radial engine. The pilot could well be
standing up to get a better view over that massive
nose! (Vought)

Center right

VF-12 was the first Navy squadron to receive the
Corsair, getting its first examples during October
of 1942. However, the USMC was to have priority
on getting the fighter since it could not be used
immediately on the carriers and VMF-124 was
formed during September. (Vought)

Bottom right

Taxiing out along Marston-mat perimeter strips,
these F4U-1s head for the main coral-surfaced
runway of Henderson Field on a mission against
Japanese troops dug into the jungle of
Guadalcanal. As a concession to the Corsair's new
role as a land-based fighter, the arresting hook
originally fitted for carrier operations was
removed, but solid rubber tires were left on the
planes' tail wheels. Normally pneumatic tires
replaced these for shore use, since solid ones
tended to tear up easily on rough surfaces.
(USMC/55449)

Top left
The pilots of the F4U-2N were seasoned veterans, each pilot selected for the squadrons had to have at least 2,000 hours flying time as taking a Corsair up into the night off a carrier was a tricky proposition at best. Two of VF(N)-101's night fighters are seen preparing for a launch during February of 1944. The early radar sets were extremely primitive and equipment failure was common. (USMC/307777)

Top right
A mystery paint scheme on a Corsair. This F4U was apparently the property of VMF-122 and the photograph was taken in the late part of 1944 on Peleliu. The most obvious oddity about the Corsair is that it is painted overall Aluminium, a curious practice for an aircraft in a combat area. Secondly, the Corsair appears to have part of its 1943-style red surround still around the national insignia. The insignia trim was only used for a few months during 1943 and all aircraft were supposed to have it painted out or over. Thirdly, the coding SS11 on the side does not correspond to any known USMC coding. Lastly, the name Sally is painted on the nose. The nice finish was a rarity for aircraft operating in the South Pacific. (R.W. Dietz)

Center left
Marine ace Captain Joe J. Foss in a Corsair over the San Diego area. Foss finished the war with twenty-six aerial victories, making him the second highest ranking Marine ace. He later went on to become Governor of South Dakota. (USMC/48604)

Bottom left
Line-up of Marine Corsairs on Guam belonging to MAG-21 including 'Screaming Meanie' and 'Peace Ever After'. Marine operated fighters were more often to have personal names and insignias painted on the aircraft than their Navy counterparts but it was still nothing like the flying billboards of Army Air Corps pilots. (USMC/110061)

Construction of the prototype had to bridge a number of new technologies and the aircraft was the first to utilize a new spot welding technique which had been developed at the Naval Aircraft Factory and Vought. This technique enabled a frame of heavy aluminium skin and thick supports to be built, resulting in an airframe that was exceptionally strong. The wing structure was manufactured in three sections: the outer wing panels were fabric covered (a curious fact considering just how advanced the XF4U was) from the main spar aft, the front part of the wing panels were metal covered, and the inverted gull stubs were integral with the fuselage. The landing gear was fitted into a bay on each of the inverted gull stubs and the gear would rotate 90 degrees and then fold back into the bays to be enclosed by twin doors.

Special attention was paid to the cowl of the aircraft to ensure that the cowling would be of extremely close fit to have the least amount of drag. The huge powerplant generated a great deal of heat and it was important that the heat was bled off so that the engine would not be damaged by the high temperatures. The engineers found it difficult to construct a cowling unit that would be both tight and cool; however they did do it and the resulting unit was a masterpiece. A generous ring of cowl flaps allowed regulation of the temperature by an efficient system of cooling airflow. The XF4U-1 was also the first fighter aircraft to utilize the principle of vectored thrust in which the exhaust gases were channelled for propulsive thrust.

The armament of the prototype F4U-1 was a bit curious. Two 0.30 caliber synchronized Browning machine-guns were mounted in the top of the engine cowling while one 0.50 caliber Browning was mounted in each outer wing panel. The cowling guns had 750 rounds of ammunition per gun while the wing guns carried 300 rpg. The strangest part of the armament consisted of anti-aircraft bombs that could be carried in ten compartments located in the mid-section of the outer wing. The rather pulp novel idea behind this curious installation would see the XF4U-1 fly above an enemy bomber formation and release the small bombs with the hope of knocking down a number of bombers. Fortunately, this curious concept was dropped with the prototype and the twenty 5.2 lb bombs were never used. It should be noted that the Germans attempted to use this idea during World War Two when Europe was being overrun with thousands of Allied heavy bombers. The Germans achieved a few victories but flying a straight-in bomb run with

thousands of machine-guns pointed at the attacking pilot left something to be desired and the procedure was dropped.

Pratt & Whitney had been applying all possible talent to the design and construction of the XR-2800. The -2 version was used for running in the Navy's test stand and the actual powerplant installed in the prototype was the -4 which was capable of putting out 1,850 hp for takeoff with 1,600 hp at 2,400 rpm available at 15,000 ft.

The first flight of the prototype went smoothly, lasting just under 40 minutes. The gear was not retracted and Bullard was pleased with the way the aircraft handled. Early in the testing program the test pilot noted that the engine was giving some problems. Poor fuel flow was causing fluctuating engine temperatures that resulted in some damage. Pratt & Whitney was very concerned that their pet powerplant ran correctly so they were on the spot with suggestions and modifications. The company's own test pilot was the second person to take the XF4U-1 around 'the

patch', trying to trace the problem. Another Vought test pilot, Boone Guyton, assumed the role of test pilot for the XF4U-1 program. During the fifth flight of the prototype something went wrong and Guyton suddenly found himself low on fuel and in very poor weather. Guyton knew that he was not going to make it back to main base so he set down at a nearby golf course. The smooth wet grass of the golf course offered little or no resistance to the fighter which landed at over 100 mph. The aircraft sailed over the course, ran into a rough, and then smashed into a wooded area, cartwheeling into the trees that surrounded the course. A shocked Guyton managed to clear himself from the wreckage of the prototype and wandered out on to the wet grass to wonder how so many factors could have been working against him. The XF4U-1 had sustained extensive damage that probably would have been fatal for any other aircraft. The prototype was to prove that the design was one tough bird.

Guyton surveyed the fighter and bleakly noted that the right wing was gone, the propeller was folded back along the cowling and the tail assembly was crushed. Engineers from the plant were quickly on the scene to get the aircraft disassembled and on trucks for the trip back to the factory. A full-time effort went into the rebuild and the 'ruined' fighter was back in the air within three months! Guyton went on to write several interesting books on flying and his chapters on piloting the F4U are gems.

The Navy, even with the accident, knew that they had a winner by the tail and that all future fighter proposals would have to match up to or surpass the XF4U-1.

The Chance Vought prototype was to make world-wide news after its rebuild when the aircraft achieved an incredible speed of just over 400 mph while on a straight and level test flight, becoming the first American combat machine to go over that speed and give the Navy considerable prestige and a reason to feel smug about their choice of a 'round' engine. At the time, 400 mph was a figure that carried some weight like the term 'sound barrier' during the late 1940s and early 1950s. It was, in fact, just a number but it was also a figure that the general public could relate to and feel safe knowing that '400 mph fighters' were protecting them.

Pratt & Whitney was freed from their burden of developing a liquid-cooled engine for the Army when General Hap Arnold, after poring over the XF4U-1's performance figures and engine output, told the company to concentrate all efforts into developing the R-2800 and other radial engines.

The performance of the XF4U-1 was actually better than expected due mainly to the fine degree of external finish on the airframe and to the added power from the vectored thrust exhausts. However, several problems were starting to rear their ugly heads as the testing program continued at a fast pace. The lateral stability and aileron control were found to be not what they should have been and it took almost 100 modifications to correct the problems. Tests in the giant NACA wind tunnel revealed that the new fighter would have an interesting spin characteristic that could cause non-recoverable situations.

The prototype was transferred to the huge naval test center at Anacostia for continued testing during October of 1940. The Navy was keeping a close eye on the war situation in Europe and, by the time Chance Vought was approached with a production proposal during November, extensive changes were in store for the fighter. The deadly battling between the Royal Air Force and the *Luftwaffe* had shown that certain requirements had to be met right from the start otherwise a fighter design could be doomed

CV-17, the USS *Bunker Hill*, **heads through the Panama Canal with a load of Avengers and Corsairs. When teamed with the Corsair, the Avenger torpedo bombers and Helldiver dive bombers made an unbeatable team. (USN/80-G-81849)**

to failure in the harsh classroom of combat over Europe. British Spitfires and Hurricanes were carrying batteries of eight 0.303 caliber machine-guns into combat to face an enemy that included heavy caliber cannon in their stable of aerial armament. The eight rifle-caliber machine-guns could hose out a lot of lead but, if they did not hit a vital part of the aircraft, little damage was often the result. Also, heavy armor plating and self-sealing fuel tanks reduced the chance of the 0.303 ammunition doing much damage. The RAF quickly added armor windscreens to their aircraft when direct or glancing hits in that area would often kill the pilot and destroy a valuable aircraft. The Germans had perfected the use of the aerial cannon and great damage was usually the result if an RAF fighter got trapped in the gun sight of a Messerschmitt Bf 109 for any length of time.

The XF4U-1's armament, considered heavy for its day, was quickly revised. The 0.30 caliber nose guns were done away with completely and the final armament consisted of six 0.50 caliber Brownings mounted in the outer wing panels. Six ammunition boxes were also located in the wing with 400 rounds for the two inner guns and 375 rounds for the outer weapons.

The fuel tanks in the prototype were also reconfigured on paper to provide a safer means of fuel storage. The four integral wing tanks were eliminated in favor of one huge tank of the same capacity directly behind the firewall. This led to the only major airframe modification on the F4U series. The placement of the fuel tank caused the pilot's position to be moved 32 inches to the rear. This repositioning had its good and bad points for the move improved the pilot's vision of the ground but the further aft position resulted in an even more difficult view over the front fuselage and huge engine cowling when the aircraft was taking off or landing. The F4U-1 would, therefore, feature a revised pilot's cabin and a new fuel system that would offer a much more positive fuel feed to the hungry Pratt & Whitney up front. The giant gas tank held 237 gallons while two leading edge tanks in the wing added a further total of 126 gallons. The main tank was protected with bullet proofing while the wing tanks contained a fire extinguishing system.

On 2 April 1941, Vought received a Navy contract for 584 aircraft, to be called Corsairs after the company's famous series of biplanes, and the first deliveries were to start in February 1941. The aircraft, now carrying the Vought designation of VS-317, would have the Navy designation F4U-1 and would mount an improved version of the P & W engine, the R-2800-8 Series B. Other modifications included the addition of armor plate to all vital systems, armor glass for the windshield, installation of an improved tail hook assembly, addition of the new Identification Friend or Foe radar unit, increased aileron span, reduced inboard flaps, addition of NACA slotted flaps, and a canopy that could be jettisoned in flight. Thus the first true fighting Corsair was born.

The first production Corsair left the assembly lines on 25 June 1942. Pearl Harbor had come and gone and America was still being hit hard in the Pacific. The Navy wanted its new fighter and they wanted it as soon as possible but little did the Navy know that the Corsair would not be flying from its carriers for several years to come!

The Navy decided to have the Brewster Aeronautical Corporation, makers of the portly Buffalo, set up a Corsair production line so more of the inverted gull wing fighters could flow to the battle areas. Under the Naval designation system the Brewster-built Corsair would be designated F3A-1 but, rather than thousands of new fighters, Brewster manufactured just over 700 before poor production techniques, shabby quality

Top
**Line up of FG-1D and F4U-4 Corsairs at Iwo Jima
on 18 April 1945. Note the long-range tanks. The
aircraft were on a stopover while engaged on a
ferry flight to Okinawa. The wide variety of
aircraft in the background makes for an aircraft
enthusiast's delight. They include PB4Ys, B-29s,
P-51Ds and C-47s. (USMC/120172)**

Top left
**Marine Air Wing 2 was eventually to exercise
administrative control over nine day and three
night fighter squadrons on Okinawa. Here the
'Hell's Belles' of VMF-441 are silhouetted against
a barrage of anti-aircraft fire put up against a
Japanese air raid on the night of 16 April. The 16th
saw a total of 270 Japanese aircraft destroyed,
thirty-eight by USMC pilots flying from Yontan
and two carriers, *Bennington* and *Bunker Hill*.
During the raid which produced this tracer
tapestry, three attackers fell to the pilots of
VMF(N)-542 and 543, the first kills of the Okinawa
campaign for the night fighters. (USMC/118775)**

Bottom right
**Detail view of the 20mm cannon armament on
the F4U-1C. The Navy preferred the 0.50 caliber
machine-guns and only 200 examples were built.
Note how the muzzles of the Hispano cannon
protruded from the leading edge of the wing.
(Vought)**

Top left
With the mighty R-2800 at take off power, the
pilot of this F4U-2N of VF(N)-101 gets the takeoff
signal from the deck officer on the USS *Enterprise*
during 1944. Twelve F4U-1s were taken from stock
and modified by the Naval Aircraft Factory into
the first single-seat Naval night fighter. (Vought)

Top right
F4U-1Ds equipped with 1,000 lb bombs on the
fuselage centerline position. The Marine Corsairs
are heading for a strike against Japanese targets
in the Marshall chain. The Corsairs of the Fourth
Marine Air Wing undertook a large part of the
burden of keeping the Japanese troops burrowed
in their caves and their airstrips cratered with
bomb damage. These F4U-1Ds were equipped
with six 0.50 caliber machine-guns with 400 rpg.
The F4U-1D did not attain production until April
1944. (USMC/86946)

Center right
A crew chief sits on the canopy of another Corsair
as he awaits the return of his own aircraft to
Guam during November of 1944. Note the canteen
belt slung over the Corsair's pitot tube.
(USMC/110057)

Bottom right
Located on the island of New Georgia (Munda) an
airstrip built by the Japanese in the middle of a
copra plantation (the trees left standing until the
very last minute to serve as living camouflage),
had served as the springboard for continual
attacks against American forces on Guadalcanal.
During June and July of 1943 an incredibly
complex series of landings on the islands which
make up the New Georgia group chewed up the
Japanese defenders and brought Munda under
American control at last. Here, on 26 August 1943,
an F4U-1 from an unidentified Marine squadron
taxis along the runway, still being widened and
improved by Sea Bees, throwing up a cloud of
coral dust and pulling condensation trails off the
propeller tips, evidence of extremely high
humidity which caused everything to rot or
corrode instantly. The aircraft is still finished in
the Blue Grey and Light Grey; White side bars
have only recently been added to its insignia,
which lacks the Red surround used between July
and September of 1943. (USMC/59974)

Top left

Corsairs earned the nickname 'Sweetheart of Okinawa', being flown by the 'Death Rattlers' of VMF-323 who destroyed 124.5 Japanese aircraft without loss to themselves. Re-engined with the 2,450 hp R-2800-18W, the F4U-4 made its combat debut during this campaign, three of these new versions are seen here taxiing out for a strike. The White number on the cowling is a temporary ferry number. (USMC/127915)

Top right

Although a pilot receives most of the publicity, without his ground crew he would be only one more infantryman. Here an F4U-1C from an unidentified MAG-31 squadron is pulled down for an engine change, its run out Pratt & Whitney being set aside for an overhaul while a new powerplant is hoisted into position. The Okinawan campaign seemed to be conducted under particularly foul weather conditions, mud and cloudy skies being the rule. (USMC/123932)

Center left

Landing on Peleliu was one thing, securing it was another. After attacking Japanese defenders on neighboring Ngesebus, the 'Death Dealers' of VMF-114 turned their attention to the dug-in survivors of the island's garrison. Here an F4U-1A drops a napalm tank on one of the reinforced cave complexes which riddled 'Bloody Nose Ridge', a defensive system which enabled the Japanese to hold off both Marines and Army troops from the 81st Infantry Division for over two months. The airstrip was so close to the ridge – within 15 seconds flight time – that often pilots would not even bother to retract the gear on their Corsairs. The Japanese, hearing the Corsairs come over day after day, dubbed them 'Whistling Death', because of the strange noise the airframe made as it passed through the air and the deadly load that the aircraft carried. (USMC/98401)

Bottom left

FG-1D with a flat tyre is quickly pushed out of the way on the flight deck of the USS *Block Island*, CVE-21. Deck crews would man-handle damaged aircraft off the flight deck to keep the way open for active aircraft landing or taking off. Sometimes, if the aircraft was badly damaged, it would be dumped over the side. (USMC/43747)

and monetary rip-offs forced the company out of business in a governmental scandal. Years later, one ex-Marine pilot remembers the Brewster-built Corsairs with something less than fondness: 'When we were at Goleta (near Santa Barbara, California) we had a number of different models of Corsairs out on the line in which we would take our training. All the Brewsters were red-lined for speed and prohibited from aerobatics after several shed their wings during flight training and combat maneuvers. We were all a bit apprehensive towards the Brewster machines. I lost a friend in one of the crashes. The cause of the wings coming off was later traced to poor quality wing fittings. I remember noting in my log book that the Brewsters were unsafe to fly and always looked at the Bureau Number and designation block to make sure that I would not draw one for a flight.'

As the production of the F4U-1 began to spool up at Vought, the problems of getting the Corsair settled down on Navy carriers began. On 25 September 1942, the first series of carrier qualifications began aboard the *USS Sangamon*. The pilot made a few landings and take offs and then declared that the Corsair was not yet fit for carrier operations. One can well imagine the feelings of the test pilot as he approached the pitching deck of the carrier. The pilot sat so far back that his view forward was virtually obscured and the view downward was not much better. Oil from the hydraulic cowl flaps spattered against the windshield, further reducing visibility. Trying to raise himself in the seat to see over the nose, the pilot kept banging his head against the low-set canopy frames.

The Corsair had a nasty stall characteristic

of rapidly dropping its port wing and a pilot needed to be very aware of the fighter's characteristics as the big plane slowed down to carrier landing speeds. Also, if the throttle were suddenly advanced, the torque from the engine and propeller could actually flip the plane upside down. The test pilot also complained of the tricky Corsair landing gear which, if landed upon with some force, would cause the oleos to compress rapidly and then extend rapidly, thus making the plane go bouncing down the deck with each bounce becoming more out of control. These characteristics could, and did, cause many young Naval aviators nightmares so modifications were undertaken in an attempt to correct the situation. In the meantime, rumors began to spread around the training bases that the new fighter was a pilot killer and extremely difficult to fly.

The pilot's seat was raised seven inches to provide better visibility and the canopy was disposed of and a new unit installed that offered almost a bubble configuration. To help with the stall problems, the Vought engineers added a stall strip, only about six inches long, on the leading edge of the starboard outer wing panel near the gun ports. This helped the wing to stall at the same time as the other by disturbing the airflow just enough to give the desired effect. The tail wheel strut was also decreased in size to give the plane a better sit. The United States Marine Corps, who felt that they were always given castoffs, were quick to grab the Corsairs coming off the production line that could not be sent aboard the carriers. The Marines felt that they could tame the Corsair ... and they did, making combat history in the process.

The war had progressed for nearly a year by the time the first combat squadron began to receive the 'bent wing bird' as the Corsair had been dubbed. The first unit to receive the Corsair for combat duty was not an elite Navy fighting squadron but rather VMF-124, a Marine unit that had been formed during September of 1942 at Camp Kearney, California. The squadron had been put together from what was left of VMF-122 and the pilots were most anxious to prove their new mount in combat.

The men and aircraft of VMF-124 were sent, after Camp Kearney, to a combat upgrading center where the Corsairs were thoroughly examined before being declared ready for combat. The aircraft were overhauled and updated with the latest factory modifications before being prepared for shipment to the Pacific battle front. By the end of December 1942, VMF-124 had been declared combat ready and the next stop was to be Guadalcanal.

Since time was short and officials were very anxious that the Corsair be sent into combat as soon as possible, pilot training was held to a minimum and the men of VMF-124 averaged only about 20 hours of flying time on the Corsair before they arrived at the combat front! This was an exceptionally low time, especially since the young Marine aviators would be facing the dreaded Mitsubishi Zeke fighters. VMF-124 arrived at Guadalcanal during February of 1943 and quickly set up their operational base so additional hours could be flown before the fighters were committed to combat.

VMF-124 had a total of twenty-two F4U-1s ready for combat patrol and the first action was seen on 14 February when the Corsairs were to accompany a mixed bag of Navy Liberators, and Air Force P-38s and

'The Sinner' lumbers down the taxiway on Guam while the crew chief stands on the wing and guides the pilot to the revetment area. The Corsair was returning from a mission to Rota Island in the Marianas where it had dropped 500 lb bombs on the Rota airstrip. (USMC/98879)

P-40s on a strike to the hornet's nest at Kahili Field, Bougainville. The Japanese were more than ready for the combined American raid; over fifty Zekes had climbed well above the advancing formation. With the advantage of height and with the sun at their back, the Japanese broke into the top cover formation of four Lockheed P-38 Lightnings. The twin-tailed fighters never knew what hit them and they were destroyed in a matter of seconds. The next layer of aircraft consisted of the Corsairs and part of the Japanese force detached themselves to tangle with the new fighter while the remainder went after the Liberators and the bottom cover of Curtiss P-40s. The Zekes appeared to be unstoppable and two Liberators, two P-40s and two Corsairs fell to the onslaught. To make matters worse only four of the enemy were knocked down so it was a decisive victory for the Japanese and not a very good combat debut for the Navy's newest fighter.

The pilots of VMF-124 examined their tactics and made changes that would take advantage of the Corsair's strong points of high speed and heavy firepower while playing to full advantage the various weaknesses that had been showing up in the Japanese Zeke. They talked to the combat-hardened pilots who were flying the outdated Wildcat against the Zekes every day and holding their own. From these changes in tactics and discussions with veterans, the Corsair was to be placed in a position of superiority that would never be challenged by the Japanese empire.

Pilots from VMF-122 pose in front of the Officers' Club on Peleliu on 11 October 1944. By the time the print had been developed four of the pilots in the photo had been killed in action. The group was typical of the Marine Corsair units in the Pacific.

The Vought factory continued its steady supply of Corsairs to the rapidly equipping USMC squadrons and, by July 1943, eight squadrons of Corsairs were ready for action in the South Pacific. In the meantime, VMF-124 had gone on to rack up victories of over seventy-eight enemy aircraft while losing eleven aircraft and three pilots of their own.

The big radial engine fighters were soon slugging their way to Rabaul on a regular basis, taking on the best that the Japanese had to offer . . . and winning. The pilots liked the reliability of the R-2800 engine and the crews of the bombers appreciated the Corsair's long range which meant that the fighters could escort the bombers all the way to the target and back, something that the Wildcats could not do. With the heavy combat flying it was just a short matter of time before the first Corsair ace emerged. The man to do the trick was USMC Lieutenant Kenneth Walsh of VMF-124. Walsh started out his Marine career in 1933, enlisting as a recruit. He worked his way up to the position of aviation mechanic and radioman and was transferred to Pensacola, Florida, for pilot training in March 1936. Walsh went on to fly observation aircraft for four years off carriers such as the *Wasp*, *Ranger* and *Yorktown*. Walsh, at this time, was an enlisted pilot. At the time of

the Pearl Harbor attack, Walsh was serving with VMF-122 with the rank of Marine Gunner. He was then transferred to VMF-124 and promoted to Second Lieutenant and his military career really began to take off.

After a dangerous trip in an unescorted transport ship, the pilots of VMF-124 off loaded at New Caledonia while their Corsairs were sent to the growing Navy base at Espirito Santo. After joining their aircraft, the pilots immediately went to work to gain more flying hours before their first combat mission, which was to be only a couple of days away. The inexperienced pilots had their hands full trying to control their powerful mounts and Walsh nearly killed himself when the big P & W suddenly quit during a training flight. Ken Walsh pointed the long nose of the fighter straight ahead and set down in the ocean. However, the fighter sank so quickly that Walsh did not have time to get out of the aircraft's cockpit. Walsh got his straps loose underwater and bobbed to the surface – with not a moment to spare – where he was rescued.

On April's Fool Day of 1943, Walsh and his squadron intercepted a large force of Japanese fighters and dive bombers that were heading for an attack on the Solomons. A huge dogfight resulted and, when the skies cleared, Walsh had destroyed two aircraft. A few days later he once again had the unnerving experience of heading towards the ocean in a powerless fighter. Walsh pulled this crash landing off with less difficulty than the first and he was rescued by a small boat that

was passing the area. On 13 May, Walsh was in the thick of combat again and he destroyed three Zekes, becoming the first Corsair ace. But Walsh was not content to let his score settle on five and, by 15 August, he was a double ace with ten Japanese aircraft destroyed. Soon after this milestone Walsh was involved in a deadly air battle when his Corsair formation was jumped by a superior number of Zekes. Walsh quickly scored one victory and then was repeatedly attacked by the enemy. Upon returning to home base, his aircraft was so badly damaged by enemy fighters that it was junked for spare parts.

Ken Walsh went on to prove his bravery in an incredible dog fight that took place on 30 August 1943. VMF-124 joined up with Bell P-39s and Curtiss P-40s to protect a B-24 raid in the Solomons. After landing in the Russell Islands for refuelling and briefings, they were once again on their way. Walsh's aircraft developed engine trouble and he returned to base. He quickly rounded up another fighter and headed for the combat zone. He thought he saw the B-24 formation on the horizon but, to his surprise, the formation turned out to be fifty Zekes heading towards an attack on the Liberators. Walsh, not thinking of his own safety, immediately attacked the enemy formation destroying two fighters. The bombers and other fighters were alerted and a huge aerial battle quickly developed. Walsh kept the Zekes off the bombers as best as he could, scoring two more victories. An experienced enemy fighter pilot latched on to the ace's Corsair and a deadly battle developed. Walsh could not shake the excellent enemy pilot who was pumping cannon and machine-gun fire into the F4U. Suddenly the engine was hit and the Corsair headed towards the deck with a dead engine. The Japanese were determined not to let the pilot get out of his aircraft alive and they closed in for the kill. Another Corsair and a P-40 dived to the rescue and fought off the enemy. Walsh smashed the Corsair into the waves and was out of the cockpit before the ripped-apart fighter began to sink. Walsh floated in his life vest until the evening when he was rescued.

For his daring exploits Walsh was ordered back to the United States where President Roosevelt awarded the veteran Marine the Congressional Medal of Honor. Ken Walsh was then promoted to Captain and assigned as a flight instructor. He was later made Assistant Operations Officer of Marine Air Group 14, a non-combat job, but the irrepressible Walsh destroyed his twenty-first enemy aircraft on a test flight in a late model Corsair. This was the last victory for the Corsair ace who went on to serve a full career in the USMC, retiring as a Colonel in the early 1960s.

Meanwhile, other USMC Corsair pilots had been quickly carving aerial combat history in the skies over the Pacific. Corsair pilots aggressively attacked the enemy whenever they appeared and multiple victories in single combat by individual pilots were not uncommon. The tremendous horsepower of the P & W engine and the six 0.50 caliber guns caused havoc on the once invincible Zekes. Corsair pilots were able to engage and destroy the enemy over his own airfields and then continue the attack by strafing the airfield and destroying aircraft on the ground. This is not to say that the Zeke was no longer a threat, it was still a deadly opponent if the Corsair pilot was lured into a trap that encompassed the Zeke's best performance spectrum which was at a lower altitude. Other Japanese combat aircraft came off much worse than the Zeke, especially the dive and level bombers. Bettys and Vals were regularly decimated by Corsair attacks, the unarmored aircraft usually exploding after one firing pass. It was becoming suicide for

Japanese aircraft to venture against the American fleet or land bases but what the American military did not realize was that suicide was perfectly acceptable to Japanese thinking.

Back in the States, decisions were undertaken to increase Corsair production even further. At the end of 1943 almost 2,000 Corsairs had been manufactured by Vought. The 862nd F4U-1A introduced a new version of the R-2800, the -8W which featured water injection that gave a brief, but extremely powerful, boost in engine performance when the throttle was shoved all the way into the war emergency rating. Such a burst of power proved to be extremely valuable to Corsair pilots for getting out of a tight situation. Production lines at Brewster and Goodyear Aircraft Division were tooling up and they had added 136 and 377 fighters respectively although the Brewster production line was in dire trouble as mentioned earlier. Goodyear-built Corsairs were designated FG-1 and FG-1A and were similar, but minus a number of naval features, to the F4U-1 and F4U-1A. Vought was constantly

experimenting with the Corsair design to produce improved versions. Such modifications included two FG-1As with bubble canopies which were to be useful in the design of the later F2G. During August of 1943, Vought produced the first F4U-1C that was equipped with four 20mm cannon but only 200 examples were produced, the Navy preferring the machine-gun armed variant. Other improvements included the addition of a center line drop tank position that could also be used for bombs.

The Navy was still not pleased with the Corsair's carrier compatibility and it fell to the Royal Navy to be the first service to operate the fighter off carriers. During April of 1944, the first combat missions by Fleet

A Corsair gets into the movies. This movie was not being shot in Hollywood on a set but 'somewhere in the Pacific'. Marine Major W.A. Helpern is seen going over the script with some Warner Brothers employees that were now in uniform. The propaganda piece was called the 'Fightin'st Wings' and further served to identify the Corsair as the 'only' USN/USMC fighter in the public's mind. (USMC/78167)

Cockpit of an F4U-4 Corsair. The cockpit was well-laid out being both compact and comfortable for the pilot. (USN)

Air Arm Corsairs were launched off the HMS *Victorious* in support of attacks on the German battleship *Tirpitz*. Britain was to receive just over 2,000 Corsairs that comprised F4U-1, F4U-1A, F4U-1B (specially ordered version supplied directly to the FAA by Vought), F3A-1D, and FG-1D models. The British redesignated these aircraft to fit their aircraft classification system and they became the Corsair Mks I, II, IIA, III and IV. Enough aircraft were eventually delivered to equip nineteen combat squadrons. Training for the British pilots was undertaken at Quonset Point, Rhode Island, and Brunswick, Maine, where familiarization with the aircraft was stressed. Full training continued in Britain. Slight modifications were carried

out on the Corsairs to make them more suitable for British operation including the clipping of wing-tips. The British had their own problems in trying to tame the Corsair on a carrier deck. A number of crashes occurred, one in which a popular squadron commander lost his life when trying to come aboard the HMS *Illustrious*. New landing procedures were developed for the FAA Corsairs and improved canopies were fitted for better vision while landing. The British soon realized that safe carrier landings would never be achieved until the cockpit seating had been raised and the built in bounce of the Corsair's landing gear could be done away with but they were pressed into combat anyway. This information was relayed back to America where similar problems were being encountered by the Navy and Vought began to make the corrections that would prove the Corsair to be a true Naval fighting

machine.

Fleet Air Arm Corsairs were to see a great deal of action, particularly in the ground attack role. The Corsairs joined with other Fleet Air Arm aircraft such as the Barracuda and Swordfish in attacks against heavily defended enemy positions in both the Atlantic and Pacific battlefields. British pilots that had been trained on American aircraft found transition to the Corsair much easier than their comrades who had taken their flight training in British aircraft. The Corsair cockpit was full of 'Americanisms' that took a bit of getting used to by the British pilots.

Japanese intruders, unable to operate in the deadly anti-aircraft fire of a daylight attack, were beginning to take their loads of death into the black night sky. The night intruders were extremely dangerous and often did considerable damage when a chance bomb would find an American gas or bomb dump. Other damage was caused by keeping the troops awake all night and leaving them groggy in the morning. A Corsair variant was built to combat the danger of night attack. The F4U-2 was a conversion of twelve F4U-1s that were drawn from stock. The Naval Aircraft Factory undertook the modification and dropped one of the 0.50 caliber guns in the right wing while adding the radar pod on the starboard wing. Two units were formed to operate the night fighters, VFN-101 off the *Essex* and VFN-75 out of Munda. The aircraft went into operation during the latter part of 1943 and soon began blasting surprised Japanese from the night skies. The Corsair was the first single-engine, single-seat Navy night fighter and it was a 'hot' bird. Requirements were quickly drawn up that would allow only experienced pilots to fly the aircraft and pilots with a minimum of 2,000 flying hours were the only ones considered.

The Navy finally tamed the Corsair for shipboard operations during late 1944 with the addition of a new oleo strut that reduced the dangerous bouncing on the carrier deck. The new canopy and higher seat level also helped get the plane to where it belonged. Every Corsair in service was quickly modified and the carrier-ready F4U was on its way.

Extensive testing had taken place between the Corsair and other types of Allied fighters to determine the future direction of Naval fighter aircraft procurement. The Corsair was tested against just about every fighter the Navy could get their hands on. Heavy opposition was expected from the famous North American P-51 Mustang, which was the darling of the Air Force, but after the tests were concluded it was found that the Corsair, which outweighed the Mustang by almost 3,000 lbs, was superior to the Mustang in all respects. It was also discovered that the Corsair was superior to the newer Hellcat in both fighting and bombing ability, a distinct surprise to Navy officials. The Navy, therefore, decided to increase Corsair production and standardize on the type as its main fighter-bomber.

Corsair development was continuing and, with further improvements at Pratt & Whitney, a new version of the fighter was to emerge. P & W had been working on the Double Wasp and had increased its horsepower to 2,500 for take off. The company had strengthened internal components, improved the cooling and added water injection. The new engine was designated the R-2800-18W. Some F4U-1s were converted for use as test beds for the new powerplant, being designated F4U-4X and flying on 19 April 1944. The major recognition feature of this modification was the fact that the air intake ducts were removed from the wing roots and added in a chin scoop on the bottom of the cowling. This gave the Corsair a larger cowling that only added to its already powerful features. The tests were very successful and Vought added some other features such as an improved clear vision canopy, new armor plating for the pilot and various other small improvements that eliminated drag and added to the top speed. The new model was designated F4U-4 and the prototype first flew during October 1944 when it was also accepted by the Navy.

The F4U-4 was to become the ultimate Corsair version for World War Two. Its huge four-blade 13 ft 2 in diameter Hamilton-Standard propeller and new cowling made the aircraft look quite business-like and gave the fighter a rate of climb of over 4,000 fpm and a top speed of almost 450 mph. Other versions of the basic -4 were soon to follow: the -4B with four 20 mm cannon in place of the 0.50 caliber machine-guns, attachments on the wing of both the -4 and -4B that would allow carriage of eight five inch rockets along with two 1,000 lb bombs, two 150 gallon drop tanks, or two huge 11.75 in Tiny Tim rockets. The F4U-4 was to blast what was left of Japan's forces out of the air while helping to lay waste to the cities of the homeland. By the start of 1945, the Vought plant was cranking out one complete F4U-4 every 85 minutes for a total of 300 aircraft per month!

At the end of 1944 and the start of 1945, the Corsairs were rapidly being deployed on America's carriers. The Corsair deployment proved to be at a very wise time, for the Japanese, their backs being pressed closer and closer to the home islands felt the stirrings of a breeze in their collective memories. The breeze was soon to turn into a wind ... a divine wind that would carry the sting of the *kamikaze*, an airborne *samurai*

A Corsair pilot gets ready to turn up BuNo 04676 in order to blow a layer of snow off the machine. The photograph was taken at MCAS Mojave, in sunny Southern California, during 1944 when the training base was covered with a rare snowfall. Mojave was used extensively for a testing and training base for the Marines. Today the abandoned base is used for unlimited-class air racing and the old wooden hangars once more echo with the sounds of World War Two aircraft, including a few Corsairs in flight. (USMC/44400)

that would slash at the invaders until they could take no more and bow their heads in retreat.

The dream of Imperial Japan involved the sacrifice of thousands of young men flying the most advanced and the most primitive aircraft that were left, the type of aircraft did not matter for as long as it could carry a bomb aloft it was to become part of the Divine Wind that would sweep the heathen enemy from the surface of the sparkling sea.

During the second week of October 1944, the Japanese War Ministry ordered arrogant Admiral Takijiro Onishi to take over command of the First Air Fleet in the Philippines. The Japanese knew that the steady advance of the American juggernaut was going to overwhelm the Philippine Islands in the very near future, thus cutting off one of the most important supply lines to the Home Islands as well as taking over one of the last important Japanese bastions.

Onishi, who figured prominently in the Pearl Harbor attack, was now faced with an entirely different situation. The United States was no longer a 'sleeping giant' but an active war machine that was moving to devour him. Onishi knew that drastic action had to be taken as the assaulting American forces were rapidly nearing and the closest Japanese battle fleet was over a week away. Deep within their hearts, the Japanese military men must have known that the war was over but, with the rather stupid display of typical Japanese hard-headedness, the military leaders were very willing to shed the blood of thousands of their troops in order to save a collective Japanese 'face'.

Onishi had a terrible idea that he rather fancied and that vision was straight out of hell: his dream consisted of hundreds, no thousands, of suicide aircraft and ships attacking the American fleet, especially the aircraft carriers. The carriers were always a sore point for Japanese strategists as they had completely escaped the attack on Pearl Harbor. When Onishi proposed the idea to his fellow commanders, he saw their eyes light up with fanatical gleam for here was an idea that would save face and might, just might, stop the advancing Americans.

Called the *Shimpu Tokubetsu Kogekita*, the Divine Wind was to be a strong blow to the American fleets. The first group of *kamikazes* consisted of twenty-four Zeke fighters armed with 500 lb bombs. The pilots were young volunteers and their assignment was to dive into American ships totally disregarding any hope of evasive action or self-survival. The deaths of the pilots were to be for the glory of the Homeland and to honor the Emperor.

The new idea was not ready for operation when American aircraft spotted the battle fleet of Admiral Kurita as it sped towards the Philippines. On 24 October 1944, the reconquest of the Philippines began as Helldivers, Avengers, and Corsairs smashed at the enemy fleet. The Japanese were hit as they steamed into the eastern waters of Leyte Gulf. The huge battleship *Musashi* took thirty bomb hits and twenty-six torpedo strikes, going to the bottom with 1,200 of its crew. The *Myoko* was knocked out of action from torpedo hits. The Japanese commander retreated but then turned back, attacking a group of American destroyers and destroyer escorts that were decimated by the heavy guns of the Japanese warships with seven ships sunk or knocked out of action. Kurita's battleship fleet withdrew again for the second time. This had been one of the most violent of naval battles and both sides were licking their wounds.

The American aircraft had acquitted themselves well in the action, sinking and damaging the Japanese ships. The Corsairs flew close cover on the dive bombers and torpedo attacks, silencing Japanese anti-aircraft fire with repeated strafing runs against the giant warships.

However, on 25 October, the next day, came a nasty surprise for the Corsairs. Nine Zeke fighters took off from Mabalcat airfield and headed over the Pacific. Their target was the American fleet and these pilots *were not* going back home after the raid. Five of the

An F4U-1 ground crew make final adjustments on a screw jack supporting the tail, a line running through the tail gear to secure the plane for upcoming gun bore sighting tests. Although designed as a carrier-based fighter, the Corsair displayed unacceptable characteristics, resulting in its gaining a bad reputation among Navy pilots. The Marines, flying Grumman F4F Wildcats, were equally cautious of their new mounts at first, but soon came to realize that in the F4U they had a machine which was equal of anything the Japanese had available. The solid rubber tail wheel tire which was to give considerable trouble, is visible as is the lack of an arresting hook, removed from land-based USMC fighters. (USMC/55427)

aircraft would be the suicide vehicles while the other four would act as escort protection. This mission would introduce one of the strangest weapons in the long history of warfare, the human bomb. The nine young pilots wore a traditional *hachimaki* scarf wrapped around their hands. Samurai warriors once wore these headbands to keep their long hair out of their face during combat. The pilots had taken last rites before the missions and had been told personally by Onishi that: 'You are already Gods without earthly desires!'

The pilots attacked four American escort carriers that were launching aircraft to protect the Leyte beachhead. The alarm went up as the Zekes dived on the American ships. Corsair pilots raced to their aircraft as the deck crew furiously positioned the fighters and started up their engines. A few minutes later Lt Seki dove his Zeke into the flight deck of the *St. Lo*. The explosion was devastating, blowing deck crew and fully loaded fighters into hundreds of pieces. The fuel tanks of the *St. Lo* began to burn and huge explosions rocked the ship. Flames shot over a 1,000 feet into the air, drawing the other *kamikazes* like moths. The *St Lo* took two more hits while three other escort carriers were hit in the frenzy. The *St. Lo* went to the bottom. The Corsair air cover did not have time to tangle with the lightning attack of the aggressors. The Americans were stunned. In all the terrible Pacific fighting, they had never seen action such as this. How

would the attacks be stopped? The new F4U-4 with its powerful engine would be the hope that the American fleet would rely on for rapid response to the *kamikazes*.

With their throttles shoved all the way forward and the water injection system engaged, the Corsair pilots chased after the attacking enemy formations, hoping to blast each and every invader from the air before they got near the American ships. The Corsair pilots also had to be careful of the deadly anti-aircraft screen that would be thrown up by the fleet for, after the first couple of *kamikaze* attacks, the American gunners would shoot at anything that looked marginally threatening and nothing could ruin a Corsair pilot's day like being shot down by his own ship.

The suicide attacks began to appear everywhere as the Japanese High Command became more and more convinced that the attacks could cause more damage than engagements with what was left of the Japanese fleet. Corsairs and Hellcats went after the attackers with every possible effort but the enemy was willing to pay the ultimate price and this fanaticism was hard to stop. The Japanese soon threw everything that they could into the battle, bombers, fighters, and even training aircraft. Most fell as blazing torches, hit by the fighters or by the incredible anti-aircraft wall put up by the defending ships. Still, some of the enemy got through. During the heavy fighting of the Okinawa Campaign, seventeen American

Initial landings on Okinawa were relatively lightly opposed by the island's defenders. Response from the Home Islands, however, was another matter entirely, pilots of the *kamikaze* special attack corps attacking United States warships in seemingly unstoppable waves. Stiffening resistance by the Japanese – dug into the southern tip of Okinawa – turned the campaign into a bloodily drawn-out fight which lasted from 1 April to 3 July 1945. Thirty-four ships were sunk or so badly damaged that they had to be scrapped. Another 368 were damaged, some being knocked out of the war, positive evidence that the *kamikaze* concept, while virtually incomprehensible to a Western mind, was militarily acceptable to the enemy. Marine Corsairs were ashore and operating from Yontan and Kadena airfields by the 4th, only three days after the amphibious landings. Here an entire squadron of 2nd MAW F4U-1Cs – armed with four 20 mm cannon rather than the usual six 0.50 caliber machine-guns – waits in the mud of Yontan to provide cover for American forces advancing down the length of the island. (USMC/117901)

warships were sent to the bottom by suicide attacks and 198 were damaged by the will of the *kamikaze*. In these attacks the Japanese lost 930 aircraft, an incredible toll but the American fleet had been hit harder than it had since Pearl Harbor.

American military planners saw that the F4U-4 was not the ideal aircraft for interception of these lightning attacks. The Corsairs stopped many of the enemy but a lighter and more responsive aircraft was needed that could quickly be scrambled and head at high speed towards the oncoming attackers and destroy them before they neared the ships. It was a tall order but the Vought designers gave the problem much

Top left
A perplexed USMC mechanic peers into the
accessories section of the Corsair's R-2800 engine.
The Corsair was the most mechanically complex
fighter in Navy and USMC service and created
some headaches for the ground crew.

Top right
Even in the midst of combat, American personnel
observed their Holy Days. Here Catholic Chaplain
Joseph J. Garrity uses a Jeep for an impromptu
altar as he conducts Mass for the men of the
'Hell's Belles', their cannon-armed Corsairs
visible in the background, identified by squadron
by the 300 series of modexes painted on the nose.
(USMC/118869)

Center right
This airfield on the Marianas was captured by the
USMC and quickly rebuilt to handle Allied
aircraft. The Marines in the photograph are
taking a break to examine the then-huge Douglas
C-54 Skymaster transport that had arrived fresh
from the factory in a gleaming polished metal
finish. The Corsair in the foreground is of
extreme interest as its markings are some of the
more extensive carried by a Marine fighter. The
Marine pilots and ground crews got away with a
lot more 'artworks' when compared to their Navy
team mates. The name 'Ring Dang Do' has been
painted in large white script on the fuselage sides
while a nude female has also been added.
(USMC/92384)

Bottom right
This F4U-1A Corsair of the 'Devil Dog' Squadron,
VMF-111 of the Fourth Marine Air Wing, was
photographed on 26 September 1944. At this time
the machine had flown 100 attack missions and
seventy-eight other assorted missions during a six
month period with the same R-2800 engine. At
this time VMF-111 was commanded by Major
William E. Clasen. (USMC/96634)

Top left

The F4U-4 was powered by a Pratt & Whitney R-2800-18W delivering almost 2,500 hp. Almost 200 lbs of armor was added to the cockpit and essential systems. (Vought)

Top right

Powerful portrait of an F4U-4B. The -4 version of the Corsair could immediately be distinguished by the intake in the bottom of the cowling. These aircraft were to have been originally delivered to the Royal Navy but none reached that service. Note the underwing armament of eight 5 in HVAR. Finish is Overall Glossy Sea Blue. (Vought)

Center and Bottom left

In June of 1945, *Life* magazine photographer David Douglas Duncan crawled into a modified auxiliary fuel tank slung under the port wing of an Army Air Force Lockheed F-5 Lightning and took off to photograph Marine Corsairs striking Japanese positions in the mountains of southern Okinawa. Here the planes, at least two four-plane sections of F4Us, approved their target, the Kushi-Take strongpoint. The Corsairs are armed with two napalm tanks on their center section stubs and 5 in rockets on the wing launchers. The pilot of the P-38 positioned Duncan where he wanted to be, behind one of the Corsairs when the F4U fired its rockets. He figured that the folks back home would like the dramatic view. However, Duncan and the P-38 pilot got more then they expected when the Corsair salvoed its rockets. The turbulence from the launching was so great that the following P-38 was knocked out of control and nearly crashed. Duncan went on to continue his photographic career, testimonial to a man who would willingly strap himself inside a converted fuel tank to take a photo! (USMC/126436/USN/24987)

thought. Teamed with the Goodyear engineers, Vought began planning a modified Corsair airframe that would be mated to a massive radial engine, the 26 cylinder Pratt & Whitney R-4360 four row engine. An example of the engine had been tested on an early F4U-1 airframe and an FG-1 that had been redesignated XF2G-1. Goodyear was awarded a contract for a development of the concept and orders for 418 F2G-1s soon followed. A follow-on contract for ten folding wing F2G-2s was also given to Goodyear. The first group of F2G-1s would be rigid wing models for operating off land bases. The fuselage of the F2G was a different departure as a bubble canopy was fitted and the turtle deck was eliminated. Water injection would boost the F2Gs engine to 3,600 hp. Alternate armament of four or six 0.50 caliber machine-guns could be carried while under wing hard points could carry bombs or rockets as well as extra fuel tanks. Problems with the design were soon encountered when the prototypes began displaying marked instability in the lateral axis. Pratt & Whitney was also having problems developing the huge engine and production schedules soon began to cause trouble. The prototypes were also falling short of their projected top speed of 450 mph at 16,000 ft. It was soon clear that the F2G would not be available when needed and the contracts were drastically cut back. Only five F2G-1s were completed along with the same number of F2G-2s which were equipped with the R-4360-4 engine for shipboard operations. The F2G-2 did hit 400 mph on the deck with a climb rate of 4,500 fpm.

Other versions of the Corsair, especially stemming from the -4 version, were produced. These included the F4U-4P with recon. cameras, the F4U-4E with APS-4 radar in a wing pod, the F4U-4N with APS-6 radar, while the XF4U-4 sported, for a period, an experimental contra-rotating propeller installation that did not do much except decrease top speed and rate of climb.

By the conclusion of the Okinawa campaign, virtually *every* American carrier was equipped with the Corsair which is an excellent testimonial to the greatest aircraft that Vought ever produced.

The last wartime variant of the Corsair was the -5 although the prototype did not fly until 21 December 1945. This aircraft was designed as a high-altitude fighter and was equipped with the new Pratt & Whitney R-2800-32 W E Series radial that could pump out 2,500 hp courtesy of a two-stage variable-speed supercharger. The canopy was completely revamped with a new bulged hood added for pilot visibility. The cockpit was completely redesigned and modernized for efficiency of operation. Spring tabs were added to the elevators and rudder to decrease the work load on the pilot and other goodies such as electrically heated cannon bays for the four 20 mm cannon and a completely retractable tail wheel were also added. One trademark for the Corsair series bowed out with the new -5, the fabric covered aft wing, a throw-back to the 1930s, was finally deleted and replaced with a metal covering.

The first production F4U-5 did not fly until 12 May 1947 as military contracts were placed on the back burner after the end of the war. An immediate distinguishing feature of the F4U-5 was the addition of two cowl inlets that provided air for the superchargers. The -5 had a top speed of 450 mph with a rate of climb of 4,500 and it could out perform the early jet fighters. The -5 was also built to carry a full complement of eight 5 in rockets, bombs, Tiny Tims, and the new deadly napalm. Other versions of the -5 included the night fighting -5N with a large radar pod mounted on the starboard wing and the -5P photo recon. aircraft which retained its cannon armament so it could fight off attackers while on photo missions.

The next version of the Corsair was the AU-1 (originally designated F4U-6) that was developed during 1950 by Vought. This version was aimed specifically for the Korean War theater and was optimized as a ground attack aircraft. The prototype first flew during January 1952 and the redesignation was a way of getting around a growing Congressional reluctance for purchasing more 'antiquated' F4Us, this way the Congress thought that they were getting a new close support aircraft. All of the high altitude equipment featured in the -5 was stripped out and a low-altitude R-2800-83 WA was stuck on the front end. This engine had a single-stage, two-speed, manually controlled supercharger that would be particularly efficient at low altitude. Much more armor was added to vital areas to protect them from the heavy ground fire that a close-support machine would encounter. The four 20 mm cannon were retained but the disposable load was greatly increased. Ten 5 in rockets could now be carried or armament could include ten 250 lb or six 500 lb bombs. Napalm, Tiny Tims and extra fuel tanks could also be carried. The centerline pylon could also carry a 2,000 lb bomb. Only 111 AU-1s were produced. Although it is outside the scope of this volume, the Corsair's service during the Korean War was as outstanding as it had been during World War Two. Corsairs smashed enemy human wave attacks time and time again as they nearly overran Allied positions. Corsairs blasted the enemy's rolling stock,

making it unsafe for the North Koreans and Red Chinese to have transport by day. There was even a Corsair night fighting ace that specialized in destroying the annoying Po-2 'Bed check Charlie' raiders that made life so difficult for the Allied servicemen. The last AU-1 was delivered on 10 October 1952.

The final version of the Corsair was the F4U-7, a variant especially produced for the French *Aéronavale* for use in that country's growing military problems in Indo China. The -7 was essentially an AU-1 airframe with an F4U-4 engine, the P & W R-2800-18W. The first example of the F4U-7 flew on 2 July 1952 and the last of 94 aircraft was delivered in January 1953. These aircraft saw extensive action during the Indo China campaign and later went on to fight in Algeria and during the Suez crisis. The French retired their Corsairs in 1964.

The Corsair had the longest production run of any piston engine fighter aircraft and the following statistics perhaps sum up its contribution to the American victory in World War Two:

> Enemy Aircraft Destroyed: 2,140
> Operational Sorties: 64,050
> Corsair Losses:
>   190 in aerial combat
>   350 from anti-aircraft fire
>   230 from other causes
>   692 on non-operational missions
>   165 in crash landings
> Chance Vought Built Corsairs: 7,829
> Brewster Built Corsairs: 735
> Goodyear Built Corsairs: 4,017
> British Operated Corsairs: 2,020
> New Zealand Operated Corsairs: 430

Corsairs were constantly being experimented with to increase their efficiency. This example is seen with three overload fuel tanks during a test to increase the fighter's already long range to something beyond pilot comfort! (USN/409234)

Corsair Bureau Numbers

XF4U-1: 1443
F4U-1: 02153–02736; 03802–03841;
17392–17515; 17517–18191;
49680–50359; 55784–56483
F4U-1D: 50360–50659; 57084–57983;
82178–82852
XF4U-3: 02157; 17516; 49664
XF4U-4: 49763; 50301; 80759–80763
F4U-4: 62915–63071; 80764–82177;
96752–97295; 97297–97531
XF4U-5: 97296; 97415
F4U-5: 121793–122066; 122153–122206;
123144–123203; 124441–124560;
124666–124724
F3A-1: 04515–04774; 08550–08797;
11067–11293
FG-1/1A: 12992–14685
FG-1D: 14686–14991; 76149–76739;
67055–67254; 87788–88453;
92007–92701
XF2G-1: 12992; 13471; 13472; 14691–14695
F2G-1: 88454–88458
F2G-2: 88459–88463
AU-1: 129318–129417; 133833–133843
F4U-7: 133652–133731; 133819–133832

Specifications

Chance Vought XF4U-1

Span	41 ft
Length	31 ft 11 in
Height	15 ft 7 in
Wing Area	314 sq ft
Empty Weight	7505 lbs
Loaded Weight	9360 lbs
Max. Speed	405 mph
Cruise Speed	185 mph
Ceiling	35,200 ft
Rate of Climb	2660 fpm
Range	1000 miles
Powerplant	Pratt & Whitney XR-2800-4 of 1850 hp

Chance Vought F4U-1

Span	41 ft
Length	33 ft 4 in
Height	16 ft 1 in
Wing Area	314 sq ft
Empty Weight	8982 lbs
Loaded Weight	14,000 lbs
Max. Speed	417 mph
Cruise Speed	182 mph
Ceiling	33,000 ft
Rate of Climb	2300 fpm
Range	1015 miles
Powerplant	Pratt & Whitney R-2800-8 of 2000 hp

Chance Vought F4U-4

Span	41 ft
Length	33 ft 8 in
Height	14 ft 9 in
Wing Area	314 sq ft
Empty Weight	9205 lbs
Loaded Weight	14,670 lbs
Max. Speed	446 mph
Cruise Speed	215 mph
Ceiling	41,500 ft
Rate of Climb	3879 fpm
Range	1000 miles
Powerplant	Pratt & Whitney R-2800-18W of 2100 hp

Chance Vought F4U-5

Span	41 ft
Length	33 ft 6 in
Height	14 ft 9 in
Wing Area	314 sq ft
Empty Weight	9583 lbs
Loaded Weight	15,079 lbs
Max. Speed	462 mph
Cruise Speed	190 mph
Ceiling	44,100 ft
Rate of Climb	4230 fpm
Range	1030 miles
Powerplant	Pratt & Whitney R-2800-32W of 2300 hp

Chance Vought AU-1

Span	41 ft
Length	34 ft 1 in
Height	14 ft 10 in
Wing Area	314 sq ft
Empty Weight	9835 lbs
Loaded Weight	19,400 lbs
Max. Speed	438 mph
Cruise Speed	184 mph
Ceiling	19,500 ft
Rate of Climb	3700 fpm
Range	500 miles
Powerplant	Pratt & Whitney R-2800-83W of 2300 hp

Goodyear F2G-2

Span	41 ft
Length	33 ft 10 in
Height	16 ft 1 in
Wing Area	314 sq ft
Empty Weight	10,249 lbs
Loaded Weight	15,442 lbs
Max. Speed	431 mph
Cruise Speed	190 mph
Ceiling	38,800 ft
Rate of Climb	4400 fpm
Range	1200 miles
Powerplant	Pratt & Whitney R-4360-4 of 3,000 hp

Pappy Boyington – Leader of the Black Sheep

Colonel Gregory 'Pappy' Boyington, Marine Corps ace credited with the destruction of twenty-eight Japanese aircraft, was awarded the Medal of Honor 'for extraordinary heroism above and beyond the call of duty' while in command of Marine Fighting Squadron 214 in the Central Solomons area from 12 September 1943 to 3 January 1944. He was shot down over Rabaul on the latter date and his capture by the Japanese was followed by 20 months as a prisoner of war.

Gregory Boyington was born at Coeur d'Alene, Idaho, on 4 December 1914. He graduated from Lincoln High School in Tacoma, Washington, and majored in aeronautical engineering at the University of Washington, graduating in 1934 with a Bachelor of Science degree. He is a member of Lambda Chi Alpha fraternity. Always an athlete, he was a member of the college wrestling and swimming teams and is a one-time holder of the Pacific Northwest Intercollegiate middleweight wrestling title.

During his summer vacations he worked in either a mining camp or a logging camp in his home state. One summer he was employed by the Coeur d'Alene Fire Protective Association in road construction and lookout work.

The famed flyer started his military career while still attending college. As a member of the Reserve Officers Training Corps for four years, he became a cadet captain. He was commissioned a second lieutenant in the Coast Artillery Reserve in June 1934, and served two months of active duty with the 630th Coast Artillery at Fort Worden, Washington. On 13 June 1935 he enlisted in the Volunteer Marine Corps Reserve. He went on active duty on that date and returned to inactive duty on 16 July.

In the meantime, the Colonel had become a draftsman and engineer for the Boeing Aircraft Company of Seattle.

It was on 18 February 1936, that Boyington accepted an appointment as an aviation cadet in the Marine Corps Reserve. He was assigned to the Naval Air Station at Pensacola, Florida, for flight training. Years before, he first flew when he was only eight years old with Clyde Pangborn, who later flew the Pacific non-stop.

He was designated a Naval Aviator on 11 March 1937. He was next transferred to Quantico, Virginia, for duty with Aircraft One, Fleet Marine Force. Boyington was discharged from the Marine Corps Reserve on 1 July 1937, in order to accept a second lieutenant's commission in the regular Marine Corps on the following day.

Detached to the Basic School, Philadelphia, in July of 1938, Lieutenant Boyington was transferred to the Second Marine Aircraft Group at the San Diego Naval Air Station upon completion of his studies. With that unit he took part in fleet maneuvers off the aircraft carriers USS *Lexington* and USS *Yorktown*.

Promoted to first lieutenant on 4 November 1940, he went back to Pensacola as an instructor the next month.

Lieutenant Boyington resigned his commission in the Marine Corps on 26 August 1941 to accept a position with the Central Aircraft Manufacturing Company. CAMCO was a civilian organization formed for the protection of the Burma Road. The unit later became known as the American Volunteer Group, the famed Flying Tigers of China. During his months with the Tigers, Boyington became a squadron commander and shot down six Japanese aircraft to secure an appreciable lead over other American aces who did not get into the fight until after 7

Boyington and his Black Sheep faced primitive operating conditions on the Pacific islands. This F4U-1 rumbles down the powdered coral taxi way at Espiritu Santo on 8 March 1944. Espiritu Santo is an island in the New Hebrides chain. In the Guadalcanal theater, all land-based aviation – including Navy, Marine Corps, Royal New Zealand Air Force and USAAF – was controlled under the command of Vice Admiral John S. McCain, Commander, Aircraft, South Pacific (ComAirSoPac). McCain's first job was to find and secure an airfield that would be closer to Guadalcanal than Efate which was 707 miles away. The decision was to construct an airfield at Espiritu Santo which was almost 150 miles closer to Guadalcanal. The airfield was constructed in the amazing time of sixteen days by the men of the 4th Defense Battalion. The strip was ready for fighters on 28 July 1942. Espiritu Santo would have the distinction of becoming one of the Navy's great wartime bases. (USMC/81655)

December 1941. He flew 300 combat hours before the AVG disbanded.

He returned to the United States in July 1942 and accepted a first lieutenant's commission in the Marine Corps Reserve on 29 September 1942. He reported for active duty at San Diego Naval Air Station, California, on 23 November and was assigned to Marine Aircraft Wings, Pacific. The following day he was temporarily promoted to major in the Reserves, which is the rank in the regular Marine Corps he would have held had his service been continuous. Within two months he was on his way overseas again.

Major Boyington joined Marine Aircraft Group Eleven of the First Marine Aircraft Wing and became Commanding Officer of Marine Fighting Squadron 214 after a short tour in the Solomons with another squadron. The new squadron was made up of a group of casuals, replacements, and green pilots and was dubbed the Black Sheep Squadron.

Before organizing the Black Sheep, Major Boyington had done some combat flying at

Guadalcanal in April 1943, as Executive Officer of Marine Fighting Squadron 122, but he had added no enemy aircraft to his score at that time. However, during those two periods of intense activity in the Russell Islands–New Georgia and Bougainville–New Britain–New Ireland areas, Pappy, so named because of his age (28) compared to that of his men, added to his total almost daily. During his squadron's first tour of combat duty, the major personally shot down fourteen enemy fighters in 32 days. On 17 December 1943, he headed the first Allied fighter sweep over impregnable Rabaul. By 27 December his record was twenty-five. He tied the then–existing American record of twenty-six aircraft destroyed on 3 January when he shot down another fighter over Rabaul.

Typical of Major Boyington's daring feats is his attack on Kahili aerodrome at the southern tip of Bougainville on 17 October 1943. He and twenty-four fighters circled the field persistently where sixty hostile aircraft

Baseball bats and caps for Japanese. Marine Corps pilots in the South Pacific effected the wearing of baseball caps as part of their flight equipment, not unlike USAAF bomber crews in the area. When beset by a shortage of the caps, members of Major Gregory Boyington's Black Sheep Squadron, during October of 1943, offered to shoot down a Japanese aircraft for every cap sent to them by players in that year's World Series. Twenty caps arrived during December from the St Louis Cardinals. These twenty original members from Boyington's squadron accounted for forty-eight enemy aircraft, the majority from October on. The photograph was taken on Vella Lavella on 4 December 1943. Boyington is standing on the left side of the cowling. Corsair '740' offers some interesting markings details. Note the star and bar insignia under the right wing while the left carries the older star and circle insignia. Also note the tape used on the wing panels to help improve smooth airflow. (USMC/68317)

were based, goading the Japanese into sending up a large numerically superior force. In the fierce battle that followed, twenty of the enemy were shot out of the skies. The Black Sheep roared back to their base without the

loss of a single Corsair.

On 3 January 1944, forty-eight American aircraft, including one division (four aircraft) from the Black Sheep Squadron took off from Bougainville for a fighter sweep over Rabaul. Pappy was the tactical commander of the flight and arrived over Rabaul at eight o'clock in the morning. In the ensuing action the major was seen to shoot down his twenty-sixth aircraft. He then became mixed up in the general dogfight and was not seen or heard from again. Following a determined search which proved futile, the major was declared missing in action.

The major had jumped from his burning Corsair, taken to his life vest and been picked up by a Japanese submarine. While a prisoner of the Japs he was selected for temporary promotion to the rank of lieutenant colonel.

With mid-August 1945, came the atom bomb and the Japanese capitulation. Major Boyington was liberated from Japanese custody at Omori Prison Camp in the Tokyo area on 29 August and returned to the United States shortly afterwards. On 6 September,

the top ace who had been a prisoner of the Japanese for the past 20 months accepted his temporary lieutenant colonel's commission in the Marine Corps.

At the time of his release it was confirmed that Colonel Boyington had accounted for two Japanese aircraft on that fateful 3 January. That set his total at twenty-eight aircraft which remains the highest Marine Corps score of the war.

Shortly after his return to his homeland, Colonel Boyington was ordered to Washington to receive the nation's highest honor, the Medal of Honor, from the President. The medal had been awarded by the late president, Franklin D. Roosevelt, in March 1944 and held in the Capitol until such time as the colonel was able to receive the award. On 5 October 1945, 'Nimitz Day', he, together with a number of other Marines and Naval personnel appeared at the White House and was decorated by President Harry S. Truman.

On the previous day, he was presented the Navy Cross by the Commandant of the

A Marine F4U-1A snarls away from Barakoma fighter strip on Vella Lavella, home for the Black Sheep, for a mission out over the Vella Gulf and Bougainville. Lt Alvin J. Jensen, a Corsair pilot from VMF-214, performed one of the great single-handed feats of the Pacific war while operating out of Vella Lavella. During a sweep over Kahili on 28 August, Jensen became separated from the other Corsairs in his squadron by a weather front. Jensen lost control of the plane in the storm and came out of it upside down in a spin. The interesting part is that he was right over a Japanese airfield! He righted his Corsair and began an immediate attack on the base. He managed to destroy eight Zekes, four Vals and twelve Bettys before heading home. Aerial recon. proved his claim of destroying twenty-four enemy machines on the ground. Jensen was awarded the Navy Cross for this daring exploit. After the war, Jensen decided to stay in the Corps but his luck ran out when, on 20 May 1949, before thousands of spectators at NAS Patuxent, Maryland, the wing came off his F2H Banshee while recovering from a dive that started at 40,000 ft. (USMC/65924)

Marine Corps for the ace's heroic achievements on the day he became missing in action.

Following the receipt of his Medal of Honor and Navy Cross, Colonel Boyington made a Victory Bond Tour. Originally ordered to the Marine Corps Schools, Quantico, he was later directed to report to the Commanding General, Marine Air West Coast, Marine Corps Air Depot, Miramar San Diego, California.

Colonel Boyington was retired from the Marine Corps on 1 August 1947 and, because he was specially commended for the performance of duty in actual combat, he was advanced to his present rank.

In addition to the Medal of Honor and the Navy Cross, Colonel Boyington holds the American Defense Service Medal; Asiatic-Pacific Campaign Medal; and the World War Two Victory Medal.

★　★　★　★　★　★

Our interview with Colonel Boyington took place at the dusty California air strip of Indian Dunes where Universal Studios was busy filming a TV series entitled *Black Sheep Squadron* that is loosely based on the wartime exploits of the Colonel. The air strip had been made up to look like something out of the World War Two Pacific and the dirt ramp was covered with restored Corsair fighters and T-6 trainers converted to look like Japanese Zekes. In other words, it was an ideal spot to interview the Marine Corps' greatest ace.

Q: It's been 36 years since you were shot down and taken prisoner.
A: Gosh, it doesn't seem that long ago. Looking at all this stuff on the replay here . . . it kind of jogs my memory, yet it almost seems like yesterday when I see some of these pilots carrying on.

Q: Now that someone is finally doing a television series on your story after so many years, when we went out on location and you watched those old Corsairs making their simulated strafing runs, what went through your mind?
A: When those Corsairs taxiied one by one out on to the field and they started giving it the old gun to take off . . . that peculiar howl of those engines . . . a little shiver went right up my old spine. It was just like 36 years ago . . . almost as if I was taking off with them.

Q: Did you have the desire to climb in the cockpit one more time and fly the Bent-Wing Bird?
A: Oh, I've had that desire many times. I guess most ex-fighter jocks have. Kind of a

mad sensation. You never give up completely. I guess I'm the kind of guy that never gives up. Maybe I should have.

Q: Why did you join the Marine Corps to begin with?
A: I guess the same reason that a lot of people did. Hell, I'd heard about all the old famous Marine Corps characters and I didn't want to end up polishing brass someplace during the war.

Q: When you joined the Marine Corps, did you fully intend to become an aviator?
A: Oh, yes. I went in as a private. Eventually I took the exam. for my regular commission . . . I think there were about eight of us that made it out of about 100 . . .

Q: You first came into the Marine Corps in 1935 and wasn't it during 1939 or 1940 when you were first approached by Chennault's people?
A: It was early in 1941 and it was the State Department . . . they didn't have the CIA then but they were developing something like that. There was an old guy who came around . . . I guess there were several of them from what I understand . . . he was a former member of the Lafayette Escadrille and he was a retired First Lieutenant from the Air Corps and he painted this glorious picture. 'Course I really had no business joining except that I was about one jump ahead of the sheriff. I owed everybody under the sun money and I had a marriage that was dissolving . . . and it was just a beautiful out for me and I wanted to keep my Marine Corps career and the only way I would be able to pay this mess off was to go on a junket like the Flying Tigers. Of course at that time it wasn't yet called the Flying Tigers . . . it was still the AVG. The Flying Tiger name came from one of Madam Chiang's fiery speeches in China.

Q: At the time you were recruited by the Chinese, what was the arrangement with the Marine Corps? Were you discharged or were you on loan or what?
A: Well, we weren't at war with Japan so anyone who wanted to go on the mission had to resign from the Marines. However, each of the pilots recruited from the Marine Corps and the Navy was a party to a secret document that was kept in the personal safe of Admiral Nimitz indicating that upon our return we would be reinstated to our former service 'without loss of precedence'. This, of course, meant that when you came back in, you would be placed at the rank that you might achieve by that time. As it finally wound up, I skipped the rank of captain. I was stymied for a while . . . Chennault wanted to keep the guys that made his reputation and

he was trying to have me inducted into the Air Corps as a second lieutenant. When I finally escaped all that by running all over the Himalayas and finally making my way back to the States, I ran into another guy that was just about like Chennault in the Director of the Marine Corps Aviation Office. He had all the Marines who had left the scene over there classified as deserters in time of national emergency. I could never understand why they never called me up. Hell, I finally wound up stuck in the reserves and unable to get a job. I was pigeon holed. I couldn't go to work for the Ferry Command flying aircraft over to Europe as a free agent where I could have made some money. So I wound up parking cars at a garage in Seattle.

Finally I couldn't stand it anymore. I kept getting letters from the HQMCA telling me there was nothing doing yet and signed by the direction of some second lieutenant. So finally I got madder than hell, drank a couple of fifths of bourbon and composed a four page letter to then Secretary of the Navy Frank Knox. Thank God he was a two-fisted man, otherwise he'd have thrown this thing in the ash can. It was sarcastic . . . oh, God. I went on that I understood about how America was having a rough time aviation-wise and reinformed him of the fact that I was already an ace. I told him that, like many people, I believed that the US always kept its word. In this case, if it wanted to keep its word, I told him to look in Nimitz' personal safe for the letter of guarantee. Damn it or not, four days later I got wired orders to proceed to San Diego from where I would be shipped immediately overseas. There was, however, no mention of joining a squadron.

Once I got to San Diego, I was treated as a second lieutenant even though it had been indicated I was to be promoted to major. Finally, just before leaving North Island, the commission came through so I finally made it.

When I got to Honolulu there was no squadron, nothing. And boy, it didn't look like I was ever gonna get to fly. So I got my head working and waited for the proper timing and got in touch with Colonel Sandy Sanderson, a great guy and a great pilot, and he was in desperate need for two squadrons who were supposed to have come out on small flattops and they hadn't arrived. I told him I could get him one within a week. Of course he was full of booze and I said I'll show ya sir. Anyhow, I had nothing to lose 'cause I figured that if this deal didn't work, at least I'd get away with a big load of Scotch as we were drinking it up in his tent.

He was the kind of guy, even though he was half-looped, who kept his word good the

following day. I found that most Marines were that way.

'I owe you this?'

'Yes sir, you do.'

'OK then, I don't remember it but if you say so...'

Q : How did you go about keeping your word?

A : Actually I had a hard time because once he consented, all the burden was on me. I had to go and pick out these guys who were sittin' in the pilot pools and waiting court martials, getting ready to be shipped back home, people who had been kicked out of squadrons. That's the only thing I had to draw from. Colonel Sanderson asked me about the squadron number as there was none and I suggested that all we would have to do was borrow numbers and aircraft. Every time a squadron came out of action for rotation, we would slip in, borrow their number, use their aircraft (after all, they were already in the combat zone) and, by the time that squadron was ready to go back to action, we could borrow somebody else's number. So he went clear up the line and got permission for this.

Q : Did you have all these details worked out in your head?

A : No, not really. Once you got started on a deal like this, you couldn't quit. Now I'm a psychopathic liar which helps and I just sort of winged my way through it. The more I talked, the more it unravelled and the more

ideas I came up with.

Q : Squadron 214 still bears the name Black Sheep. How did you end up with a name like that and with the number?

A : That happened to be the first squadron going out of combat after this thing was OK'd. We were just borrowing the number for six weeks is all it amounted to.

Q : Didn't they already have a nickname?

A : Oh, they had a name, an insignia and the whole works. Unfortunately they'd been in combat once and they got the hell kicked out of 'em. When we took the thing over, we happened to luck out. We just knocked everybody down. So when the powers to be saw this they figured good God, let's send the original 214 back home. Naturally there was a big fight over this with the commanding officer, a Major Buhl. He was livid and I couldn't say that I blamed him, but hell, I wanted the squadron and I wasn't going to argue with him.

We wanted our own name and some of the boys came up with the name Boyington's Bastards. Being formed overseas like we were, we didn't have anything, not even so much as a typewriter. Most of the guys were misfits and leftouts, so the name seemed fitting.

Once we got over there, we got to talking with a war correspondent who told us that he couldn't write about us because they wouldn't print the name. So the cor-

Marine air power in the Pacific. This photograph typifies the USMC aviation effort during World War Two. Endless tiny islands infested with insects, palm trees, sharp coral, and Japanese. This photograph was taken on 25 October 1943 as USMC Corsairs taxi out from their revetments in answer to a 'scramble' call to intercept enemy bombers coming in from Bougainville. Boyington and his Black Sheep answered many of these scramble calls, blasting Japanese bombers out of the sky to add to their impressive victory scoreboard. (USMC/61335-B)

respondent along with a couple of the pilots, came up with the name Blacksheep and designed a shield with a flower like they used to do in the medieval days which is called a bastard shield. 'Course to draw the thing was kind of a comedy. One of the guys in the squadron could draw anything if he had a picture to go from. So we went through magazines and articles and so forth and finally found a cartoon that came close enough to what we wanted.

Q : Then came the famous first mission....

A : Yeah, on the first mission we knocked down eighteen aircraft ... which is a hell of a lot of planes. It was all really quite by accident. We could have missed the enemy all together. We were escorting some bombers over Bougainville and flying between two layers of thin clouds. We dropped down through the bottom layer and happened to find ourselves flying right in the back of a formation of Japanese fighters. We charged our guns and started there.

Q: Now you were flying the Corsair. What did you think about the aircraft? Had you had any Corsair time prior to this?

A: Hell, I had never even seen one until I got overseas. Naturally I had heard about the Corsair and how much time it had spent in prototype form. Several people I knew in the Corps had been killed in the plane.

Q: How many of those eighteen kills from that first mission were you personally responsible for?

A: If I'm not mistaken, on that particular mission I think I got five planes.

Q: So you made yourself a double ace?

A: That's correct. I kind of lost count but we also found a Japanese fighter a few days later that had crash-landed on the beach of an island named Choiseul. Whether or not that was mine, only the Good Lord knows, but I am reasonably sure that it was.

Q: And from that time on your kill rate continued to grow until ...

A: 3 January 1944, when I took a hit and my main gas tank caught fire. Of course I bailed out and became a prisoner of the Japanese. At that time Foss was already established and, as I recall, shortly before I was shot down, Bong and I were even with twenty-five kills each. Then I got three more to reach twenty-eight before being captured and of course Bong continued to fly with the Army and ended up with forty kills. Interestingly enough, I ran into Bong once over Rabaul. He was flying his P-38 out of New Guinea and we talked over the radio for a while.

Q: That day you were shot down was it one bandit that got you or were there several planes involved?

A: Well, my wingman had evidently been mortally wounded because he went into a 45 degree dive and he had pulled back on the throttle. I was screaming and cussing at him over the radio to get out but he finally dove into the water. Never even fluttered an aileron. And all the time I was kicking planes off of him but there were also planes behind me, so I dove down and levelled out over the water and poured on the coal. Just about that time the gas tank exploded.

Q: One thing you never mentioned, were you burned at all?

A: Hell no, I was out of that aircraft in a split second ... at about 200 feet over the water.

Q: Did your parachute open fully?

A: It caught, luckily, but I didn't even complete one swing before I hit the water which, incidentally, was just like hitting concrete.

Q: How long were you in the water?

A: It was an early morning raid and I got knocked down a little before eight o'clock in the morning. The Japanese submarine picked me up some time during the late afternoon.

Q: Were you injured very badly?

A: I wasn't in too good a shape. Most of my right ear had been shot off and that hurt. The burst from a 20 mm cannon shell had knocked out a few of my teeth and I had been hit in the thigh with machine-gun fire. I had also been shot through the calf of the leg and my ankle was shattered by another 20 mm cannon burst. Other than that, I was OK.

Q: Well, you had some ear problems prior to this anyway, hadn't you?

A: Yes, when you'd wake up in the morning, your ears would be plugged solid with the material that would form in there. It was like plaster of Paris being poured into your ears. Every morning the surgeon would drill down through those plugs and then pour something through the hole to dissolve the crud enough so that we could hear over the radio in the air.

Q: Once you became a guest of the Japanese, how long were you aboard the submarine?

A: It was just a few hours or so. We weren't far from Rabaul and they stayed on the surface and cruised right into the harbor. That night I was blindfolded and had my hands tied behind my back and they paraded me around naked. At one point I kind of hobbled through the town and I could hear the tinkling of glass and laughter from women. I figured someone was having a cocktail party and of course I had been stripped naked and I wasn't sure whether the women were laughing about my lack of manly efforts or what. But in the condition I was in, that was no time to try to improve upon things.

Q: We were obviously doing a lot of bombing at Rabaul during this time.

A: Oh, yes. During the time I was there our planes were bombing the daylights out of the place. At least they would let us go down into bomb shelters while I was there which is more than what they would let us do once we got to Japan.

Q: What was it like being on the ground and watching your own bombs coming at you?

A: It was certainly a mixed feeling. On the one hand you knew that it had to happen if you were ever going to get out of this place but at the same time you were hoping to God that one of those bombs didn't have your name on it.

Q: At the time of your capture, were the Japanese aware of who you were?

A: Well, I don't think so at first. At the time I was shot down I planned to lie and tell them I was just an operations officer along on this one mission to see what was going on and that I wasn't a regular pilot and this is exactly what I did. What I didn't realize was that some enterprising recruit back at the squadron had painted my name on the back of my life jacket. I thought they believed me and it wasn't until later in Japan when it became obvious they knew.

Once every two weeks I would be interrogated by an officer and on one of those occasions the officer commented about how interesting it was that a flyer by the same name as mine had been awarded the Congressional Medal of Honor. I mentioned something to the effect that that was good for him and then the officer asked me if I knew a woman by the name of Grace Hallenbeck. I remember thinking that, my God, something's happened to my mom. The Japanese Commander noticed my reaction and said, 'Don't worry, she's fine. We just got a radio report that she recently christened a new aircraft carrier.' I grinned and told him that the old lady was still in there pitching even if I wasn't. At that point he reached over and grabbed my shoulder and said, 'Listen fella, even though you're captured we appreciate a guy who's done something for his own country,' I thought that was a real nice gesture and certainly true to life.

Q: How was your treatment generally at the hands of the Japanese?

A: On the whole, not bad at all. Oh, there were a few heels here and there but then the Marine Corps had its heels too. What the hell, you run into heels wherever you go. One of the first things I was told after joining up was that there would be times when I felt like resigning because of some heel but that no five or six heels could ever destroy anything as great as the Marine Corps. And that was the case with the vast majority of Japanese. A few heels and they can make life pretty miserable if they want to.

Q: There have been a lot of stories about the legendary Pappy Boyington and I suppose many of them have been blown way out of proportion. One of the stories was that you were the only man ever to be captured by the Japanese who weighed more when he was released than he did when he was captured.

A: That definitely is not true. At one time during my early captivity I had dropped from my normal weight of 170 lbs down to around 90 lbs. Later, however, I was allowed to work in their kitchens stoking fires and was able to steal enough food to get my weight back up to around 130 lbs by war's end.

Q: How did you feel at the time when they told you that you had been awarded the Medal of Honor posthumously?

A: Well, there's a long story behind that. Twice before in my Marine Corps career I had been written up for the Medal of Honor and it had not been approved. Even the Air Corps had written me up for a Silver Star and the Marine Corps' reaction to that was 'To hell with you, we'll decorate our own people.' The net result was that I got nothing. So at the time I was shot down and given up for dead, I hadn't received a single decoration, not even a Purple Heart, after twenty-eight victories.

Had it not been for a piece by columnist Ed Sullivan with the *New York Times*, I probably wouldn't have received anything. They hadn't even sent a Purple Heart to my home. Well, Roosevelt had read the article and let it be known that I would be a recipient of the Medal of Honor. When the Marine Corps got wind of this, they figured God we'd better do something too so General Vandercliffe ordered his boys to write me up for the Navy Cross, posthumously of course.

After the war, when I returned to Washington, Roosevelt had, of course, passed away and it was Henry Truman who hung the Medal around my neck. There were a number of men receiving medals in the ceremony and Truman used that saying for which he was quite well-known to everyone but me. He used to say, 'I'd rather have this honor than be president of the United States.' I was all ready to tell him that I'd trade my medal for his job. I often wondered why he never said it.

Q: I understand that while you were standing there waiting to be decorated by the President, someone came up and made a rather amusing comment.

A: Yeah, we were all standing there at attention out in the back of Truman's office on the White House lawn – he was such a quick little character they never knew when he was going to pop out so we had to stand at semi-attention and then they'd call us to brace when he appeared – and an old friend of mine from the early days who had since been made General snuck up behind me. Of course I couldn't turn around, but he said, 'Hey, Ratsoff', which was my nickname, 'you know you're not supposed to be here.' His meaning was that while nothing was too good for a dead guy, they never would have awarded me anything had they known that I was still alive. I turned my head slightly and said, 'Yeah, I know General, but I sure (expletive

deleted) 'em, didn't I?' He just smiled and walked on.

Q: So you were decorated with the Congressional Medal of Honor and the Navy Cross . . .

A: And that was it. About ten years after the end of the war, I got a letter from Marine Corps headquarters and they said that if I would kindly note down all the missions I had been on, they would award me the Distinguished Flying Crosses and Air Medals to which I was entitled. I got to thinking about it and it came out to something like fifteen DFCs and fifty or so Air Medals and they never had even sent me a Purple Heart. So I wrote them a letter and told them not to send me a goddamn thing. If they couldn't give it to me when they were supposed to, forget it. I never heard another word from them.

Louis H. Wilson, Jr, the current Commandant of the Marines was standing there in line with me (on the White House lawn to receive the Medal). And I'll tell you that he is a beautiful guy. My wife and I were down in Los Angeles for part of the Marines' Bicentennial

celebration and Louis did something that is just typical of a great man. Here he is Commandant, he broke ranks during the ceremonies and came over to me, and I'm just there as a spectator, to shake hands and say, 'Remember me? I was junior to you standing in that line waiting for Harry Truman.' That was over 30 years ago and I'll tell you it takes a real man to do that, to break ranks and come down with the guys.

Q: You just recently attended a reunion of VMF and VMFA 214. How many of the men that you commanded in your squadron were there?

A: Unfortunately there were only five of the members from my squadron period on hand but that's because there had not been sufficient time before hand to contact all of the surviving members. It takes a lot of tracking down names, addresses and phone numbers, and there just wasn't enough time.

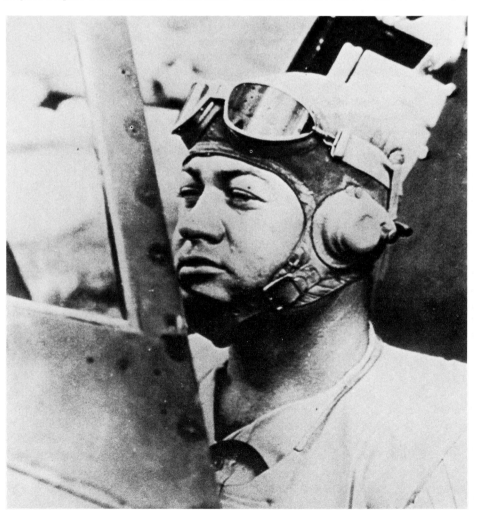

The scrappy Boyington in the cockpit of his faithful Corsair before taking off on yet another mission against the Japanese. Boyington's personality clashed with many higher ups yet he had what it took to take on large numbers of the enemy and defeat them over their own territory.

But there were over 300 members there from the beginning of the squadron right up to the present. The squadron still exists at MCAS El Toro, California, flying A-4 attack aircraft.

Q : What do you do for a living now?
A : I'm an oil painter ... have been for a number of years now. I do mainly desert landscapes, sunrises, sunsets, etc. I suppose with my appearance and all, I should be a retired construction worker or something but a great deal of learning and effort has gone into my current occupation. it seems rather incongruous but I think of myself as a genuinely delicate, artistic person. And that sort of thing is reflected in one's flying. I didn't say it, but Marion Carl who was an ace and later a test pilot for the Marine Corps and Navy, when asked about me, said that I was the most delicate, natural pilot he had ever seen.

Q : Do you make a good living by painting?
A : I do. Actually, I'm three paintings behind right now. I could do better by painting more but, hell, I only do what I want.

Q : Let's get back to the television series for a moment. Of course after the war you were a national figure for a time and then it happened all over again with the publication of your best selling book *Baa Baa Blacksheep* in the late 1950s. It would seem as though the logical follow on, a movie about your exploits is long overdue. How do you feel about this current recognition that you are being given?
A : I know that you don't mean it that way, but I want to make it clear that I don't consider that anyone is *giving* me *anything*, say, in the manner that they would have an old timer's night at a baseball park for a retired player. The producers are in it for the money and that's it. Of course, it is something far more personal to me than that. Fifteen or so years ago when Columbia bought the movie rights to my story, the script they came up with was terrible! I'm happy about the fact that this time they are doing it right. They are doing their best to capture the flavor of what it was really like back in the old days. Of course, you have to consider that the movie will be shown on television and will therefore be subject to certain restrictions as far as graphic representations of events are concerned, but at least they are doing their best to tell the truth in the TV movie version that will lead off the weekly series. Later, the series will focus on fictional plots but the program will strive to maintain authenticity in terms of showing 'what it really was like'.

Q : What about the young actors that are portraying pilots in the series?
A : They all seem pretty dedicated. They come over to me and ask for pointers on achieving realism in their action scenes. I think one of the best examples was when James Whitmore, Jr, a fine young actor who is following in his father's footsteps and plays a character in the movie named T.J., came over to me while we were out on location and asked, 'Why was it that you guys fought so much between yourselves? Why did you drink so much? Was it because you were scared to death underneath it all?'

I told him hell no, that he had to understand we were a strange breed of cat. We were all there because we chose to be. No one had forced us to be flyers. We could have done many other things in the Marine Corps, but we wanted to do this. When they worked us for seven or eight missions a day and on into the night, and they did do this frequently, we were exhausted. We'd fall asleep under a wing on the coral dust and someone would have to come by and kick us to say it was time for another mission. We'd grumble, get in the plane, crank it up and fly off. But when things would let up, our adrenalin would still be in high gear. We would have loved to have fought the neighboring squadron out in a coconut patch, but when we couldn't do that, we'd just go after each other. That was just the way we lived. The philosophy was simply to live one day at a time because that was all you could be sure of. They'd threaten us with general court martial for things we'd do by the day. But we knew that would take six months of paperwork and none of us knew whether we were going to be alive six months from now and didn't really care. That was a Marine pilot for you.

Q : You talk about threatened court martial and so forth, this Colonel Lard is one of the prime characters in the script and, as such, is Boyington's nemesis on the home front.
A : He was a real enough character but of course I can't reveal the real name of the person – I didn't do that in my book. But when I wrote the book, I naturally got tons of mail and the vast majority of it was in reference to this Colonel Lard who was the 'fictional' character I had in the book. Most of the letters were from ex-service guys who would comment about how they, too, had known their own Colonel Lard and how similar the characters were.

As I look back on it, I truly feel sorry for this man. He had everything going for him. He was an Academy graduate, a good flyer in his time, but he was an insecure person. And he tried to make up for this somehow by

being a great disciplinarian. No matter what situation I happened to be in at the time, I don't think I ever suffered from insecurity in the sense that I doubted myself and I thank God for that.

Q : Another interesting phase of your career was your relationship with General Claire Chennault during your stint with the Flying Tigers.
A : Well, you know he was retired from the Air Corps as a First Lieutenant and a couple of his flying sergeants got him a job with Chiang Kai-shek. It was only thereafter that he promoted himself to General. He was always a great talker and it was Madame Chiang that put his words into being by starting the American Volunteer Group. It wasn't Claire. She made it a money thing. The Chiang Kai-sheks turned everything into money.

Actually, I could never blame poor old Claire. I felt sorry for him, too. But I couldn't help but needle him. Christ, he threatened to have me court martialled and shot so many times. I remember when I told him that I finally figured out his angle, I said you've got a monetary deal with the Chiang Kai-sheks that won't quit. All your tactics are phoney, you're a phoney. You're just trying to keep the guys around that made your reputation out here and a lot of them are sick and tired. I told him I figured he was in for several million dollars. Well, it turned out to be ten million. He married a Chinese woman finally and they inherited her father's estate but that didn't fool me. This was all shortly before I left.

Q : Did you get along with him at all?
A : I didn't. There were several reasons why not. I think one of the main reasons was due to a fella there who was second in command. He was a guy who had resigned from the Air Corps rather than be court martialled and he had come over and married a White Russian, a very beautiful woman. This was the reason that Chennault hired him, because of his wife who was kind of a free woman. Then of course I came along and I was a lot younger than he was. Naturally, as years went on and I shaved in front of the mirror, I got to understand why he hated me so much.

Q : One of the things I wanted to ask you about that we have kind of overlooked is your nickname ... 'Pappy'. How did you come by that name?
A : Well, it was the pilots who gave me the name, but originally it was worse than that ... it was 'Grandpappy'. It got shortened to 'Gramps' and then finally the newspapers turned it into 'Pappy'. It all revolved around

the statistic at the time that the average military pilot's life expectancy from the time he started flying was seven years and I was long past that. So that's why I was considered so old.

Q: Even as a young man you were what many would call a paradox. You were a scrapper who never walked away from a fight yet you had the temperament and finesse of an artist and I imagine it was this unusual combination that went a long way, along with being a natural pilot, toward your becoming a leading ace.
A: Yes, it did.

Q: You retired shortly after World War Two, then along came Korea. Did you feel the urge to do anything about that?

A: There wasn't much I could do. I was medically retired from the service. One thing I did volunteer for was to talk to pilots about the prospects of becoming a prisoner of war. I told them I'd do it for nothing, but no, they wanted some well-educated idiot who had never been anyplace to instruct the guys.

Q: Do you hold any malice for the Japanese?
A: Not a bit. In fact I never really did while I was there as a prisoner. Hatred takes something out of you.

Q: The Japanese pilots you came up against were they good, green, or what? You were operating roughly during the mid-point of the war.
A: They varied of course. Some of them were very, very good and you discovered those right

off the bat.

Q: I suppose there was always that one that got away?
A: Oh, certainly! Due to time, ammunition, gas, whatever. There always had to be somebody getting away. I guess the main thing I had going for me at the time I got into action in the Pacific was my earlier combat experience. You come to learn that you don't have anything to fear unless an enemy is in a certain position. When you first go in there, hell, you're afraid of a meatball way up there that couldn't even shoot at you. But it's just like boxing. Finally, you get to where you force the other guy to throw a punch and then you counter punch them. But you could never do that unless you knew what the other guy was capable of.

Q: During the Vietnam War, our pilots had a tendency to break to the left. This, of course, was due to the fact that they had been taught to drive with their right hand. The enemy gunners became quite aware of this and it cost us. Did you ever observe anything like this with the Japanese pilots?
A: There were certain things that one learned to look for. But, more importantly, one planned ahead for certain situations. For example, one of my pilots came to me one day and asked how the hell to get away from a Tony? That was an inline engine Japanese fighter that could dive with a Corsair. And if you turned left they're going to get you. I told him to get 'em started going down hill to the left and then jerk it on over to the right and they can never stay with you. And that, I guess, was due to the different effects of torque and the designs of the airframes, whatever, but you didn't worry about that . . . it worked. Then if you wanted to go get him, you just turned back around to the left.

Q: You flew the inline engine Curtiss P-40 in China.
A: That is where I learned most of this stuff. Finally, I kind of got used to gunfire and . . . you learn that, hell, a guy can be flying formation with you but unless he gets in a certain position, there's nothing he can do to you. But that sort of thing would scare a green pilot to death. It was just a matter of familiarization.

A current Boyington and actor Robert Conrad, who plays the commander of the Black Sheep in the television series of the same name, on location during the filming of one of the episodes. Boyington acted as technical advisor to Universal Studios on the series.

Q : It's certainly an understatement that you have led a full life. It's an age-old question but what would you do differently if you had it to do again?

A : I don't even think about things like that. No man is entitled to a second go around and I am sure that if I were to do it all again, I would stumble over the same pitfalls given my personality and temperament. In other words, it wouldn't be so much a matter of the breaks as it would be the person's makeup. Say somebody offered me a job ... the unknown ... combat ... the chance to pit your skill against another guy's skill. Hell I'd be a sucker for that.

Ira Kepford – Corsair Ace of VF-17

Ensign Ira Kepford was sweating in the cockpit of his Vought Corsair as he scanned the horizon over a vast stretch of the Pacific. It was 11 November 1943, and the intense tropical sun beat through the plexiglass canopy of the Corsair making Kepford feel as if he were in a greenhouse. Kepford belonged to VF-17, 'Blackburn's Irregulars' as they had been dubbed in honor of their commander, Captain John T. Blackburn.

VF-17 had picked up quite a reputation stateside as the unit worked up to combat-ready status. High-spirited pilots were known to run trucks off the local roads as they made *inverted* passes down the roads. Nothing was sacred and race tracks, official ceremonies, farmers, and local citizens all became targets for hedgehopping pilots as they enjoyed the enormous power of their newly acquired fighters. Needless to say, the Navy did not look on this conduct very kindly, indeed buzzing was considered a serious offense, but Blackburn insisted that his pilots were all the more ready for combat and, instead of being punished, they should be sent directly into combat. The Navy, only too glad to be rid of such flying maniacs, happily agreed and VF-17 head for the Pacific where they were to set an amazing record of eight enemy aircraft destroyed for every Corsair lost. The scoreboard would total 8,577 combat hours, 156 enemy aircraft destroyed over the Solomons, five ships sunk, and *twelve* aces, more aces than any other Navy unit. It must be remembered that this incredible score was achieved in the space of 76 days!

Ira Kepford, who would become one of the stars of VF-17, grew up in Illinois where he became a star football player at Northwestern University. As a student, Kepford found himself interested in the military life and, accordingly, he joined the Naval Reserve during the middle of 1941. After graduation from school, Kepford obtained an honorable discharge from the Reserves and took up an appointment as an Aviation Cadet with the United States Navy.

Following training he was assigned to VF-17 at Norfolk, Virginia, which was to be the first Navy squadron equipped with the Corsair. A good number of the pilots making up the squadron had combat experience and Kepford eagerly listened to their accounts of tangling with the Japanese fighters. Many of the pilots had been flying the antiquated Wildcat and looked forward to taking the Corsair into combat ... they had a lot of scores to settle.

November of 1943 found Kepford adjusting the throttle of his Corsair, leaning back the mixture to achieve the best fuel flow as VF-17 cruised over the Pacific in support of a Task Force that included the *Bunker Hill* and *Essex*. Flying from Ondonga, New Georgia, the Corsairs were able to add a good measure of protection for the ships. The Navy still had not cleared the Corsair for carrier operations so 'Blackburn's Irregulars' had to mix with USMC and USAAF units and take a good deal of ribbing about sailors being stranded on land. As the Task Force steamed into Empress Augusta Bay the action began with a bang. Japanese torpedo bombers, flying low to the water, made straight for the carriers. Fuelled by the typical Japanese 'do or die' attitude, the bombers were a serious threat. The pilots of VF-17 saw the carriers putting up an intense anti-aircraft barrage as they maneuvered to avoid the incoming attack. Kepford shoved the throttle forward and the big R-2800 bellowed as the squadron dived to the rescue. The Corsairs fell among the eighteen torpedo bombers like chickens on a June bug. In the first blazing pass, seventeen of the attackers were blown out of the air and the surviving bomber was polished off on the second pass. The gunners on the carriers cheered as they saw the amazing feat of aerial combat and the pilots of VF-17 were even a bit stunned. However, the enemy was not to be stopped and attack after attack was pressed home by courageous pilots whose aircraft were just not a match for the powerful Corsairs.

Kepford was in the thick of the fighting, twisting and turning, as he went around and around with Zekes and Vals. As the Corsairs began to run low on fuel, they came down and *landed* on the carriers, an unprecedented move that was not officially sanctioned. The carrier crews could not have cared less about official permission as they rapidly refuelled and rearmed the F4Us for they knew that the fighter pilots were stopping the enemy's concentrated attacks.

By the end of the day's fighting, an exhausted Kepford had destroyed four of the enemy and damaged a fifth. For such an outstanding performance the young ensign was awarded the Navy Cross.

VF-17 found itself transferred to Bougainville during January of 1944 as that is where the heavy fighting was taking place and 'Blackburn's Irregulars' knew where they wanted to be! Kepford, by this time, had been promoted to Lieutenant (jg). During the latter part of January, the squadron was out protecting a bomber strike against Rabaul when they were jumped by a superior number of Zeke fighters. Kepford and his wingman attacked a formation of twelve enemy aircraft and, when the smoke had cleared, four of the Zekes were added to Kepford's score. It was commented that Ira liked doing things in a big way! For his aerial marksmanship Kepford was awarded the Gold Star.

VF-17 settled into the difficult grind of existing in the primitive living conditions of Bougainville and of the daily grind to Rabaul and back. Rabaul was a nightmare of flak and enemy fighters flown by pilots who knew that there would be no retreat and were only too happy to sacrifice themselves for the emperor. On 19 February 1944, while on a strafing mission to Rabaul, Kepford commanded a flight of four Corsairs to fly as protection for the Corsairs that would be doing the strafing.

On the way to the target, Kepford's wingman was forced to turn back to home base with engine problems. Normally, Kepford would have been compelled to cover his wingman's withdrawal as the area over Rabaul was not safe for just one aircraft. Each Corsair needed the other for protection. Kepford realized that the Corsairs in the ground attack mission needed to be protected so he continued without a wingman. However, once over Rabaul, the resistance was extremely heavy and Kepford was ordered to head back to home base.

As he headed back to Bougainville, Kepford spotted a Rufe float-plane skirting near the ocean. He attacked at once and blew the enemy out of the air with a single burst of fire from the six 0.50 caliber Browning machine-

guns. As he climbed back to altitude, the young ace noticed a large formation of Zeke fighters heading in the same direction that he needed to take to get back to Bougainville. Some of the fighters spotted Kepford at low altitude and broke formation as they headed after 'easy game'. The Zekes excelled in aerial combat at lower altitudes where the Corsair was not as maneuverable.

The Zekes roared in on the low-flying Kepford, intent on blasting the American into the ocean. In a desperate attempt, Kepford dumped the flaps on his Corsair, the bent-wing bird shuddered and immediately slowed as the speeding Zekes flashed by. Kepford pressed the firing button and watched in satisfaction as the slugs from the Brownings tore one of the enemy aircraft apart. Kepford immediately cleaned the flaps back up and shot the throttle forward but he was heading in the wrong direction with more of the enemy now in hot pursuit! Shoving the throttle all the way forward, Kepford cut in the new water injection system that was intended to give tremendous surges of power for just a few minutes. The Corsair shuddered and then roared forward as the Pratt & Whitney engine pumped out well over 2,000 hp. The Japanese fighters were still behind him but they were dropping. Kepford realized that fuel was getting low and he *had* to head back in the direction of the enemy. Racking the F4U into a violent turn, Kepford tried to head away from the pursuers but the nimble Zekes were able to turn inside the Corsair's violent turn. The high-speed turns continued at wave-top height, the threat of a high-speed stall a constant possibility, as one of the Zekes began to close the gap and open fire. However, the Japanese pilot was cutting things just a bit too fine and the wing tip of his fighter made momentary contact with the top of the waves and, in the next instant, all that was left of the enemy was a huge plume of ocean spray and a few bits of debris. Kepford's Corsair had taken a number of hits but he was now rapidly gaining on the enemy and he made it back to Bougainville. There was not much fuel left by the time he touched down and the ace was shaking from the exertion of the combat and drenched in sweat from the heat and enormous concentration required in the deadly conflict.

Kepford increased his score to seventeen official victories, becoming the fifth highest ranking Navy ace of World War Two. In December of 1944 Kepford was sent back to a stateside position where he stayed until the end of the war.

Magnificent aerial formation of five Corsairs from VF-17 with ace Ira Kepford's F4U-1 in the lead. The aircraft is finished in the tri-color camouflage scheme which was adopted on 1 February 1943. The upper portion of the fuselage was painted Non Specular Sea Blue with Non Specular Intermediate Blue applied to the fuselage side, vertical tail and rudder surfaces. The upper surfaces of the wings and horizontal tail were painted Semi-Gloss Sea Blue. All under surfaces were painted Non Specular Insignia White which did not extend up the fuselage sides nor beyond the shadow of the horizontal surfaces. The Intermediate Blue used on the fuselage sides was blended into the upper and lower colors so as to leave no definite demarcation line. The lower surface of the folding portion of the wing was also painted Non Specular Intermediate Blue. Leading edges of the wings were painted Non Specular Sea Blue and blended into the upper and lower wing surface colors. White tape was used to cover the panel lines over the gas tank and instrument access panel. Codes were in White and the national insignia carries a Blue surround. VF-17's skull and crossbone insignia can be seen on the cowling and was painted in Black and White. Victory marks were White and Red. Photograph was taken on 15 April 1944. (USN/80-G-217817)

Robert Hanson – The Terror of Rabaul

Twenty victories in just six missions covering a period of 17 days—an outstanding accomplishment that was not to be equalled by any other Allied flyer during World War Two. The one man air force who achieved this fantastic record was a young Marine fighter pilot – First Lieutenant Robert Murray Hanson.

This superb combat flyer was to have an unusual beginning in life, being born in Lucknow, India, on 4 February 1920, the son of Methodist missionary parents then stationed in that country. Hanson was to spend his early childhood in India, only occasionally returning for short visits to the family home in Newtonville, Massachusetts. When ready for college in the spring of 1938, he decided to return to the United States by way of Europe, bicycling his way through the continent. It was a broadening experience for the young man, the highpoint coming when he was in Vienna at the time Adolf Hitler's troops marched into Austria. With a talent for linguistics gained from contact with other missionaries in India, Hanson was able to speak fluent Hindustani, Spanish, German and French and was to have no language difficulties during the trip.

He enrolled at Hamline University, a small Methodist-sponsored college in Saint Paul, Minnesota, in the fall of 1938. While in school Bob Hanson, a husky six-footer, was to achieve no small amount of fame by becoming the conference light heavyweight wrestling champion. A natural athlete with quick reflexes, he was also to star on the school's football and track team. Despite a busy schedule of studies and athletics, Hanson found time to pay his own way through college by working in the school cafeteria during the day and as a night club bouncer at night.

Only a few days after graduation in May of 1942, Bob Hanson enlisted in the Marine Corps and was accepted for flight training. He won his wings and commission in the spring of 1943 at Corpus Christi, Texas, becoming a fighter pilot. By the Fall of the year he was ready for a combat assignment. Ordered to the South Pacific as a replacement pilot, he arrived there on 6 October 1943. Joining Marine Fighting Squadron 215,

stationed at the time at Vella Lavella, Hanson was to fly the powerful new Vought F4U-1 Corsair and to take part in air operations against the Japanese forces in the Bougainville-New Britain area.

On 1 November 1943, VMF-215 was among the aviation units assigned to provide air support for the Marine amphibious landings at Empress Augusta Bay on the south coast of Bougainville. While flying with the squadron high above the landing force, Hanson suddenly broke away and single-handedly attacked a formation of six Japanese Val dive bombers he had spotted on their way to hit US Navy ships supporting the landing. So aggressively did Hanson go after the Japanese planes, they were forced to jettison their bombs and flee. During the ensuing battle, young Bob Hanson was able to shoot

A Marine fighter pilot hunches over the controls as his Corsair lifts off the airstrip at Cape Torokina, Empress Augusta Bay, Bougainville. The F4U-1s of the Marine flew daily combat missions against the heavily defended Rabaul area. Some of the fiercest aerial fights of the Pacific war took place over Rabaul. Lieutenant Robert Hanson scored 20 victories in just 17 days during this period of intensive fighting. (USMC/71422)

one of the enemy dive bombers down. The Val was to be his first official victory of the war.

Bob Hanson showed an early dislike for the discipline and teamwork so strongly stressed as fundamental to success in the air by Marine commanders. At every opportunity or excuse he would break away from the formation to go after an enemy aircraft on his own. In particular, he disliked the job of flying as a wingman, feeling too vulnerable to an enemy attacking from the rear, whereas only the leader had an opportunity to down enemy planes. At first this independence was to bring sharp reprimands. But later, as he began to achieve a number of victories, his superior officer Major Robert G. Owens, put up with this tendency to break off on his own in a fight as long as it brought results.

Flaps down, power back, canopy open ... a Marine Corsair comes in for a landing after a combat patrol. Since the Navy did not feel that the Corsair was suitable for carrier operations, it was left to the Marines to prove the powerful fighter's worth and prove it they did. In Marine hands, the Corsair was almost unstoppable and it was just as good in the ground attack role as it was as an aerial interceptor. The Corsair could easily carry a bomb and rocket load that was equal to what the famous de Havilland Mosquito twin-engine bomber could lug into the air. (USMC/81363)

While flying with VMF-215 on a protective patrol for the US Navy task force supporting the landing on Bougainville a few days later, a large formation of enemy aircraft, between twenty and thirty Zekes, Hamps and Kates, were heading for the Navy ships. The Marine flyers went after them and were to shoot down five of the enemy planes, Bob Hanson getting three himself before the badly mauled Japanese broke away from the fight and headed back for their base. But Bob Hanson was not content to let them get away, chasing after the fleeing enemy planes. The rear gunners of one of the Kates scored a number of hits on Hanson's Corsair as he swung in behind. The engine sputtered to a stop and Hanson nosed the Corsair down toward the water. He brought the crippled aircraft down to a safe ditching and then quickly got out the life raft before the plane sank. The rest of the day was spent drifting lazily on the ocean.

In the late afternoon a number of Japanese warships passed close to Hanson in the water but fortunately did not see him. Then, recognizing an American destroyer in the distance, Hanson paddled furiously toward it while singing a popular song of the day, *You'll Be So Nice To Come Home To*. The

destroyer was the USS *Sigourney*, on its way to Guadalcanal. An alert seaman spotted Hanson in his little yellow life raft and the destroyer moved in to pick him up. Back at his base on Vella Lavella a few days later, he found he had been reported as missing in action. No one had seen Hanson go down during the fight. But he also learned that he had been credited with the three enemy aircraft he had shot down that day. His total now stood at four victories.

During November and early December of 1943, VMF-215 continued to operate from Vella Lavella as the Marine landings on Bougainville were brought to a conclusion. A new airfield was being prepared at Torokina, located on the east side of Empress Augusta Bay and some 200 miles closer to Rabaul. The new field was ready by 16 December and VMF-215 began to operate from there. During this period Bob Hanson was to score another victory and bring his total to five, along with the title 'ace', by the end of the year. At this time the Japanese High Command, following the fall of Bougainville, decided to greatly reinforce their position at Rabaul on New Britain Island with naval and air forces from Truk. Their plan was to build an impregnable fortress from which to strike

Husky Bob Hanson was born in India, the son of missionary parents. In a meteoric combat career he was to threaten the record of Boyington and Foss as the top Marine ace of World War Two.

back at American forces gathering strength on Guadalcanal and other island bases in the Solomons group. The main job of Marine air units in the area was to effectively counter this potential threat by the Japanese on Rabaul.

Marine flyers, shortly after beginning their intensified campaign against Rabaul, received a severe shock on 3 January 1944. Major Gregory Boyington, along with his wingman, were reported lost over Rabaul while on a fighter sweep (it would not be known until the end of the war that 'Pappy' was a prisoner of the Japanese). It appeared that Boyington had had the best chance of becoming the leading Marine ace of the war. Lieutenant Bob Hanson, with only five victories at the time, could hardly have been considered a serious contender for the title.

Yet in his first air battle over Rabaul on 14 January, Bob Hanson, with this one mission, was to double his score. VMF-215 was to be part of the Marine fighter force assigned to protect a squadron of US Army B-25 Mitchell medium bombers of the 13th Air Force on a raid to Simpson Harbor. The bomber formation was attacked by seventy Japanese fighters as it neared Rabaul. The Marine Corsairs came plunging down to protect the bombers and in the wild swirling aerial battle Bob Hanson was to be credited with downing five of the enemy fighters. This brought his score to ten victories.

On his second flight over Rabaul, Hanson was again flying fighter cover but this time for Navy carrier bombers on a strike at the enemy bastion. Only a few Japanese fighters came up to contest the bombers. During the fight Hanson was able to knock one of the enemy planes down in flames.

His third mission to Rabaul was to take place on 17 January 1944. The strike consisted of twenty-nine SBDs and eighteen TBFs escorted by seventy Marine, Navy and Army fighters. This time the Japanese opposed the Americans in force. A total of seventy-nine enemy aircraft were shot down, eleven by the Marine fighters. Bob Hanson was credited with knocking down three of the enemy before the rest were scattered. Five ships in the harbor were sunk. It was judged to be the most successful bombing mission carried out against Rabaul up to this time.

A week later, on 24 January, VMF-215 was again assigned to protect a formation of eighteen TBFs from VC 40 and VMTB 143, sent to hit shipping in Keravia Bay at the south end of Rabaul. The weather was none too promising with huge thunderheads and torrential rains to obscure vision. Over the target area, Hanson became separated from the formation in the bad weather and began to climb. Above the clouds he found a large force of Japanese Zekes, using the clouds for concealment, preparing to dive on the American bombers. Hanson tore into the enemy formation with devastating fury, knocking four of the Zekes down, and probably a fifth, in only a few minutes. The enemy fighters, scattered by Hanson's vicious attack, quickly withdrew leaving the bombers unaware of the danger that had been lurking above them. The bombers, carrying 2,000 lb bombs with delayed fuzes, continued on their mission and sank five enemy ships in the harbor.

Only a couple of days later Hanson took off on his fifth mission to Rabaul. The Japanese there had recently been reinforced with sixty-two Zeke fighters and thirty-six dive bombers from Truk to bring their total estimated air strength to around 300 aircraft. A large number of the Japanese fighters again came up to intercept the Marine bombers and fighters. In a wild and savage air battle Bob Hanson was to down three of the enemy planes to bring his total to twenty-one victories.

A reconnaissance flight reported a number of Japanese ships had recently arrived in Simpson Harbor and a hastily assembled air strike was ordered for the late afternoon of 30 January. A formation of eighteen TBMs from VMTB-233, protected by the Corsairs of VMF-215, headed for Rabaul. Nearing the target area the Marine flyers ran into a strong force of Zekes. As the Avengers went down to hit the enemy shipping, the Corsairs tangled with the opposing fighters. A Japanese freighter, the *Iwate Maru*, was sunk and several other enemy ships seriously damaged by the Avengers. In the air battle raging above, two Corsairs and one Avenger were shot down, but the Marine flyers were to claim twenty-one Zekes destroyed. Bob Hanson got credit for four of the enemy, bringing his total to twenty-five, only one short of Foss's and three short of Boyington's record. Bets now began to go down among the Marine flyers on Bougainville that Bob Hanson's next trip over Rabaul would see him emerge as the Marine Corps' top ace.

The next mission to Rabaul was scheduled for 3 February, the day before Bob Hanson's 24th birthday. He was to be part of a patrol, led by Captain Harold L. Spears, on a fighter sweep over Rabaul. Arriving over the target area, they found Rabaul hidden under a layer of clouds, common in that area of quickly forming tropical storms. The Marine flyers had no choice but to return to their base on Bougainville. On the way back, Hanson called Spears on the radio and asked for permission to strafe a lighthouse used by the Japanese as an early warning post and flak tower on Cape Alexander, a piece of land jutting off the southern tip of New Ireland. This lighthouse had been particularly annoying to the Marine flyers since repeated attempts to knock it out had failed. Spears gave his OK and Hanson dropped his Corsair down into a dive, guns firing at the lighthouse. Pulling up and then over in a sharp turn, Hanson was coming back over the lighthouse on his second pass when his Corsair was hit by an enemy anti-aircraft shell from the ground, tearing off part of the fighter's wing.

Spears watched from above as Hanson attempted to ditch the badly damaged Corsair in the storm-churned sea. He was skimming over the surface about to set down when a wing dipped into the water and the Corsair viciously cartwheeled several times into a giant splash. When the water settled, all that remained on the surface were bits of debris and an oil slick. Passing slowly over the spot, Spears searched the water hoping to see Hanson's head come bobbing to the surface but nothing appeared on the choppy sea. It was evident Bob Hanson had been killed, trapped in the Corsair as it sank to the

Top

Armorers work on the 0.50 caliber machine-guns of the Corsair. Virtually all of the maintenance on the Corsairs had to be done in the harsh heat, humidity, and insects of the South Pacific. The well-worn finish on this Corsair, named 'Bubbles', is testimony to the rigors of the climate in which the tough fighter had to survive and function. (USMC/A55431)

Bottom

Marine mechanics pull the propeller of an F4U-1 through a couple of revolutions prior to starting the massive Pratt & Whitney R-2800 radial engine. Engine policy in the Air Corps settled on sleek inline powerplants while the Navy chose the bulkier-looking radials for their aircraft. It worked out that the radials were able to develop more horsepower, were without a vulnerable cooling system, and could absorb a tremendous amount of battle damage, all important factors when operating a single-engine fighter over vast stretches of water occupied by the enemy. (USMC/55442)

bottom.

A few weeks later, the middle of February, Rabaul was considered to be effectively isolated. Japanese air power, estimated at up to 400 aircraft, had been whittled down to only a handful and these were withdrawn to Truk. From that day on not so much as a postcard was to come in from Japan as the large enemy force, nearly 100,000 troops, was abandoned to its fate. Marine, Navy and Army flyers would continue to bomb Rabaul, but more as practice for newly arriving flyers before they moved on to the serious fighting further north. No attempt was made by the American forces to capture Rabaul, which would have resulted in heavy casualties, since it was no longer considered necessary. Much of the credit for this victory was to go to the Marine flyers, such as Bob Hanson, whose bravery and tenacity in carrying out these missions was responsible for knocking Rabaul out of the war. Hanson's squadron, VMF-215, was to receive the first Navy Unit Commendation Award for the 137 Japanese aircraft shot down in an 18 week period. The squadron had also produced ten aces during the campaign against Rabaul.

Seven months later, on 1 August 1944, First Lieutenant Robert Murray Hanson was posthumously awarded the Congressional Medal of Honor in recognition of 'his great personal valor and invincible fighting spirit in keeping with the highest traditions of the United States Marine Corps'. In just over three months in combat he had achieved 25 victories, 20 in just 17 days, to rank behind Boyington and Foss as a leading Marine ace of the World War Two. Even though the war was to continue on for another year and a half, no other Marine flyer was to surpass him during this time.

Corsair Crack-Ups!

Even after the Corsair was finally adapted to an aircraft carrier's deck, it still had its share of problems.

At this point the pilot of a Navy F4U-4 probably is wondering whether it's all worth it. The high-speed cameras have caught the Corsair in the act of balancing on its striped propeller boss. The aircraft, aboard the USS *Coral Sea*, on 2 August 1950, is in the act of falling on to its back. The pilot emerged shaken but unhurt.

Top left
The pilot on an F4U-1D botches up his approach and attempts to go around but the carrier's island looms in front . . .

Top right
The Corsair hits the island with a tremendous impact, shattering the fighter and sending the right wing flying off . . .

Center right
The fighter continues its forward progress. Note fires breaking out as the fuel tank ruptures. The wing has fallen into the gun emplacements, sending the crews scattering . . .

Bottom right
Fire crews douse the main fuel tank and cockpit with foam. Note how the forward portion of the Corsair is balanced against the island . . .

Top left
The foam clears away and the bloody but basically uninjured pilot is seen in the cockpit from which he was pulled to safety.

Top right
The pilot of this F4U-1 is frantically unbuckling his harness as flames begin to spew from fuel spilling out on the flight deck. The rescue crewman on the right is adjusting his helmet before heading into the inferno to pull the pilot to safety. Accident took place on the USS *Bataan*, CVL-29.

Left
Marine F4U-4 of VMF-322 goes over the side of the USS *Sicily*, CVE-118, on 14 October 1949. The pilot had attempted to do a go around. The deck crew always faced the hazard of an out of control aircraft crashing in their midst, as often did happen.

5 TIGERCAT –
The Elegant Killer

Grumman's Tigercat had everything a twin-engine high-performance fighter could offer but the Navy did not want the aircraft!

Major E.A. Van Grundy, United States Marine Corps, retarded the throttles of his Grumman F7F-3N Tigercat night fighter a bit more and felt the airframe shudder slightly as the powerful twin-engine fighter protested the slow flight. Van Grundy eased forward on the thick control column just a fraction of an inch to build up the speed a couple of more knots. The Tigercat wallowed through the air, protesting every inch of the way – it wanted to go fast with the speed for which it was designed. Van Grundy's radar operator's ghostly voice came through the headset, giving changes in course for the elusive target they were pursuing.

Suddenly Van Grundy spotted a target directly ahead, its lines vague in the blackness. Almost in a reflex action, he centered the target in the F7F's gunsight and punched the firing button on the control column. The Tigercat gave a mighty shudder as the four 20 mm cannon, mounted two in each wing root, belched explosive shells into the 'bandit'.

The target, a primitive Po-2 biplane of the North Korean air force, literally disintegrated under the impact of the heavy shells, dropping the two shrieking 'gook' airmen on a one-way elevator ride to infinity. Seeing the target destroyed, Van Grundy shoved the throttles forward and felt himself pushed back into his seat as the Tigercat picked up

The magnificent lines of the Grumman F7F-3N Tigercat night fighter are shown to particular advantage in this view. The F7F-3N came along too late to see action during World War Two and the design itself was a victim of rapidly changing requirements. The USAAF's long-range B-29 bombing to Japan had eliminated any requirement for a long-range naval night fighter along with the fact that the modified Corsairs and Hellcats were doing a good job in the night intruder role. All Tigercats, except for the prototypes, were painted Glossy Sea Blue as the new naval specification issued on 7 October 1944 decried. The F8F-1 Bearcat in the background is flying chase on the Tigercat while on a sortie from Grumman's Bethpage, Long Island, 'ironworks'. (Grumman)

speed and roared upward towards the cold stars.

Van Grundy's kill was one of only *two* victories scored by what was, perhaps, the most elegant twin-engine fighter ever built. The kill took place over Korea rather than the skies of World War Two for which the F7F was designed. The target was certainly not worthy of the hunter for the Po-2 looked like something left over from World War One and was used by the North Koreans as a 'Bed-check Charlie' to drop small bombs on American bases to keep troops awake and on the odd chance that some real damage might be caused. The Po-2s were hard to define on radar because of their tube, wood, and fabric construction and their extremely low speed rendered the biplanes almost invulnerable to the fast night fighters that were equipped to handle much more modern and powerful opponents. In fact the USAF had just lost a Lockheed F-94 Starfire, its most modern night fighter, on a Po-2 interception. The Po-2 was destroyed but the Starfire was going so slow that it stalled and spun into the ground killing both of the 319th Fighter Interceptor Squadron members. A high price to pay for such a questionable victory.

The Tigercats of VMF-513 were forced to go after such game and the pilots un-doubtedly grumbled, wanting to hunt the more modern MiGs, but time takes its toll and the Tigercat, the ultimate development of the piston-engine night fighter, was out-moded by the arrival of the newer jets.

The United States Navy and Grumman had some experience previous to the Tigercat with twin-engine fighters. Grumman had constructed the XF5F (along with the some-what similar USAAF XP-50) as part of three new fighter projects for the Navy which were launched during 1938. The other two aircraft were the Vought XF4U-1 and the Bell XFL-1. The XF5F-1 was the first twin-engine single-seat fighter built for the Navy and was flown on April's Fool Day of 1940. The XF5F-1 was extremely unusual for its time, with two Wright R-1820-40 Cyclones mounted ahead of the short fuselage which featured twin rudders. Grumman labelled the design G-43 and gave it the name Skyrocket. Originally armed with two Danish Madsen cannon, the aircraft was eventually con-figured to carry four 0.50 caliber Browning machine-guns. The prototype experienced a number of teething troubles and did not complete its tests until the early part of 1941. It was then returned to the factory and emerged with a longer nose and spinners added to the propeller hubs. The Army's XP-50 featured a nose gear but both aircraft suffered technical problems (in fact the XP-50 crashed on its *first* flight) and were discontinued. The XF5F-1 was scrapped

The Grumman XF5F-1 Skyrocket was certainly a startling concept for the late 1930s. The abbreviated fuselage was flanked by two large radial engines mounted on a broad wing. The fuselage terminated with twin horizontal stabilizers and mounted a large canopy that gave the pilot excellent vision. Carrier operation was foreseen and the wings could be folded from their 42 ft span down to 21 ft. The XF5F-1 made its first flight on April Fool's Day of 1940 with factory pilot Bud Gillies at the controls. The Skyrocket offered performance that made heads turn with a top speed of 380 mph at 16,500 ft and an initial rate of climb of 4,000 fpm. The aircraft was designed originally for a pair of Danish Madsen 25 mm cannon but, on paper, this was substituted for four 0.50 caliber machine-guns. As was common Navy practice in those days, ten light bombs could also be carried.

Despite the Skyrocket's performance, the conservative Navy officials had some doubt about the new concept. Several problems such as engine cooling, some instability in certain conditions, and the fact that the position of the wing would blank out the pilot's view during carrier landings helped deflate the Navy's initial enthusiasm for the project. The nose was eventually lengthened and the engine nacelles redesigned along with contra-rotating propellers being added to the engines, but the Navy had completely dropped the idea. However, the concept of a naval twin-engine high-performance fighter had been aired and would be drawn on for future reference when Design G-51 began. (USN/465058)

after completing 211 test flights, most of fairly short duration.

Grumman and the Navy benefited greatly from the lessons learned in the construction and operation of the two prototype fighters and, in the early part of 1941, the Navy issued a directive for the development of the XF7F-1. The requirement called for a fighter that was powered with two 2,100 hp Pratt & Whitney Double Wasp engines and armed with four 20 mm cannon and four 0.50 caliber machine-guns along with provision for a torpedo under the fuselage or two 1,000 lb bombs beneath the wings. The aircraft was to be carried on the proposed 45,000 ton *Midway* class carriers but production F7Fs *never* operated from carriers.

On 30 June 1941, the Navy authorized Grumman to proceed with its G-51 and the two XF7F-1 prototypes were ordered on 30 June 1941. It is interesting to note that the Army beat the Navy to the initial order when, on 20 May, it ordered two modified G-51s to be designated as XP-65s. These aircraft were to be equipped with two-stage Wright R-1820-67/69 engines. Turbo-superchargers were later added to the specification and the performance was expected to pass that of the XF7F-1. However, Army and Navy specifications clashed and it was

thought that the bi-service fighter would be overweight with the different modifications required for operation by both services hence the Army bowed out and let Grumman continue its tradition as a naval aircraft supplier.

The prototype XF7F-1 lifted off from Grumman's Bethpage, Long Island, facility on 2 December 1943 as test pilot Robert Hall pushed the throttles forward and felt the exhilarating acceleration of the thoroughbred fighter. BuNo 03549 unfortunately led a short life when it was destroyed in a non-fatal crash but, by then, the second prototype was flying and carrying on the research duties. Soon after the flight of the second prototype, the Navy placed an initial order for 500 aircraft.

As the first examples of F7F-1s, now designated Tigercat to keep with the tradition of Grumman's airborne felines, began to leave the production line, a radical change in Navy thinking took place. During April of 1944, the Navy decided that the Tigercat should be operated by land-based squadrons only so the bulk of the Tigercat production was transferred to the United States Marine Corps. It was felt that this move would eliminate lengthy carrier qualification trials as well as provide the Marines with a hard-hitting fighter-bomber that would be well suited to their operational definition.

Accordingly, plans were set in motion to equip twelve USMC squadrons with the twin-engine Cat while the Marines would give up an equal number of squadrons of Corsairs that would be taken back by the Navy and added to the carrier forces in the Pacific.

The production F7F-1, as its designation implied, was classified as a fighter aircraft but the Tigercat was also expected to operate as a tactical ground attack aircraft in support of Marine ground movements. Accordingly, the F7F-1 was very heavily armed with four 20 mm cannon in the wing roots and four 0.50 caliber machine-guns in the nose with 200 rpg for the cannons and 300 rpg for the nose weapons. In addition, under wing stations were designed to carry standard 1,000 lb bombs and a fuselage station could accommodate a torpedo, bomb, or long range fuel tank. A number of nagging technical problems and a rapidly changing situation on the Pacific battlefront brought the production to the -1 Tigercat to a sudden halt on 31 December 1944 with only thirty-five examples manufactured.

As the Navy and Marine air arms began to venture over the home islands, the Tigercat's role began to drastically change. The third production F7F-1 (BuNo 80261) became the prototype XF7F-2N night fighter. Most obvious modifications included a second seat for the radar operator located over the middle of the wing and the AN/APS-6 radar in the nose and the deletion of the four machine-guns located under and behind the nose cone. Further modifications included the addition of rocket launching stubs under the wings and provision for the huge Tiny Tim 11.75 in rocket under the fuselage. The rocket had to be dropped from the Tigercat before ignition could take place so that the blast would not damage the metal skin. A short umbilical cable rolled out with the rocket which was fired by electrical impulse breaking the cord. The modifications of adding a second position reduced the fuel capacity by 46 gallons, down to 380 gallons.

As with the -1, the -2N was a very limited production aircraft with only sixty-five examples being produced between November 1944 and August 1945. All of the night fighters were equipped with more powerful Pratt & Whitney R-2800-34 powerplants, and the remaining operational examples of the -1 were also re-engined with this powerplant.

The Navy obtained several examples of the F7F-2N for a most unusual project. The Tigercats and a North American PBJ-1H Mitchell (an updated relative of Doolittle's Mitchells that took off from the *Hornet* early during the war to give the Japanese a taste of what was coming) were compared in an interesting series of carrier testing. The Tigercats went aboard the USS *Antietam* for a series of over thirty night landings during April of 1945. The six pilots that flew the F7F-2N during this period found that the type performed satisfactorily but the Navy took no further interest. The large PBJ-1H fared little better as it flew off the USS *Shangri-La* and the type was thought to be too large for contemporary carriers. The Navy decided to shelve its studies in twin-engine carrier night fighters in favor of continued operation of its modified Hellcat and Corsair night fighters.

The pilot of an F7F-2N pulls in close to the Grumman camera plane. This view shows the second cockpit behind the pilot, flowing perfectly with the fuselage lines. With the broad wing the radar operator would not have much of a view but his electronic eyes could search far beyond those of the pilot. Special note should be paid to the well-designed engine nacelles that contained the powerful P & W R-2800 engines and landing gear in a minimum amount of space to help reduce drag. Note the simple insignia and overall Glossy Sea Blue finish. (Grumman)

Two virtually identical views of a F7F-3N while on stores test from the Grumman factory. In one view the aircraft can be seen carrying a standard fuel drop tank that was attached to the general purpose shackle under the fuselage. Note the rocket launching stubs for the eight 5 in HVARs. The boarding ladder has been left in the down position, marring the aircraft's fine lines. The -3 series had the higher vertical fin to provide more stability. Power came from Pratt & Whitney R-2800-34W radials. In the other view, the F7F-3N is equipped with a Mk. 13 torpedo that weighed 2,150 lbs. (Grumman)

The honor of being the first Tigercat-equipped squadron went to VMF(N)-533 which arrived at the battlefront on 14 August 1945, the day before the end of the war! The Tigercats made a few patrols but saw no operational engagements in the war for which it was designed. The squadron was transferred to China where it saw service for several years with different models of Tigercats.

The only Tigercats to go to a foreign air force were two -2Ns that were transferred to the Royal Navy but virtually no information is available on their testing. The Tigercat, compared with the clunky underperforming aircraft operated by the Royal Navy, must have seemed like a space ship to the British seamen.

The next variant of the Tigercat also achieved the most fame and largest production numbers. The F7F-3 was produced as a single-seat day fighter and was powered by P & W R-2800-34W engines. A total of 250 -3 variants were built between March and June of 1946. Lockheed Air Service, well-known for their modifications to other manufacturers' aircraft, and who are still modifying military aircraft today, converted sixty -3s to the F7F-3N night fighter variant.

One of the most noticeable identifying features of the -3 Tigercat was its tall, graceful fin which was necessitated by the increase in engine power. The majority of the F7F-3Ns featured the bulged nose that housed the SCR-720 radar. The -3N also had a second cockpit added in the same position as on the -2N. A number of -3s were converted in the field to other variants. The F7F-3D was a drone controller and was immediately identified by the Bearcat canopy grafted to the turtle deck! The F7F-3P was a photo-reconnaissance modification with a number of camera positions. One -3N was converted to F7F-4N standard and featured a strengthened airframe, stronger landing gear, new radar, and arrester gear for carrier operations but only twelve examples were completed, the last leaving the Grumman lines during November 1946, thus closing down Tigercat production.

When the Korean War broke out, the Marines took their Tigercats to the battlefront. VMF(N)-513 and 542 operated both -3s and -3Ns and obtained two kills over the Po-2 biplanes as described in the opening of this chapter. Although the Tigercat only scored a marginal duo of aerial victories in Korea, it did achieve some success in the tricky night ground attack role. The Marine Tigercats would intrude at night over enemy territory and blast opportunity targets such as trains, vehicles, military dumps and bridges. However, the Tigercat was obsolete,

especially with MiGs lurking about, and they were out of active service by 1952 with a few soldiering in specialized roles or as hacks. Thus Grumman's elegant feline never really experienced the operational use that it de-

served which is lucky for Japanese pilots. A few Tigercats are preserved in museums and, up until 1978, a half dozen were still flying as fire bombers in California.

Flying the Tigercat

Even though it was a high-performance aircraft, the Tigercat was a 'pussycat' in the air.

The Grumman Tigercat, because of its tricycle landing gear, proved to be a bit unique among the Navy and Marine 'tail-dragger' fighters of World War Two. The nose wheel gave the sleek twin-engine fighter greatly improved ground handling and vastly improved pilot visibility. The cockpits were large and roomy and the aircraft offered twin-engine safety on long over-water missions.

The F7F was a fair-sized aircraft and getting into the cockpit required a minor amount of gymnastics. A retractable boarding ladder was housed in the lower part of the right side of the fuselage just to the rear of the trailing edge of the wing. The ladder was pulled down by the pilot who clambered up over the wing and gingerly eased himself through the open canopy into the large cockpit, usually putting one leg on to the cockpit cushion and then sliding himself into position. The boarding ladder was then stored by a ground crewman. If the ladder was not stored it detracted from the aircraft's top performance and did nothing for the F7F's sleek looks.

Once in the cockpit, the pilot immediately noticed the excellent visibility compared with the Hellcat and, particularly, the Corsair. These aircraft were equipped with tail wheels which meant that, while on the ground, the large engine and cowling obscured the pilot's vision. The position of the wing on these two aircraft also restricted visibility. The cockpit of the F7F was placed in front of the wing, giving an almost unobscured downward view. The cockpit and instrument panel was essentially similar to the F6F and F4U except for the engine controls and instruments which were doubled. The throttle quadrant was mounted in its traditional left-hand position and was a model of efficiency for single-hand operation. A hefty control column was also very similar to the type used in other Navy fighters. Rudder pedals were placed behind the central panel which ran between the pilot's legs and contained fuel gauges, air distributor,

and flap controls with the landing gear retraction system. Most F7Fs were equipped with autopilots which greatly reduced pilot fatigue while operating on long missions.

The climate control was quite good in the Tigercat's cockpit and the heater was most efficient in clearing the windshield and providing warmth for both cockpits, an essential item for long night missions at high altitude. The rear cockpit for the radar operator was also very roomy although visibility was extremely limited but a throw-over canopy was provided to help relieve any feeling of claustrophobia.

A reading of the F7F pilot's notes revealed few vices but several warnings had to be kept in mind. As with most high-performance twin-engine military aircraft, the F7F was a real handful when one engine failed. The lowest possible airspeed for safe control was a very high 130 to 140 knots depending on altitude. The manual stated that if an engine failed below 120 knots the pilot should immediately retard the functioning engine to prevent the aircraft from violently rolling, retract the landing gear and flaps and prepare for a straight-ahead crash landing if he was not high enough for a successful parachute escape. The normal lift-off speed for the Tigercat was around 75 knots so the pilot had to be particularly cautious during this critical period. However, with the powerful engines, the F7F accelerated very quickly and the hazardous period was a short one. The same precautions applied to landing which was carried out at about 100 knots. If an engine failed during the landing approach, the pilot was advised to immediately apply power and attempt to go around or, if the airspeed had decayed past the safety point, to attempt a 'power-off' landing immediately.

The F7F was an extremely clean aircraft and the 430 knot 'red line' was easy to exceed under the pressures of combat or training. The clean design and the powerful engines combined to make the 'top' speed one that was easy to slide past. In a dive from high altitude, the F7F quickly built up speed and elevator control gradually diminished until being completely lost and the aircraft went into a nose-down dive from which recovery could not be effected; so recovery from a high-speed dive had to be initiated almost immediately or the pilot would find himself running out of altitude and ideas at about the same time. The effects of high-speed compressibility were just being understood as high-performance aircraft advanced to the edge of the sound barrier.

In preparation to starting up the Tigercat, the pilot would make sure that his seat harness and parachute were properly attached and adjusted. Engine starting was a straightforward procedure and after the engines were sufficiently warmed up, taxiing could begin. Since the F7F's props had little clearance, care had to be taken when taxiing over rough ground. The pneumatic oleo strut nose gear was also subject to a fair amount of up and down movement and care had to be taken to prevent bottoming-out since this could also damage the propeller tips. The powerful R-2800 powerplant, even at idle, quickly built up taxi speed and the brakes had to be used to keep the speed down. The brakes were quite effective and a combination of brakes and throttles made the F7F an easy aircraft to steer while on the ground.

In the run-up area, the pilot would go through the check list, ensure that the rudder boost was in the on position, apply the brakes and run the engines up to 40 inches of manifold pressure. For takeoff, the brakes were released and the throttles swiftly but smoothly advanced to 53 inches and 2,800 rpm. The takeoff run was quite forceful as those big Hamilton Standard Hydromatic propellers bit into the air. Control from that big rudder was most effective and there was little tendency for the aircraft to wander. A slight bit of back pressure on the control column eased the nose wheel into the air and, within a couple of seconds, the Tigercat rotated and became airborne. After clearing the runway, the pilot would reach for the gear handle on the center panel and clean up the aircraft to its best climbing speed of 150 knots which ensured a sparkling climb rate of well over 3,000 feet per minute.

Once in its natural element the Tigercat had few bad flying qualities. The only qualities in the minus box were the fairly heavy controls (by single-engine standards) and the roll rate was rather low. All control pressures were well within the capabilities of the average pilot. Spinning was prohibited since, during the F7F's testing phase, the aircraft exhibited a nasty oscillating spin that became very violent and recovery was very difficult.

The Tigercat, without external tanks or

Beautiful shot of a Tigercat at rest after a late afternoon mission. This view shows many of the -3N features to good advantage. The bulged nose for the SCR-720 radar is well-defined as are the 20 mm cannon in the lower wing root. It should not be forgotten that the Tigercat was originally designed as a carrier aircraft and, as such had folding wings. Although the USMC had little requirement for a folding wing Tigercat, the wings were frequently folded to help conserve ramp space. The canopy arrangement is also evident with the front hood being slid back and the radar operator's hatch being hinged on the left side. Also note the fuel tank on the fuselage shackle. Only sixty -3Ns were converted from standard -3 single-seat fighters. (R.T. O'Dell)

weapon loads, was certified for unlimited aerobatics which it would perform with *élan*. In fact two surplus Tigercats were converted for use as skywriters and their graceful maneuvers were a most impressive sight. The pilot had to be constantly aware, however, of how easy it was to build up speed in some of the maneuvers.

The Tigercat did not show any bad vices in stall configuration, either clean or dirty. The stall was gentle with plenty of warning provided by gentle buffeting. With power off and everything down, the F7F stalled out at about 70 knots. When the aircraft was clean and power was on, the stall took place at about 60 knots. The aircraft would begin to shake and mush through the air until the pilot eased the stick forward so that speed could build up and the Tigercat would immediately begin flying once again. Stall recovery only took up around 350 feet of altitude, an exceptionally low figure for a World War Two fighter. With one engine out, rudder forces were very light but the rudder boost system kept the situation in hand.

The only problem in landing an F7F was getting it slowed down. The clean airframe did not lend itself to rapid deceleration and the usual practice was to enter the landing pattern clean, pull up into a military break, pull back on the throttle, dump 15 degrees of flap and, as the downwind leg was reached, the aircraft would be going slow enough to drop the landing gear. With gear and half flap the approach speed was around 100 knots. Throttles were eased off at about 50 feet, although care had to be exercised in not dropping the aircraft on to the runway, and the nose was brought back into landing attitude. Contact was made with the main gear and the nose gear was held off the runway until speed decayed. Brakes were applied early in the landing roll as the aircraft was not prone to slowing down and the R-2800s did not feature reversible props. High winds on landing were not a problem because of the tricycle landing gear and the Tigercat was approved for cross-wind landings at up to 30 mph and 90 degrees to the runway.

The Tigercat was a rugged and fairly docile aircraft with high performance. Its crews had nothing but respect for Grumman's twin-engine feline and there was a great deal of sadness when the final military Tigercat departed for the scrapyard and the new jets advanced to take its place.

Tigercat	Bureau Numbers
XF7F-1	03549–50
F7F-1	80259–93
XF7F-2N	80261*
F7F-2N	80294–358**
F7F-3	80359–608
F7F-4N	80548, 80609–80620***

Notes:

*XF7F-2N was modified from the third F7F-1.

**Two F7F-2Ns transferred to the Royal Navy as TT348 and TT349.

***First F7F-4N was modified F7F-3 BuNo 80548.

Surviving Tigercats ended up their service lives in the vast USN/USMC 'bone yard' at NAS Litchfield Park, Arizona. BuNo 80580 is seen shortly after its arrival for storage. The aircraft's engines would be 'pickled' with a preservative process and sensitive parts of the airframe would be sprayed with a removable coating that could be stripped off if and when the machine was needed back in military service. (R.T. O'Dell)

Grumman XF7F-1

Span	51 ft 6 in
Length	45 ft 6½ in
Height	13 ft 9 in
Wing Area	455 sq ft
Empty Weight	15,275 lbs
Loaded Weight	20,107 lbs
Max. Speed	430 mph
Cruise Speed	180 mph
Ceiling	42,000 ft
Rate of Climb	4200 fpm
Range	1160 miles
Powerplant	Wright XR-2600-14 of 1800 hp each (2)

Grumman F7F-3

Span	51 ft 6 in
Length	45 ft 6½ in
Height	14 ft 7 in
Wing Area	455 sq ft
Empty Weight	16,396 lbs
Loaded Weight	21,906 lbs
Max. Speed	460 mph
Cruise Speed	190 mph
Ceiling	40,400 ft
Rate of Climb	6000 fpm
Range	1900 miles
Powerplant	Pratt & Whitney R-2800-34W of 2100 hp each (2)

Grumman F7F-2N

Span	51 ft 6 in
Length	45 ft 6½ in
Height	13 ft 9 in
Wing Area	455 sq ft
Empty Weight	16,028 lbs
Loaded Weight	21,690 lbs
Max. Speed	445 mph
Cruise Speed	190 mph
Ceiling	41,000 ft
Rate of Climb	5200 fpm
Range	1800 miles
Powerplant	Pratt & Whitney R-2800-22W of 2100 hp each (2)

Grumman F7F-3N

Span	51 ft 6 in
Length	45 ft 6½ in
Height	16 ft 7 in
Wing Area	455 sq ft
Empty Weight	16,592 lbs
Loaded Weight	21,738 lbs
Max. Speed	447 mph
Cruise Speed	185 mph
Ceiling	40,000 ft
Rate of Climb	6000 fpm
Range	1900 miles
Powerplant	Pratt & Whitney R-2800-34W of 2100 hp each (2)

The F7F-3N was the only variant of the Tigercat series to claim a successful combat record but then that record was established during the Korean War and not World War Two. Two primitive Po-2 North Korean biplanes were blown out of the air by Tigercats from VMF(N)-513. General Schilt (commanding general of the 1st Marine Air Wing) flew a Tigercat on a Korean combat strike on 10 November 1951, the 176th birthday of the USMC. (Grumman)

Two F7F-3Ns from USMC squadron VMF(N)-542. The -3N had an empty weight of 16,592 lbs and a loaded weight of 21,738 lbs. Top speed was 447 mph with a ceiling of 40,000 ft and a sizzling rate of climb of 6,000 fpm with a range of 1,750 miles. This squadron was originally formed on 1 April 1944 at Cherry Point and served as a replacement/training squadron during World War Two. (USMC)

F7F-3 BuNo 80412 is seen after being pulled from storage at NAS Litchfield Park. The powerful Arizona sun has oxidized the Glossy Sea Blue paint but spray-on preservative prevented other decay, including the canopy's plexiglass. This machine was saved from the giant aluminium smelter at the facility by a civilian operator. The aircraft was registered N7628C, the Tigercat in the right background was also saved and became N7626C, and was eventually converted to a fire bomber in California. The speedy fighters carried fire retardent to do battle with the raging blazes that take place in California during the summer and fall. It was a deadly battle and a number of Tigercats were lost during this useful service. About a half dozen survived to be retired during the late 1970s and these aircraft were offered for sale to private pilots who had the means to feed those hungry R-2800s (R.T. O'Dell)

6 BEARCAT
The Pugnacious Contender

The Grumman F8F was designed as a high-speed interceptor that would wreck havoc among enemy aircraft. Luckily for the Japanese, they never had to feel its sting.

During the 1930s, when the sport of air racing was in its heyday, aircraft designers were obsessed with the idea of taking the largest possible engine and mating it to the smallest possible airframe. Speed was the ultimate quest and the designers felt that the combination of minimum airframe and massive powerplant would make a sure winner at the pylons. However, aeronautical design was still rather undeveloped and what looked good on paper proved to be unworkable and even deadly in practice. Most of these custom-made racing machines exhibited vicious handling characteristics and new barriers such as compressibility, flutter and high-speed stall were encountered and little could be done about these problems for

aeronautical engineering had not advanced far enough to encounter these new and unusual stumbling blocks. Several of the racing designs such as the Gee Bee series were downright killers. However, even with these dangerous mounts, daring pilots were able to race up the scale towards the goddess of speed and that was what their efforts were all about.

By the time World War Two was rapidly building to actual confrontation in Europe, racing aircraft were going past the 400 mph barrier, astounding military and civilian observers alike. True, these racing mounts were capable of flights of extremely short duration for their highly modified powerplants were literally tearing themselves apart.

Fine study of Grumman F8F-2 Bearcat BuNo 121612 on a test flight near the Bethpage factory. The -2 was the ultimate version of the Bearcat and made its first flight on 11 October 1944 with the last delivery taking place on 14 April 1949. The taller fin of the -2 model is clearly seen in this view. Note the substantial turnover structure placed behind the pilot who sat high atop the fuselage under a bubble canopy that offered just about the ultimate visibility in a fighter aircraft. (Grumman)

A head-on view of the Bearcat gives a good idea of how compact the design was. With wings folded, the span was considerably reduced. Note the size of the Aeroproduct's propeller. The wide stance landing gear gave good ground handling characteristics. Taped-over ports for the four 0.50 caliber Browning machine-guns can be seen in the wing leading edge. (Grumman)

No direct military application could be made from the racers but the techniques that were being developed from these machines certainly *could* be applied to a new and very deadly form of combat aircraft.

In England, a brilliant engineer named Reginald Mitchell had designed a series of racing floatplanes for Supermarine during the late 1920s and early 1930s that were to advance aeronautical engineering in a quantum leap. On 29 September 1931, Mitchell's S6B floatplane racer went past the timing markers at an amazing 407.5 mph and the world of aviation would never be the same. Mitchell, knowing that his racers had extremely limited application, set his creative genius at another mark, a high-performance fighter. At the time, most fighter aircraft were biplanes that did not look all that different from their World War One counterparts. Armament was usually limited to two light machine-guns and the aircraft were usually slow, underpowered and not very efficient in their role of fighting aircraft. However, the biplanes did have superb maneuverability as anyone who attended the giant air displays of the 1930s can attest. Mitchell envisioned a

fighter that would be a monoplane, carry heavy armament, have a very high top speed, and be extremely maneuverable. The result, of course, was the immortal Spitfire and the combination of Mitchell's beautiful airframe and Rolls-Royce's magnificent Merlin engine are still looked at as models of aeronautical efficency.

During World War Two Allied fighters grew heavier and more powerful and the Axis was driven from the skies. Fighting aircraft began to take on the dual role of air combat and ground attack which, for a single-engine fighter, was an extremely hazardous occupation, especially in the face of heavy enemy anti-aircraft fire. Britain and USA began to produce heavy-weights such as the Thunderbolt and Tempest, large and powerful aircraft that could fight their way through just about anything. However, the concept of a small, responsive fighting aircraft with high performance seemed to have been all but forgotten by design staffs that were eager to create machines that could haul huge bomb and rocket loads into the air.

During 1943, with Hellcat production well under way, Grumman representatives visited

A Bearcat catches a carrier's arresting wire while the emergency barrier can be seen stretched across the deck. The Bearcat did not exhibit any bad carrier operating qualities. Its small size and huge power reserves made it popular with both deck crews and pilots. (USN)

the battlefields of the Pacific and Europe. These visits enabled the company to learn what was going on in the combat zones and what the airmen wanted in the way of combat aircraft. Meetings between Navy officials and Grumman representatives at Pearl Harbor during 1944 helped lay out future naval fighter aircraft plans. The Navy knew that the Japanese were rapidly losing the war but they also knew that they were facing a foe who would literally fight to the death rather than risk the dishonor of surrender. *Kamikaze* attacks were beginning to take place against the Fleet and the Navy (not knowing of the top-secret atomic bomb development) foresaw a long and hard fight to gain control of the Japanese home islands.

Hellcats and Corsairs were racking up impressive kill ratios against Japanese aircraft but these aircraft, although extremely tough and fast, lacked the maneuverability of the Japanese counterparts. This, when combined with the overall very good performance of the two fighters, was not that much of a drawback since most fighting was done away from the carriers where the Hellcats and Corsairs could roar in and out of enemy formations at will, blasting Japanese fighters and bombers in high-speed passes then pulling up and setting up for another firing

run before the Japanese could use the maneuverability of their machines against the heavier American fighters. However, with the increasing number of suicide attacks and the fanatical determination of Japanese pilots to press home their attacks, the question arose as to the best way to defend the carriers and other naval units. A fast highly responsive fighter was needed to bridge the gap between the big naval fighters and the smaller Japanese machines. A fighter was needed that could be launched within a minimum time, close with the enemy at a high rate of speed, and engage and destroy the enemy before damage was done to the Fleet.

The old formula of huge engine and small airframe once more reared its head but this time Grumman engineers were determined to make the formula successful and give the Navy a fighter that could reliably carry out its duties. The result was the Bearcat, Grumman's last piston-engined fighter and an aircraft that was smaller than the Wildcat with more power than the Hellcat!

The company's proposal was listed as Design Number G-58 and the Navy liked what it saw so, on 27 November 1943, two prototypes, designated XF8F-1, were ordered. Construction was undertaken at a very rapid pace and the first prototype flew on 31

August 1944. Right from the first, Chief Engineer William Schwendler and his staff knew that they had created a machine with the sparkling performance that the Navy required. Test pilot Bob Hall was very favorable in his comments concerning the stubby fighter. BuNo 90460 was equipped with a Pratt & Whitney R-2800-22W Double Wasp that pumped out 2,100 hp at takeoff power. The prototype had a top speed of 424 mph at 17,300 ft and a rate of climb of 4,800 fpm. Clearly, this is what the Navy wanted and on 6 October 1944, less than two months after the prototype flew, the Navy issued contracts to Grumman for the production of 2,023 F8F-1s. A contract was also placed with the Eastern Aircraft division of General Motors on 5 February 1945 for 1,876 Bearcats that would be designated F3M-1.

Problems with stability and fuel consumption cropped up with the prototypes. That huge Double Wasp was a hungry beast and internal fuel capacity was increased from 150 gallons to 183 gallons. Underwing pylons that would accommodate a drop tank or a 1,000 lb bomb under each wing panel were also added. When the second prototype flew, a dorsal fin had been added and this helped improve stability. Planned production figures included 100 aircraft a month by June 1945 with complete phase out of the Hellcat production line by January 1946.

Testing of the prototypes and twenty-three pre-production aircraft proceeded rapidly with the first carrier operations occurring on 17 February 1945 when nine carrier landings were carried out aboard the USS *Charger*. The test showed that the Bearcat would operate off carriers with no problem. That big engine pulling the little airframe made the Bearcat literally leap off the carrier's deck.

In interests of weight, the -1 Bearcats were armed with four 0.50 caliber Browning machine-guns rather than the standard battery of six. It was thought that the four guns would do almost as much damage as the six especially when combined with the fantastic performance of the F8F.

Another unusual innovation in the Bearcat design was the use of wing tips that could be blown off in flight. These breakaway wing tips were to be used as a safety feature. When the aircraft was under high G forces during combat, the wing tips would break off rather than let the wing suffer the fatigue of bending under pressure of the combat maneuvers. The idea was tested out on a Wildcat, the tips were separated from the wing by an explosive charge that was actuated by sensing devices. Difficulties arose with symmetrical separation of the tips and the attendant problems

The Blue Angels operated the -2 Bearcat for a brief period of time. With the -2, the team's name finally appeared on the nose of the aircraft, painted in Yellow script. During 1945, a Bearcat was tested with a McDonnell FD-1 Phantom jet. The Bearcat was able to walk away in the climb-out but once the early jet gained some altitude, the Bearcat was in trouble!

Grumman F8F-1 Bearcat

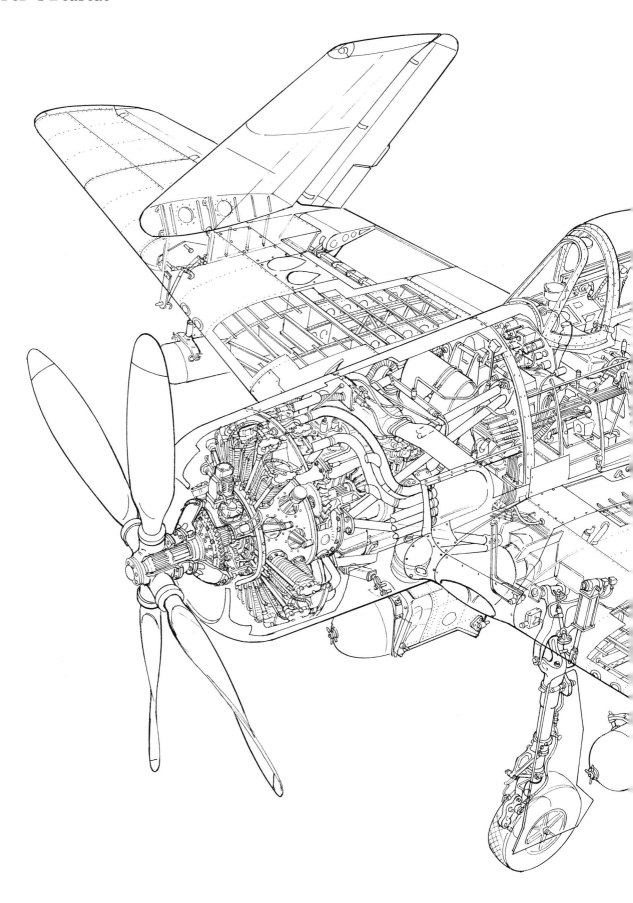

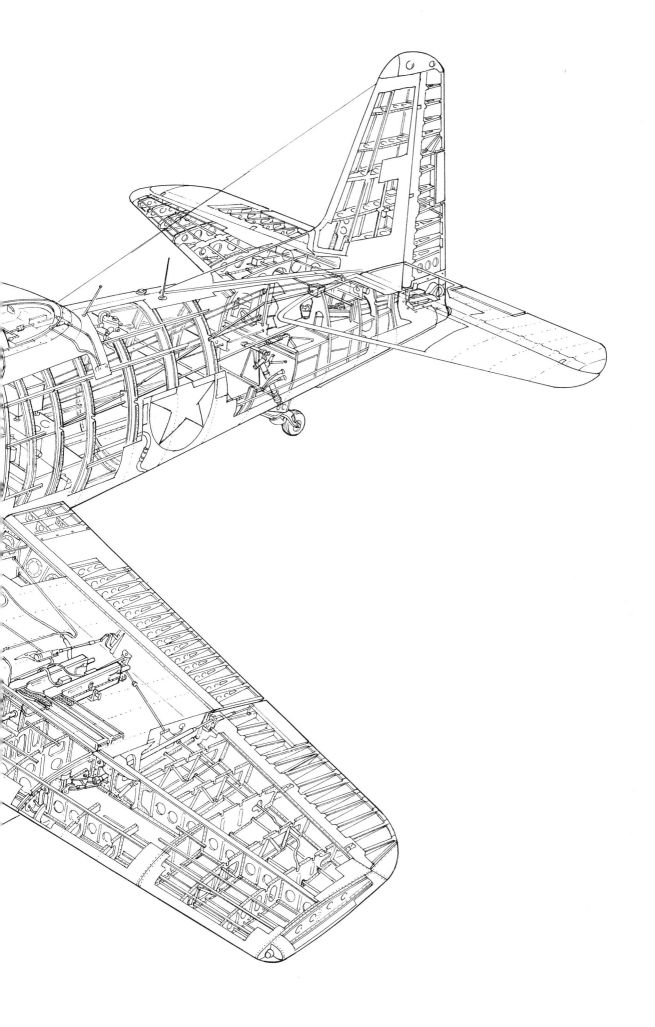

of assymetric flight so the project was dropped after one fatal accident and the aircraft that had been modified were all converted back to standard configuration.

Naval planners decided to equip a Navy squadron with some pre-production and production model Bearcats to aid in faster testing and acceptance of the aircraft. VF-19, based at NAS Santa Rosa, California, was picked as the test unit and had received its complement of aircraft by 21 May 1945. The squadron began an intensive flying schedule to train as many pilots as possible for a combat tour to begin in the late summer. More aircraft were assigned to the squadron as they became available and the ranks of Bearcat trained pilots began to grow. As with any such test unit, problems began to arise. The main stumbling block was excessive leaking from the jungle of hydraulic and oil lines that ran behind the engine compartment. A look into this area was known to

make even the most veteran naval aircraft mechanic blanch at what he saw. This engine accessory area, later to give serious problems if and when a fire occurred, was the cause of a number of complete engine failures which found rooky VF-19 pilots frantically looking for the nearest flat area near Santa Rosa. With the engine out and propeller feathered, the Bearcat's gliding habits were about equal to a P-51 Mustang so, if the pilot kept his wits about him, emergency landings were not impossible in the hot little fighter. Some complete engine stoppages were later traced to diaphragm and seal leaking problems. Other failures came from the lengthy use of lean mixture while in cruise configuration. This was overcome when Pratt & Whitney technicians suggested the use of auto-rich setting while in cruise.

VF-19's Bearcats were grounded for a brief period by the nightmare of leaks and engine failures but Grumman and P & W experts

Beautifully maintained F8F-1 flown by the commanding officer of VF-20 Lt Cmdr D.C. 'Whiff' Caldwell, over San Francisco, California, during June 1947. The campaign ribbons of the pilot were painted on the nose of BuNo 95318. The markings on the aircraft were white. (W.T. Larkins)

worked around the clock to correct the problems and the grounding was soon lifted.

The pilots and crews of VF-19 were confident that they had a fighter that could stop anything that the Japanese put into the air but fate was to take the squadron on a unforeseen turn. The atomic bomb was dropped on Hiroshima and then Nagasaki and the war suddenly ended with Japan's unconditional surrender on 14 August 1945. Almost overnight military units were disbanded and the 'shock' of peace hit the aircraft factories like a tidal wave. Grumman reeled under massive contract cancellations. Before the atomic bomb happened, Grumman Aircraft Engineering Corporation had about 20,500 employees who set a record during March of 1945 when they turned out 664 military aircraft including the Hellcat, Tigercat, Goose, Widgeon, and Bearcat. The day after surrender Grumman received massive contract cancellations from the government. Shortly after the factory opened for work on that fateful morning, the public address system announced that all work at Grumman had been suspended as of that day and all employees were to leave the area and take all personal effects with them. Grumman officials then put their heads together to plan a course of action. Over half of the wartime payroll would have to be let go immediately so, after a few days of closure, selected employees would be called back to work, letting the others go on to try to find employment in other fields.

With production drastically cut back, Grumman knew that the Hellcat production line would only go on to November, the Tigercat for another year, but the Bearcat line could run on for three or four years if production eased up. The original order book showed plans for 6,135 F8Fs but peace-time cancellations cut this down to only about 700 aircraft so plans for producing fifteen of the stubby fighters per month were set down. Further lay-offs cut the Grumman peace-time payroll down to only 5,400 employees.

Confusion, of course, was to be expected after the layoffs and, when Grumman resumed Bearcat production about a week after the initial closure, shop managers were stunned to find that not a single riveter had been rehired! Needless to say, the situation was quickly corrected but the atmosphere around the plant was one of not knowing what was going to happen tomorrow even though the company had produced 98 per cent of the Navy's torpedo bombers and 65 per cent of that service's fighters. The company immediately took steps to diversify its production and entered into the esoteric world of aluminium canoes and truck bodies.

As Bearcat production slowly continued, the engineering staff began making certain changes that would produce a better fighter. Beginning in April of 1946 around one-fourth of the Bearcat production was made up to the -1B variant which carried four 20 mm cannon in place of the machine-guns, giving the 'Cat a very deadly punch.

The United States Air Force (USAF) had been receiving quantities of the Lockheed P-80 Shooting Star jet fighter and, although just a bit too late to see combat during the war, the aircraft would have profound effect on the aeronautical manufacturing community. A P-80 was tested against an F8F-1 and the results were most depressing for Grumman. The P-80 got the upper hand over the Bearcat every time and the F8F was never able to even get a mock shot at its opponent.

The Navy decided that it needed jet fighters but a new breed of aircraft carrier would also be needed so, in the interim, Bearcat production was to continue and, by December 1947, nineteen squadrons were equipped with F8Fs.

By the end of 1947, a new version of the Bearcat had entered production, the F8F-2. A Pratt & Whitney R-2800-30W engine was fitted along with a 12 in extension to the vertical fin to help improve stability. The XF8F-2 was BuNo 95049 and 293 -2s were produced along with twelve -2N night fighters and sixty -2P recon. fighters which had the armament reduced to two wing guns.

As jets began to enter naval service during 1949 (and Grumman was right in the race with its F9F Panther which was to become the Navy's standard fighter bomber) the number of active Bearcat squadrons immediately began to drop. Some aircraft were transferred to Naval Reserve units while the USMC received other aircraft. Many were sent to the vast storage facility at NAS Litchfield where they moldered under the intense Arizona sun until being sold or scrapped.

F8F-1 BuNo 95300 is seen with a large test probe mounted on the right wing. This aircraft was used in developmental trials for the F8F-1N night fighter, of which only thirteen were built. The night fighter carried an APS-19 radar pod. (USN/405312)

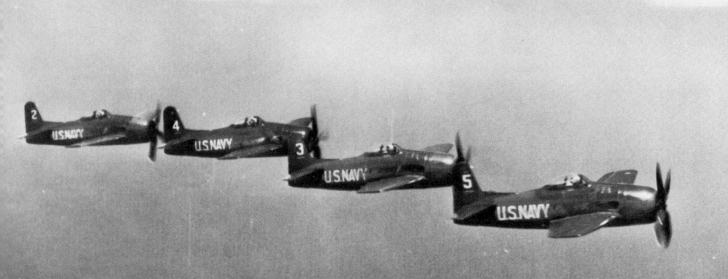

Top left

The use of orthochromatic film turns the Yellow markings dark on this Blue Angels F8F-1. The Bearcat was one of the top-performing propeller-driven fighters and it set a climb record of 10,000 feet in 94 seconds from a standing start at the 1946 Cleveland National Air Races and the record stood for ten years before it was claimed by a jet. (R.T. O'Dell)

Bottom left

The Blue Angels' use of the Bearcat was of fairly short duration for the jets were the way of the future and they were what the public wanted to see. This rare inflight view of four of the Angels' -1 Bearcats shows off the little fighter's ability to hold a close formation.

Bottom

Factory-fresh F8F-2, BuNo 122711, at the Bethpage factory. Note the Grumman use of water-based paint to apply the temporary nose numbers that were used until the aircraft was transferred to a Navy squadron.

When the Korean War began in 1950, the Bearcat was considered for active service. However, the aircraft could not carry a heavy bomb or rocket load for the ground attack role (the veteran Corsair could carry much more) and, as the tests with the P-80 had already proven, the F8F series was no match for Communist MiG jet fighters so the Bearcat was quickly phased out of service.

Even though the Bearcat was fated to miss out in the action of World War Two and Korea, it *would* eventually see action even though this was to take place in an area that the rest of the world liked to forget. During the late 1940s, trouble was brewing in French Indo-china as the Communist Viet Minh rebelled against the French colonial government and began slaughtering French and Vietnamese citizens with equal abandon. The French had no intention of letting the area go so they sent in heavy reinforcements of veteran troops and the cream of the French Foreign Legion who also began slaughtering off Viet Minh and Vietnamese citizens with similar abandon. France had been drained by the German occupation of World War Two and its factories had a long way to go in order to supply the equipment that the French Army and *Armée de l' Air* needed in the jungle war. The French were also faced with a new problem, guerrilla warfare. This was a filthy

war, as the United States would discover during the 1960s, in which it was hard to distinguish friend from foe and where the enemy could strike and fade back into the protection of the jungle before the French forces could react. French troops began taking casualties, heavy casualties, and it was realized that much more airpower was needed for ground support. The US government was only too happy to aid the French and thus get rid of tired propeller-driven fighters and attack bombers that were filling the storage bases.

A number of -1 and -1B Bearcats were supplied to the French who formed two new squadrons of the French Expeditionary Air Force. Additional supplies of Bearcats followed and the French pilots were quite pleased with the aircraft, particularly since it was replacing the totally unsuited Bell P-63 Kingcobra. The Bearcats operated from short, unprepared strips near the front line where they flew constant sorties against the rebels, blasting them with cannon fire and napalm. The Bearcats and the other surplus World War Two aircraft took a very heavy toll of the enemy but the supply of Viet Minh seemed to be inexhaustible and the final blow for the French came when the fortress of Dien Bien Phu surrendered after a long and bitter fight on 7 May 1954. A cease fire was

signed in Geneva on 27 July and the French withdrawal from North Vietnam took place.

Even after the French collapse, the Bearcat's military career still had some mileage. The surviving French Bearcats were given to the new South Vietnamese Air Force while the Royal Thai Air Force received 100 F8F-1Ds (a -1 with a new fuel system) and F8F-2s. These aircraft continued to operate for a number of years, occasionally attacking the numerous Communist guerrilla attacks that crossed those countries' borders. By 1955, all US Naval Reserve Bearcats were withdrawn and sent to the scrap heap but the Bearcat's career was still not at an end.

During the 1960s the sport of air racing once again cropped up in America and the pilots who participated in these events found that the powerful Bearcat was hard to beat. However, very few Bearcats were left and they had become virtual collector's items, demanding extremely high prices. Unfortunately, during these air races, a number of the Bearcats were destroyed in accidents and the small number of survivors became even smaller. The Bearcat's crowning moment of glory came during 1969 when veteran test pilot Darryl Greenamyer took his highly modified -2 Bearcat over a timing course at Edwards AFB in California and broke the speed record for propeller-driven aircraft which had been held since before World War Two by a German Bf 209, a specialized and advanced racing aircraft. Greenamyer's speed of over 480 mph proved that the Bearcat had earned its laurels as the last of the propeller-driven fighters. This particular Bearcat is now proudly displayed at the National Air and Space Museum in Washington, D.C.

Currently just over a dozen Bearcats still survive, many of them flyable. The stubby fighter with the big radial engine up front is one of the most popular exhibits at today's air shows where the propeller-driven veterans are treated with veneration.

BuNo 121546, a -2 Bearcat, displays a colorful set of markings. Most Bearcats exhibited very few interesting personal markings during their service life. Note the barrels for the aircraft's guns. The fuselage center pylon tank is in position. (R.T. O'Dell)

Bearcat Bureau Numbers

XF8F-1	90460-61, 94753
F8F-1	
(pre-production)	90437–90459
F8F-1	94752, 94754–95498
XF8F-2	95049, 95330
F8F-1B	122087–152, 121463–522
F8F-2/2N/2P	121523–792, 122614–708

Specifications

Grumman XF8F-1

Span	35 ft 6 in
Length	28 ft 3 in
Height	13 ft 10 in
Wing Area	244 sq ft
Empty Weight	7017 lbs
Loaded Weight	9115 lbs
Max. Speed	424 mph
Cruise Speed	185 mph
Ceiling	33,700 ft
Rate of Climb	6500 fpm
Range	2000 miles
Powerplant	Pratt & Whitney R-2800-22W of 2100 hp

Grumman F8F-1

Span	35 ft 10 in
Length	27 ft 10 in
Height	13 ft 10 in
Wing Area	246 sq ft
Empty Weight	7170 lbs
Loaded Weight	9430 lbs
Max. Speed	421 mph
Cruise Speed	185 mph
Ceiling	40,800 ft
Rate of Climb	6300 fpm
Range	2200 miles
Powerplant	Pratt & Whitney R-2800-22W of 2100 hp

Grumman F8F-2

Span	35 ft 10 in
Length	27 ft 10 in
Height	14 ft 10 in
Wing Area	246 sq ft
Empty Weight	7650 lbs
Loaded Weight	13,500 lbs
Max. Speed	447 mph
Cruise Speed	190 mph
Ceiling	42,000
Rate of Climb	6600 fpm
Range	2200 miles
Powerplant	Pratt & Whitney R-2800-30W of 2250 hp

BuNo 95387, an F8F-1, is directed from its parking space and out towards the runway by a ground crewman who was an essential part of taxiing operations since the pilot had a difficult time seeing over the bulky cowling of the huge radial engine. Note the ports for the four 0.50 caliber Browning machine-guns.

Bibliography

ABRAMS, RICHARD, *F4U Corsair at War*, Ian Allan, London, 1977.

BUCHANAN, A.R. (Editor), *The Navy's Air War*, Harper & Brothers Publishers, New York, 1946.

DANBY, PETER A. (Editor), *United States Navy Serials 1941 to 1976*, A Merseyside Aviation Society Publication, Liverpool, 1976.

GREEN, WILLIAM, *Famous Fighters of the Second World War*, Doubleday and Company New York, 1962.

GUNSTON, BILL, *The Illustrated Encyclopedia of Combat Aircraft of World War II*, Salamander Books Ltd, London, 1978.

JOHNSON, LT COL. EDWARD C., *Marine Corps Aviation: The Early Years*, History and Museums Division USMC, Washington D.C., 1977.

KILGRAIN, BILL C., *Color Schemes and Markings US Navy Aircraft 1911–1950*, Published by the author, Canada, 1976.

LARKINS, WM. T., *US Marine Corps Aircraft 1914–1959*, Aviation History Publications, Concord, California, 1960.
US Navy Aircraft 1921–1941, Aviation History Publications, Concord, California,

SHERROD, ROBERT, *History of Marine Corps Aviation in World War II*, Combat Forces Press, Washington, D.C., 1952.

SWANBOROUGH, GORDON and BOWERS, PETER M., *United States Navy Aircraft Since 1911*, Putnam, London, 1976.

THRUELSEN, RICHARD, *The Grumman Story*, Praeger Publishers, New York, 1976.

WAGNER, RAY, *American Combat Planes*, Hanover Press, New York, 1960.

Index

Photographs/captions in bold.
Specifications in italic.